MW00510733

TO:

FROM:

MINDSTIR MEDIA

Published by Mindstir Media, LLC
45 Lafayette Rd | Suite 181| North Hampton, NH 03862 | USA
1.800.767.0531 | www.mindstirmedia.com

Printed in the United States of America
ISBN-13: 978-1-7347069-2-5
Library of Congress Control Number: 2020903898

**BRIDGINGTHEGAPWITHWES.COM**

# BRIDGING THE GAP

## BETWEEN HOMEOWNERS AND THEIR HOMES

### The Quintessential Guide

to Effective and Successful
Homeownership - Vol 1

**BY WES TAYLOR**

America's General Contractor

# TABLE OF CONTENTS

# Foreword

BY PETER COLLINS - RECORD PRODUCER

Somehow, I don't think Warren Zevon had me in mind when he wrote the immortal line: "he was a credit to his gender" (Linda Rondstadt's *Oh Poor Pitiful Me*) in as much as I manage to hurt myself during the simple task of banging a nail into the wall to hang a picture.

Therefore, for such a pitifully incompetent homeowner such as myself, Wes' book is a godsend!

Not only does it cover every aspect of critical home inspections, maintenance, and how to save large fortunes, it takes you through the moment you first view the house (with or without a realtor), balancing pros and cons, the exact nature of the purchase psychologicaly, prioritizing changes needed, bad neighbors, and managing your budget. *Bridging the Gap…* is a stimulating read, that will only improve the enjoyment and appreciation of your unique sanctuary.

Wes appears to have left no stone unturned in this highly informative yet humorous masterpiece. As with his broadcasts and television appearances, his sarcastic, fun, and slightly off the wall nature keeps the information entertaining while hitting the *bullseyes* one after the other!

Peter Collins, Record Producer
*Rush, Alice Cooper, Phil Collins, Stray Cats,*
*Brian Setzer Orchestra, Indigo Girls*

"You don't stop dancing because you get old,
you get old because you stop dancing."

# CHAPTER 1
# Introduction

*"Home wasn't a set house or a single town on a map. It was wherever the people who loved you were whenever you were together. Not a place, but a moment, and then another, building on each other like bricks to create a solid shelter that you take with you for your entire life, wherever you may go."*

—Sarah Dessen, *What Happened to Goodbye*

Let me congratulate you for having a home! Strange sounding, isn't it? Big deal! Don't most of us have one? Notice I didn't write, "house" or "apartment?" Let's start by defining a few terms and getting on the same page. You can always claim where you reside as your home, and your home and rights in a home are well protected in America, whether your home is a house or apartment, deeded to you, or rented. A realtor may help you buy or sell your home, but the truth is, what you are actually buying or selling is a piece of land with the possible inclusion (addition) of an improvement, such as a house, townhouse, condo, oil well, or barn. While your house is comprised of the land and improvement, "home" includes the yard, the neighborhood, the neighbors, the streets, the larger community and the city, and the most important ingredient is you. The relationships you form with the structure, co-occupants, neighborhood, and community are really how I define "home."

Just about every big-ticket item comes with an owner's manual. Cars, computers, and dishwashers come with instructions. In most cases, the manual is specific to that particular model. In the case of the great American home, however, there isn't one. You may breathe the same smelling air as the family from which you purchased the house, have the same neighbors, and even have a dog like theirs, but your "home" will be very different from theirs. The same is true for Bob and Janet next door and the single father and four boys living down the street. Every family occupies their home **dissimilarly.** A true homeowner's manual would have to know you personally. It would have to richly address your family members, the relationships you form with Bob and Janet next door, the kids that your kids play with, and the noise coming from the rail yard a few miles away. You will create your own homeowner's manual, and it will exist in your mind and heart.

Mechanical systems or plumbing fixtures may come with an owner's manual, but building your home means you will be met with unanswered questions, frequently addressed with folklore, guessing, poor advice, and some stumbling. Sounds a lot like raising kids, doesn't it? You and many others reading this book have several things in common, such as the same failures, successes, bad neighbors, great celebrations, and grief. These elements make creating and having a home both challenging and rewarding.

This book has been created to enhance and expedite the rewards and overcome challenges found in home ownership. The sooner you master your home and everything of which it is comprised, the more rewarding and healthier the experience of home ownership will be. It is then that we, together, will bridge the gap between you and your home!

Imagine that upon returning after a night out, you walk up to your door, put the key in the lock, open the door, step inside, and think, "It sure is good to be townhouse." Silly, isn't it? You are *home*.

Empty nesters look at each other while warmly reflecting on their successes as a family and one says, "I'm so proud of the house we built." Silly again, because he was a teacher and she was a bank teller, neither were builders. What they are proud of is the *home* they created forty years ago and still create in the present. In fact, they lived in a few different parts of town along the way.

The terms "house" and "home" have different meanings at the core. A house is a structure. A home is a place. Where the two meet and succeed together, you exist. Your house or apartment is your home. It will be a huge facilitator in your life, and is so personal to you from the outside world. Your home will serve and protect you while you're naked in the shower or when you're throwing a beer can at the TV because the Crimson Tide won again. It will witness your failures and accomplishments. It will hide your tears and wild laughter. All it asks is that you protect it in return. You will help it to its feet when a storm beats it mercilessly. You will attend to scratches and bruises. You will have to keep it warm on freezing nights and cool in the blazing sun. Sounds a lot like real love, doesn't it?

Upon getting my first car, dad said the usual, "You know that this is going to require more from you than gas. You will have mechanical expenses, oil changes, things to learn, and you'll have to wash and wax it." Whew... And insurance... Your home is the same way. It will require fuel (electricity, water, gas) but also insurance, mechanical inspections, visits from plumbers, repairs from water damage, settling foundations, and the list goes on and on.

Nearly every square inch of this home is going to require your attention and upkeep at some point. Each toilet flapper, blade of grass, strip of caulk, roof shingle, and carpet fiber means that it is up to you to learn as much as possible about its structure and your lifestyle related to the structure. If you are super wealthy, then disregard that last statement. But if you are like most of us, you will need to learn much more about your property and home. With such education, you will be richly rewarded with equity, peace of mind, safety, and quality of life. Those are the facts!

On the Internet, there is a lot of informational material, such as *"How To"* and *"Remedies,"* related to virtually any subject about a house. There are nice poems about your home as well. It seems like these materials cover all of the bases, so it doesn't make much sense for me to do videos or provide instructions on how to repair a roof shingle or finish concrete... I'm not that great with plants and colors, either. I am here to address the things that are so prevalent in the life of the homeowner that nobody has ever told you. Besides, I want to appeal to 97% of you and not just the 3% who have a roof leak right now. I believe 97% of you have a pet or a bad neighbor or will benefit from home equity, and I would rather share with you the knowledge others have neglected concerning your home and pets! After all, we are only talking about the biggest liability for which you will be responsible.

Unfortunately, the house and home will consist of very steep, unmerciful, and expensive learning curves. Solid solutions and effective management of these things are the key to success in the home. Ironically, it is no place for amateurs! Most folks simply don't know much about a house or home when they make that big purchase and start out. Good thing for YouTube? If so, then I say, "Good thing for emergency rooms as well." Let's *bridge the gap* starting right now!!

*"In life, a person will come and go from many homes. We may leave a house, a town, a room, but that does not mean that these places leave us. Once entered, we never entirely depart the homes we make for ourselves in the world. They follow us, like shadows, until we come upon them again, waiting for us in the mist."*

—*Ari Berk, Death Watch*

# CHAPTER 2
# About Me

*While checking out at a convenience store, the clerk asked, "Do you have kids?" I replied, "Probably."*

People who know me will tell you that I often utilize humor. I rely on humor and sarcasm quite a bit and find comfort in being able to laugh at myself. I respect those who can deal in the business of humor without hurting others, and believe humor is a healthy outlet that helps us have some kind of control over chaos. I will weave my sense of humor into my writing. I also love horses, dogs, aviation, and western art.

I will approach sentence and gesture as if we are either in the living room together, across the hedge between our yards, or standing in the driveway together. Plain talk is where we connect. I shall try to reach you in a meaningful way. From this point forward, I am your *neighbor in the know*!

Writing and presenting material in conversational form means that I can reach more people in a far more permanent, tangible, and meaningful way. If, at any time, I get a bit technical or wordy, keep in mind that I am trying to define, describe, and convey relationships, systems, behaviors, and solutions without video or illustrations. I will also give entertaining accounts of true stories.

As the on-air "home" guy (radio), or on TV endorsing products, I base my approach to all things "home" on simple facts: everything important to you comes together in your home. The house or property you bought becomes an integral part of everything important in your life and in the lives of those you love. Your home is a member of the team. It is a part of your life, love, children, finances, pets, grieving, suffering, celebration, nutrition, prayer and religious expression, holidays, marriage, divorce, healing, injury, and even birth and death. All of these things will be made so much easier if this large team member is well cared for. Your quality of life will increase commensurately with how well you do as a property owner and homeowner.

So, how did I arrive at such a passionate position for other people's lives and the places their lives happen? Apparently the house gods have been stalking me since I was a child in Colorado. I wasn't particularly good at math nor owned an erector set. I didn't do well in English. It is interesting that as an adult, there has been a lot of math in nearly every profession of mine, and one of my hobbies is reading and writing. I love learning accurate history. Growing up, I held the usual jobs like washing cars and mowing grass. Dad had rental property, and on his way to the office, he would drop me off at these places once a tenant vacated. Before pulling off, he would hand me a bag with lunch and a drink and say, "Do a good job. Call me if you need me." He left me with drywall mud, paint, hand tools, and trash bags. He would return at the end of the day and say, "Wow, you did a great job." He was a positive, fair, successful, and consistent man. It meant a lot to me that he approved of my handiwork. As I look back at those times through the lens of a now Master Builder, I am certain that the work I did then was terrible, which makes him an even better dad.

Neighbors would ask for my help around the house doing specific handyman chores. It paid better than making pizza, and I had my choice of hours to work (or not). I learned a house quickly. In college, I excelled at soccer and music, but to make money, I worked at a bank in Denver, and later as a ranch hand near Laramie, Wyoming. Later, I worked on a framing crew in the Rockies. After moving to the south, I worked for a builder and eventually became a General Contractor/Real Estate Developer.

Contracting and real estate development was, for the most part, destroyed in 2008-2012 due to the Great Recession. During that time, I became America's General Contractor on TV and Radio. Most homeowners and contractors were severely hurt, if not financially ruined. Nearly two generations of people saw their net worth evaporate. Lives were destroyed, and often with little chance of recovery. A highly skilled labor pool was decimated and replaced by foreigners who would do poor quality work at a fraction of the cost. It was also during this time that I noticed homeowners were spending record amounts on their *existing* homes. That's right! Instead of buying a place, experiencing soaring property values, then selling and getting rich, they were staying put. They were buying new bathrooms, kitchens, hardwoods throughout, or new windows to help strengthen the value of their houses. It was then that I decided to dedicate my experience as a homeowner (end user of goods and services) and contractor (provider of goods and services) with those who could benefit from it.

Given that the economy was in shambles, the relationship between contractors and homeowners became strained and out of balance. Shady contractors, or those who were starving, were taking huge sums of money up front from homeowners then disappearing. Likewise, homeowners would come up with terrible and creative reasons they simply couldn't pay contractors for work completed. I found myself helping both sides to solve these problems, hence my calling as a consultant. It made more sense to help each side agree to several items prior to the exchange of money or purchase of material. You will read about those items/guidelines later.

Homeowners would call on me to build budgets, map out timelines, develop specific rules that workers needed to follow, and supply them with names of reliable contractors.

The homeowners trusted me because I had nothing to sell them (such as a new roof or HVAC system). I fell in love with two aspects of the deal. First was the *forensics*. In the world of crime investigation, the term *forensics* is used to describe evidence that better helps them to understand a crime. Evidence can lead them to the cause of a crime and, hopefully, the perpetrator of the crime. Police investigators use everything from fingerprints, to the time of day, to DNA, to ascertain certain facts about a crime. Factual evidence in the hands of a highly experienced investigator helps him catch the crook! When I use the term *forensics* related to problems at a structure, I refer to being presented with a problem and using my experience and evidence gathering in order to determine a cause. It helps to understand the degree of damage it created or could create if left unattended. My experience would allow me to then determine what measure should be taken to remedy the problem. I also developed a deep passion not only for the homeowners, but for the contractors as well. Both sides were terribly hurt in the recession. I had walked in the shoes of both for a long time and could speak their respective languages. I paid close attention to the dynamics of the relationship between the two. When does it work and why? When doesn't it work and why? Getting to the bottom of that meant that I had to be present at many meetings between the two. I made a lot of discoveries that I will share with you in this book.

I wish that I could tell you that I am tall, talented beyond description, and a master of the homeowner niche. Like anyone else, I do have a few gifts but I have a lot more scars and wrinkles. It seems like just when I think I have seen everything related to a house and home and owners and contractors, I am caught, puzzled again and chasing something down another rabbit hole. But I have been deeply entrenched in the subject for a long time now. I have fallen flat on my face, been terribly wrong when critical answers were needed, and been dead broke a few times as an adult. I have been ripped-off by both contractors and homeowners. I have also been richly blessed with success, home ownership, truly knowing love, and the toughest lesson of all: *forgiveness*. I have simply paid attention and not been afraid to ask questions.

Keep in mind that the guy who wrote the book about surviving the wilderness when lost in the arctic didn't do so because he is a genius, was well versed in meteorology, and was able to push the envelope of human genetics. He wrote it because he survived the bad, the ugly, and the deadly. He is the guy you want with you on that particular expedition. Take my knowledge and experiences with you on your expedition of owning a house and building a home!

If the guy who hypnotizes me asks me to close my eyes and take my mind to the most peaceful place, it would be my front yard in

Green Hills, Nashville. The time is 4:00pm. It is early October. It is still warm but the humid heat is gone. I am standing under the large maple that turns fluorescent yellow in the fall. I am facing west with my eyes closed. The sun forces its rays through the leaves and then my closed eyelids, and I can see this God-like light across my face and feel it on my chest and legs. There is no other earthly light with this magnificence. It cannot be created by man. The street is quiet with the exception of a distant lawn mower and dog barking a few blocks over. It is at this place and point in time where and when I am perfectly centered. Just feet from that physical spot is the open lawn and driveway. It is there that I will wave at neighbors, or visit or joke with them. At some point in our relationship, they will each bring up an issue at their house or in their home. I have counseled on subjects like exterminator contracts, codes and zoning, how to throw a football, and for those simply needing an ear. I listen with an open mind and heart. Those experiences were a great prerequisite for handling caller questions when on the air as the *home* guy. I suppose the experience is the same for the doctor, mechanic, lawyer, or preacher on any street in America. There is always that one *quick* question! I didn't mind because I am called to increase the quality of life for those I care about and where my gifts or talents can lend themselves.

Speaking of keeping things light, conversational, and ENTERTAINING - imagine how successful Elvis would have been had he walked onto the stage in a business suit, gently taken the microphone, and read a poem with a lonesome harmonica in the background. Imagine, if you will, *Painting with Bob Ross* if Bob had a crew cut instead of a fro, and demanded that you do this or that? In a Drill Sergeant's voice, he would yell, "What the hell is that? A painting? A cadmium freakin' white tree? You smeared the magenta into the stream you idiot! That tree was supposed to be your little friend, you MORON!" Well these might be bad examples because even Elvis would have made a hit out of it. Yeah… And I guess it would have been entertaining to see Ol' Bob come unglued. Talk about ratings. Dude had a resting heart rate of like… 12. RIP.

# CHAPTER 3
# Bridging The Gap

*"No other success can compensate for failure in the home."*

—*J.E. McCulloch*

When it comes to all things home, there are several *how to* videos on the Internet. There are even magazines and TV shows dedicated to the topics of the home. Yet, despite being bombarded with information, most homeowners are virtual amateurs when it comes to maintaining and repairing a house or structure correctly. Most of you are teachers, lawyers, doctors, pilots, and store clerks. You know your jobs well, and you can watch videos and ask home store clerks questions. However, unless you have the tools, money, skill set, physical ability, and stamina/muscle memory, it is best to allow experienced professionals to do what they do best. Trying to go it alone (and failing or creating a bigger problem) is a huge gap between homeowners and their homes.

Did you know that the *home* genre is among the most popular on television? Ratings prove it year after year. I was asked to host one of these home TV shows. At first I was excited, but after filming the pilot and reading future scripts and show topics, I knew it wasn't a fit. I couldn't pull it off. I was very unnatural while trying to make it work on camera. The premise of the show was untrue. The world of home ownership, interacting with contractors, and the role I would play doesn't happen in the real world. I found it curious that I was chosen for the part based on the fact that I was a real contractor (and not an actor). No matter what you see in commercials or in shows, just know that it took a lot of writing and editing before it got to you. The same thing is true with reality shows. I wasn't surprised that, as home genre TV programming caught fire, the number of average people wanting to get into the house-flipping and construction business increased dramatically. I understand how we can get inspired by seeing a kitchen or porch remodel in 16 minutes of airtime. Getting to pick out the tile, faucets, or paint colors is a poor representation of what it takes to remodel a kitchen correctly. Transforming almost any space can cost a lot of time and money. Injuries, codes violations, legal trouble, and even death are often a possibility when doing your own home projects. All the while, your soffit is falling down from water damage because nobody in your home cleaned the leaves out of the gutters. By the way, a soffit is the wood trim underneath the gutters. We turn a blind eye to the basics of simply maintaining the place. The joy of having the new blue tile and appliances pales with the misery of having to replace water-damaged soffits, roof trim, and gutters. **This thinking is a gap between homeowners and their homes.**

No matter how experienced and knowledgeable we are about our properties, chances are good that at one time or another, we are going to have to rely on experienced professionals for help. I don't know about you, but I don't want to be a slave to my house. I get tired. I hate back pain. I don't want to have to keep up with the latest and greatest structural findings out of Japan. So I ask, how experienced are you at interacting with contractors and sub-contractors? How often do you interact with the various trades? How extensive your understanding is of the various systems and materials at your house will determine the degree of success you will have interacting with the professionals (or nonprofessionals). Knowledge is good insurance. **Ignorance is a large gap between homeowners and their homes.**

Seasoned and successful contractors have mastered their relationship with homeowners. The good ones interact with homeowners daily or weekly. The sooner you and the contractor are in agreement with accurate scope of work, price, and timeline, the better your working relationship will be, and your projects and repairs will turn out better as a result.

Both you and the contractor are equally responsible for the outcome of projects and repairs. Merely blaming a contractor for a poor result doesn't always represent reality. Sometimes, a contractor does terrible work or rips you off. Even then, you still bear some responsibility. Perhaps you didn't check references. Perhaps you weren't thorough enough to explain your need or provide a description of your expectation. He cannot see what you picture in your mind. If he is skilled at communication, he will ask a lot of questions that better define your expectations. He may know how to lead you there. Likewise, if a project turns out amazingly well, you don't have to thank him repeatedly. Stop and give yourself a big pat on the back (and a cold beer). You were successful in picking the right contractor, defining your expectations, articulating the end goal, and upheld effective relationship management. **Not knowing that effective communication between you and a contractor will**

**determine the success of your projects is a gap between home-
owners and their homes.**

There are usually exceptions to rules. Good relationships
between people are all about communication, gut instinct, trust,
not being petty or prideful, and going the extra mile in a selfless
way. The payoffs, in whatever form, are what keep us coming back
for more. All successful relationships, like marriages, are built on
something larger than the individuals. Some people bind through a
hobby or religion. Successful golf partners put the integrity of the
game ahead of simply winning at all costs. Many marriages begin
at the altar, and God is placed as priority #1. In the case of home
projects and repairs, a good communal quality of life should remain
the fulcrum when approaching those who will provide the services.
Homeowners who *cheap out* and rely on *low bids* rarely attain value
and peace of mind. Contractors who show up merely for a paycheck
will let you down every time. They often have little pride, and it
shows in their work. I don't want anyone working for me if he is
watching the clock and doing the minimum just to get the check.
I am not increasing his quality of life, nor is he mine. If a project/
relationship is all about an individual, then both the individual and
the project are likely to suffer because of it. My home and quality
of life is important. I do not mind paying for value, and a good
contractor deserves to be paid for delivering that value.

Most of my experience is the product of having one foot firmly
in the contractor camp, while the other is in the homeowner camp,
just like you. Most of my contracting experience is in real estate
development, which can mean a host of things. In my case, it was
as the spec (speculative) builder. I bought the land, designed the
structure, then built the structure with the use of subcontractors.

Like the average homeowner, in my line of work, I had to pay these contractors/subcontractors to do the work at my property/project, just like you. I know exactly how it feels to make the decisions, learn materials and processes, hire people, and have to pay them. I have done it on a massive scale and subsequently mastered it. But keep in mind that most contractors are not builders. They are plumbers, roofers, brick masons, etc. The only skin they have in the game, usually, is their time, but there are contractors who will buy materials and pay their labor, but they know you are going to pay them (if you don't and they are licensed, then they can sue you and will likely win if they are organized). For the most part, they are paid for their knowledge, skill, and time. Meanwhile, the homeowner/payer is completely reliant on that contractor's skill, knowledge, and integrity. See how this works?

**Choosing the cheapest labor and materials while expecting a good outcome is a large gap between homeowners and their homes.** Remember, if you think a good contractor is expensive, consider how costly a lesser one could be. There is no project more expensive than the one that has to be done twice.

In closing, I am often witness to an amazing phenomenon when it comes to decisions made by house buyers, as few buyers really understand what they are purchasing. I mean, they understand it is a house in which they will live, and that this is the most money they will likely ever spend on something. The criteria upon which they base their decision to buy is based on location, price, number of rooms, and on some fantasies about the future, while they completely ignore the product that they are paying for. Some of you are thinking that the home inspection took care of that aspect. Think again. That subject is coming up. Here we are standing in our new house/condo with almost zero understanding of the systems, materials, elements, and skill which will keep it in good working order.

Think of it this way: if I ask you to tell me what you bought, you will probably look at me in a confused way and answer, "Well… I mean… It is a house. It has 4 bedrooms and three baths. It has a huge basement and cool outdoor living area…" As you go on and on, you are going to tell me, with ever-growing enthusiasm, about all of the great stuff at the house. I will bet that you will not answer, "Well… I bought pretty strong soil with quick refusal at the west end of the house and more clay at the east side (imminent foundation failure). It is a Tudor style with a tall roofline, 12:12 pitch, and 4" gutters (shedding failure, rapid wood rot, and foundation and basement wall failure). The tile floor was laid by hard working foreigners who didn't understand water to powder ratios for the thinset mix (cracked tile and grout within the first few years). There is custom trim and 22 degree ceiling joints (constant movement and nail pops at all joints with any changing exterior temperature). We also have a fireplace where there is no flue liner or fire rated brick (all the cinder, sparks, and ashes are being delivered directly into your attic. Fire is imminent). Yep… We just love our new place!"

So we sit at the closing table with this huge check that cannot be cancelled and have a home inspection report. What could possibly go wrong? I understand that the framing system or roof pitch and ice-shield are boring compared to the parties we will have here, how close it is to the office, and getting to choose tile for the backsplash. But know that as you sit at the closing table, you are walking straight into a huge gap between you and this house. Let's build the bridge so that you two can meet and shake hands.

# CHAPTER 4
# New Beginnings

*"Home is where my habits have a habitat."*

—*Fiona Apple*

You got through the lengthy home searches, earnest money, credit checks, blunders, closing documents, title search, and home inspection. But there are many other proverbial medals that need to be earned long after moving your furniture in.

All of these documents related to your home purchase need to be copied and kept in safe places in case of fire, flooding, or burglaries. These days, you will receive hard paper copies along with digital ones. Saving to the cloud isn't enough and risks being hacked. Keeping a record on a thumb drive is a good idea. Put that in the safe deposit box or at a family member's house.

Over the years, you will acquire a lot of receipts and invoices related to services and goods you have purchased to maintain and repair your property. Some expenses will be for routine maintenance, while others will relate to increasing the value of your property. These receipts and invoices should also be kept in a safe place, along with related ledgers. I keep the home improvement receipts and ledger separate from the maintenance/repairs receipts and ledgers.

In these ledgers, you will keep the receipts, dates of the receipts, reasons for the repair or improvement (brief description), service providers' names, and contact information. You will also note if the items have an accompanying warranty. When the HVAC fails, it is important to know who installed or repaired it (and when). If you discover that ABC HVAC Co. did the work and offered a 10 year parts and labor warranty, then you will know who to call. This could save you from service or repair bills that a different HVAC company would have charged for. It might also remind you of a contractor who provided excellent service, work, and price.

I keep home improvement receipts and invoices for tax purposes. Laws change frequently, but home-related tax laws remain fairly constant. There are benefits to having records of expenses for the improvement of your property. Your Certified Public Accountant (and some tax preparers) know the rules related to tax deductions. If the value of my property has doubled over a 12-year span, and I sell it, I stand to make a nice profit. I also stand to be taxed on my gains. I am pocketing $255,000 at the closing table (profit from equity), and I have receipts worth $100,000 representing property improve-ment expenses. I have profited by only $155,000. This would greatly reduce my tax liability. Of course, in the world of taxes, deductions, and homeownership, it is crucial that you enlist the advice of licensed tax professionals since there are capital gains exceptions.

Remember that a house can be expensive to maintain and improve. It is easy to misplace receipts, and sometimes we forget the details. Keeping ledgers and envelopes for receipts is easy. They are easy to update as well. This is a habit that can save you a lot of money and frustration.

If, someday, you decide to keep your property as a rental (instead of selling it), there is another set of rules related to taxation and deductions. A rental property becomes a business. Even though you still own the property, it is no longer your home. You are the business owner, manager, and primary investor. Many business expenses are tax deductible. With rental property, both residential and commercial, there is an opportunity to make monthly or annual profit, but the goal is to enrich yourself through increased equity over the term of the rental. Eventually, you may elect to sell the property; however, many tax implications may come into play. In order to avoid taxation on profits, invest a portion of the profit into another property. It is a good idea to consult with a CPA for guidance prior to engaging in real estate investing. Knowing the business you are getting into and having financial strategies for the future are ingredients in a strong business plan.

While we are on the subject of new beginnings, I would like to offer a solution to an age-old problem homeowners face. Prior to getting to that, keep in mind that when we first see a house (house shopping), we see our lives in that house, while also discovering things we would like to change about the place in order to further personalize it. Such changes could be as simple as wall color or as dramatic as doubling the size of the living area with an addition. Usually, if we can afford them early on, we make the desired changes. Fortunately, having a lack of extra money to make all the changes we would like can be a good thing. "Why would Wes suggest not doing projects that would make the place your own? After all, the place is empty, and you have another place to stay, which makes now the perfect time to create the house you have always envisioned!"

The reasons people purchase houses are often driven by some very strong psychological influences. When they look at a property for the first time, they are looking at a kitchen, or a living room, or a backyard. But what they are *really* seeing is a very powerful vision in their minds of their lives when occupying that house. The visions are of interacting with people, objects, and situations at some time in the future in that new place. As they walk through the house for the first time, they envision changes that they believe will enhance their lives. Many times, such changes could have a dramatic and positive effect on quality of life. But in most cases, it is not true. For example, I have witnessed couples who argue over a gas versus wood-burning fireplace or the placement of a water heater. These things are important to them at the time of purchase. They overlook other items that become important later. Such items could include: the light fixtures, the height of a bathroom vanity, or the shape of steps to a deck. Often, at the time of move in, they allocate money toward things that they may hardly notice after a couple years. As time goes by, quality of life declines as other needs arise that really will have an impact on quality of life. Unfortunately, there is no money left to address these more important things. In other words, please move in, take a deep breath, and get used to your new home before recklessly changing things that would otherwise have no positive impact.

A new house occupant should live there for a while in order to find out how the structure feels, lives, and contributes to his life. For example, people may spend money on furniture and musical instruments for a particular room, but soon discover that the room is terribly uncomfortable due to drafty windows or too hot because of the direct sun. Or, perhaps a new owner spends a fortune on a swimming pool with plans of entertaining others, but finds that the pool area eliminated parking for future guests.

Patience in spending not only applies to large ticket items, but to medium-sized purchases as well. For example, you may want granite countertops in the kitchen. This is an item that many homeowners tackle soon after purchase. The problem is that the owner didn't have several seasons to see how light affects this particular granite and finish throughout the year. How will the granite choice interact with the wall color, cabinet stain, flooring, appliances, and overall lighting? Granite is almost always a strong upgrade choice. But if the choice in granite reveals a wrong color or pattern at different times of day or year, it could affect the quality of life in this very important room. Remember, you will probably see the granite sample in a factory yard under the midday sunshine, or in some showroom/home improvement store where lighting is bound to be very different from that in your home. Granite is costly enough to warrant purchasing only once. Giving yourself a little time (4 seasons) in the kitchen will almost certainly help you make better decisions down the road.

Here is my advice: upon the purchase of your new house, keep a notepad in the kitchen or office. Make notes about the things you like and dislike about a room (kitchen, living room, master bath, etc.). It could be related to size, flow of foot traffic and noise, color, trim, or flooring. Write down changes that you might like to see in the room. Assign an estimated price/cost to the items. Wait six months and check your list. See how much of it is still desired. Add up the dollar value of the changes you wanted then, but no longer find important. If you find that all of the changes still ring true and for the same reasons, it may be time to make the changes one item at a time. You can also elect to put the list away and check it in another 6 months. A lot can happen in your life over the span of a year that could impact your needs or desires.

Most new homeowners get a little excited at first. We allow our dream vision of the place to get the best of us. The keys to successful project decisions are poise and discretion. Buy the property, move in, and live there for a while. Your lifestyle and surroundings will almost always tell you what you need or want, versus what you think you need based on immediate emotion. A friend of mine tells young people in love to wait four seasons prior to engagement and committing to marriage. Similar advice applies here.

Owning real estate is one of the key tenets to experiencing the *American dream*. Further, it is John Doe's best shot at creating personal wealth. In a democracy, citizens can decide by popular vote as to what the rules are and change them if they have a loud enough turnout. If a large group of people decide that they don't like people who eat ice cream or paint their houses orange, they can, as a group, vote to forcibly take that ice cream or orange house from the other person. Despite what is often taught in schools today, America is actually a constitutional republic as opposed to a *popular vote* democracy. This means that we are a nation of laws, and are represented by elected officials who are entrusted to keep and protect the rules while defending our rights. This is to ensure that your rights cannot simply be taken away because others, who outnumber you, don't like ice cream or orange houses. You reserve the right to keep and maintain your personal property and choices/lifestyle as you see fit (minus hurting others or breaking laws), regardless of your age, race, gender, religion, personal choices, ice cream, etc. Many people will fight this because they believe that their own feelings and perspectives are more important than yours and the rule of law in a constitutional republic. I often refer to the form of governing in a democracy as being nothing more than *mob rule* on a grand scale. In a communist nation such as North Korea, officials may simply take your property and life if they so choose.

There is the case of *eminent domain,* whereby a government (local/state/federal) may forcibly take your property in exchange for paying you fair market value for it. It is only supposed to be used for the welfare of the general public. If the governing body of the State of Florida has made the determination that a highway, airport, or bridge is in the public's best interest and your house is in its path, then they may take your house and pay you fair market value in exchange.

I believe the case for eminent domain can be abused. There have been cases where a *for-profit* entity has used this *tool* as a means to forcibly acquire residential property and build businesses, thereby displacing residents. Claims are made that the new building will facilitate commercial business that will employ a lot of people and increase tax revenues! I find this practice to be abhorrent in America. I would expect this kind of thing to happen only in third world countries. I further believe that if eminent domain is used by the government as a means to take private property from one citizen and give it to another as a means of making profit, then 100% of those profits should be given directly to those who were forced from their homes. After all, it is for the public good, right?

# CHAPTER 5
# Why We Bought Our Houses

*"A man travels the world over in search of what he needs and returns home to find it."*

—George Moore, *The Brook Kerith*

In college, I had a professor who claimed that the things that attract us to our partners in marriage are the same things we end up resenting about them. I wonder if the same principle applies to the houses and condos we purchase.

In the beginning, we fall in love with that master bathroom and all of its furnishings! The deep tub, walk in shower with handrails and product dispensers, granite countertops, and all of the towel slots above and below are so amazing! Within a year, we begin to feel like those bathroom walls are closing in on us. That warm and rustic look with the dark colors, elaborate cabinetry, and hardware begins to look busy and cluttered. We begin to envision a large, minimalist, industrial, and well-lit master bath where we can simply relax and *breathe easy* every morning and night.

We also fall in love with that huge deck! You feel like Mel Gibson in "The Patriot" and want to walk out to the middle of the deck, raise your arms, and scream, "Freedom!!" A year later, you realize that you would rather stay inside because the deck and searing sun are just too hot. The following spring, you realize that the deck needs to be pressure washed and re-stained every year. This love-hate phenomenon can apply to many things within a house.

You purchased a house because things about this particular property attracted you. After all, you borrowed a quarter of a million dollars, are paying interest for borrowing the money, and have contractually agreed to care for it for the next thirty years. You visited a lot of other prospective properties. Why did you pick this one over all of the others? Was it the location or price? Was it the color and finishes? Was it the school district? Perhaps it was because the bedrooms were huge. Or it may be a combination of many of these. Then again, it might be, like in most cases, because the minute you pulled up to the house, your subconscious took over. It took your conscious mind on a trip down Fantasy Lane. From that point forward, you no longer looked at the property and its various offerings. You suddenly were only able to see yourself in this property. After pulling up, you opened the front door and your eyes went straight to the fireplace. This is very common. You didn't see a mantle and gas logs. Instead, you envisioned the holidays snuggling by the fire, happy kids, and hot chocolate on Christmas morning! You then raced to the kitchen, which is the heartbeat of the home! You didn't see a large stainless refrigerator. You envisioned yourself opening the door and easily finding a marinated roast for the guests who are just waiting to have dinner with you in your new dining room! As the natural light draws you to the window overlooking the backyard, you don't see the bricks, pressure treated wood planks, and grass. What you see is your spouse with the kids in a future sandbox. You picture yourself at a future grill. Your fantasies were strong enough to go to contract with a seller. You had already started making the place a home without ever spending a night or speaking to a single neighbor. So, I began with the question of why you bought this particular house and offered some explanations related to location, schools, color, or size of rooms. In the end, I believe that it was a single thing that led you to the purchase, and that it far outweighed all other things; it was the picture in your mind's eye of you and your life there and at that structure. So, now is my chance to ask you whether you envisioned only the good, or did the fantasies also envision the bad, challenging, and heartbreaking? I realize it is human nature to envision all things good as we enter a prospective new house. It is when those fantasies become arrested by wrong wall colors, splintered decks, broken shutters, or bad smells that we move on to the next prospective house. You thought that the kitchen was too small. There wasn't enough natural light. In the end, it wasn't about the kitchen size or small windows. It was the fact that you couldn't envision your life in that space. That particular property didn't facilitate your fantasies. Keep in mind that this can happen before you ever enter the property. A house purchase is an extremely emotional decision and commitment. Let me further illustrate my theory with some hypothetical (yet common) scenarios:

YOU pictured yourself in that quiet and regal home office making calls and closing deals. Did you also envision yourself sitting in the deafening silence as you create your resume and make calls in search of a job? People get laid off.

YOU pictured yourself and friends gathered around that beautiful and large kitchen island on the Fourth of July! I assume you didn't picture contractors on ladders tearing out the ceiling and identifying all of the damage from the leaking tub directly above.

YOU pictured having some cold ones and grilling on that back deck. Did you picture your spouse passed out drunk in the lawn chair every night?

YOU pictured the kids playing in that finished basement. Did you also picture the basement flooded with three feet of water?

YOU loved the open floor plan and pictured a big happy family eating pizza after the baseball game. Did you also consider searching for privacy from your spouse, as divorce is imminent?

I realize these examples are dramatic and very much in contrast with your fantasies at the time of purchase, but understand that they are extremely common and can happen to anyone. The business of buying and selling property is full of people hoping that you cling to your emotions and fantasies. Remember that in life, there is good and bad. Both happen in the home, since it is the place where all of the important things in your life come together. Make sure that when you purchase and live your life in that place, you keep one foot in reality. Do not go from day to day considering only how life can or may be; consider how life is.

# CHAPTER 6
# How Much Do You Know?

*"I came from a broken home. My bedroom window was cracked."*

—*Jarod Kintz, Seriously Delirious but not all that Serious*

You have heard the saying that nobody cares how much you know until they know how much you care. Well, let's apply that kind of thinking to this house of yours. Nobody cares how much you know except your lenders, insurance agents, family members, neighbors, and HOA members. I wonder how much you know about this thing you bought called "home." How well do you understand the nature of the expenses and the maintenance needs that come with the place? I want to increase your daily awareness about your house, and since knowledge is king, the more of it you have, the richer and more powerful you are. Being prepared with knowledge is critical to surviving the unexpected. So, here are some questions. Keep track of how many answers you get right.

- Why should you have your chimney inspected?
- Your house has a master water shut off valve. Where is it?
- What is the most infectious appliance in your home?

- What is the #1 contributor to quality of life in your home?
- Name two reasons you might use primer.
- How often should you check your fire extinguishers?
- If you notice that a nail is backing out, what should you do?
- What does it mean when tree leaves bloom and form in clumps?
- What did your builder do with the construction trash/debris?
- Should you lend your tools to a neighbor?
- If a neighbor's tree falls on your house, does his insurance pay?
- What is the difference between a *general* and *sub*contractor?
- Why should you save all house improvement receipts?
- What is the difference between caulk and silicone?
- Name 3 major events that affected housing trends in America.
- Why is it a bad idea to pressure wash concrete?
- Give two reasons a contractor might decline to work for you.
- Define the term "storm chaser."
- What is the most common do-it-yourself project?
- Name 5 tools every homeowner must own.
- Give 3 examples of bad behavior by a neighbor.
- Name the 3 most common causes of house fires.
- What is the most flammable system in a home?
- Name 5 venting systems in a home.
- Name 5 annual inspections you should perform on your home.
- What purpose do breakers serve?
- Why should you turn water valves off, then on every month?
- Name one reason why a water heater can break down.

- What is the belt buckle rule?
- What causes a yellow stain on a ceiling?
- What is the cause of a black stain on a ceiling?
- What is the #1 enemy to the exterior of your house?
- Who is responsible for repairing a broken water pipe?
- Can your homeowner's insurance policy be cancelled?

# CHAPTER 7
# The Home Inspection

*"Trust me, you can dance."*

—*Wine*

I find the home inspection to be similar to getting a physical from my doctor. I may feel pretty good and not notice any unusual aches or pains, but in the back of my mind, there is a fear that test results could come back with terrible news. We don't get physical exams because we know everything is fine. We get them in case something is wrong that we cannot see or feel. We also want to know because if something is out of whack, we can address it before it becomes worse. When we make an offer on a house, we hope that everything in the house works just fine. And just like the doctor ordering a physical exam, ordering a home inspection is imperative, just in case something is wrong. Many mortgage lenders now require a home inspection. They don't want to lend money for a disaster any more than you want to get stuck with one.

In America, industries largely operate in similar ways. Meat packing plants follow strict health regulations. Most physicians approach the physical exam in similar ways. The average physical includes a blood pressure check, height and weight measuring, cholesterol screening, and a few other tests. Mature men might be interested in kidney function, prostate, kidney and liver health, and lung strength. Physicians also have a governing set of principles and laws they must follow. The tests given to a patient during a physical exam are similar from coast to coast and doctor to doctor. Days later, the physician will consult with the patient to go over the test results. He may say that everything looks great, or he may say that you need to change your diet or get more exercise.

Home inspectors and their inspections can significantly vary from one to the other and from city to city. As a rule, there is no governing set of objective standards (as there are in medicine, the food industry, or home appraisals for example). One inspector may perform a simple "walk through," making sure the appliances work. A different inspector may examine every square inch of a property during a period of four hours. In these extreme examples, both inspections would be short-changing the buyer and the seller.

Since buyers (or their mortgage lenders) typically choose to have a home inspection, it might make sense that they should request the most thorough and toughest inspector possible, but this isn't always a good idea. A *gung ho* and exceedingly critical inspector can ruin a deal for a buyer by scaring him or her, and the potential for the sale is lost. More often than not, this breed of home inspector is driven by his own insecurity and desire to make himself appear smarter than other inspectors. Many home inspectors are failed contractors or failed codes department inspectors. I want the home inspection to reveal items that need immediate attention and those which can cause problems later. I do not want the home inspector to color a report with his personal opinions about certain brands or be hypothetical about systems that he has not mastered himself. I do not want him to intentionally scare buyers and alarm sellers. There is a saying that we are entitled to our own opinions, but we are not entitled to our own facts. Many buyers are scared out of a purchase by an unreasonable inspector and a hypercritical report. In many of these cases, the house would have made a great home and simply needed a little attention here and there. Likewise, there have been many negligent home inspections as well. These reports can leave buyers trusting that they made a great purchase, only to discover later that they are chained to a piece of junk.

Years ago, I built and marketed gorgeous and high quality historically styled houses. When I build, I am present at all phases of the project. Each project is built correctly and with premium materials. I take pride in my structures and approach each new build with the goal of the house serving the new owner, and not the other way around. A thorough marketing effort brought potential buyers. One such prospect made her offer, and we went to contract. In that contract, she included a normal contingency that was based on a successful home inspection. Her realtor secured the services of a local home inspector. On the afternoon of the inspection, the buyer and her father accompanied the inspector to the property. This particular inspector was known as "The Deal Killer" in contractor and mortgage lender circles. As this buyer and I visited in the kitchen, the home inspector went to a far corner of the living room to change into his inspection suit. He strapped *this* on his arm and *that* onto his leg. He then filled his many pockets with every imaginable gizmo and God knows what. He had a flashlight on his forehead and another strapped to his right shoulder. He wore pads that rivaled those worn in the NFL. Basically, he looked like a Ghostbuster on crack. I wish I had taken a picture. It would have certainly gone viral.

I knew that my project was flawless and had no defects. I had disclosed that the crawl space door had yet to have its lock installed. The inspector began his inspection (if that is what you want to call it). He appeared to be performing a séance in one room. He lay on the floor in another to get a better look at the new hardwoods. He rolled marbles, took measurements, and smelled the window casing at the back door. The inspector finally went outside and disappeared. He was under the house in the crawlspace. We heard a loud banging noise and felt the floor shake under us. It happened twice more. I ran to the crawl space opening and yelled for him. He didn't answer. I yelled again and he replied, "Almost finished."

He then emerged and went to his truck. He sat in his truck working on the report. Fifteen minutes later, he came into the house and addressed the buyer. He went over his report with her, showing her pictures and offering his opinions. I went to another room to offer them privacy. When they finished, I asked to see the report. He set a stack of papers and digital photo displays on the granite kitchen island. The pictures were of water supply lines that were not connected (bathroom faucet), an electrical wire that had been torn loose from its fasteners under the house, and an active air duct supply line that was on the floor of the crawlspace. Finally, there was a major support beam that had been removed, and was laying on the main air trunk line. Remember the banging noise and shaking floor? I grew furious in my disbelief over what had just happened. Rarely have I acted physically when angry. This time was the exception.

In the awkward, yet quick events that followed, both the buyer and her father became scared and left the property. I called the police and made a full report that he had vandalized my property. I also made a lengthy report to the Department of Metro Government and Housing Authority. I would later drop the charges in exchange for his agreement to never engage in the business of inspecting homes again. He was fined for not being correctly licensed or insured. The following day, I received a call from the prospect's real estate agent, informing me that the buyer had cancelled the contract based on the findings in the inspector's report. I accepted, but received another offer the following week and sold the property. What is sad about this whole situation is that the first prospect could have had an amazing and high quality home had it not been for *The Deal Killer*. Further, to date, she would be sitting on approximately $600,000 in equity because of soaring property values in that neighborhood. That event took place 12 years ago.

There is another, opposite approach to home inspections. This took place in 2009. You may remember that we were in the second year of the Great Recession. I was heavily leveraged financially, and had used banking stocks for collateral to help finance some very large and grand house builds. I had also invested a tremendous amount of my own money into the projects. Home sales were at a record low and bank stock values had tanked. All builders, mortgage lenders, and realtors were *running for the hills* as the housing and banking industries were in free-fall. Still, I believed in my projects. Since I designed and built them myself, I believed them to be superior to the *McMansions* that were my competitors. Certainly my projects would sell despite the economy. In some ways, I was correct. The last house project I had in my possession was my favorite project ever.

It was a huge American Foursquare in the most desirable neighborhood in my city. A highly creative marketing effort attracted a particular buyer. They made an offer with the usual contingencies. We closed on the property and to date, they still live there and we have become very close. Prior to the close, their realtor visited me at the site and told me that a home inspection had been scheduled for later in the week. I asked for the name of the inspector. When she told me, I couldn't believe her answer. It turns out that the home inspector was the builder of the high-end houses up the street that were also for sale. I asked, "Are you telling me that you hired my competitor to do the home inspection on my property? This is a massive conflict of interest. This is like having McDonald's do the health inspection on the Burger King next door. The answer is NO and NO is a complete sentence." She assured me that he had a great reputation as a home inspector and that he promised to be fair. I told her to find a different inspector.

The buyer and I had already formed a good and trusting relationship. He called and told me that he was aware that the house met or exceeded federal, state, and local codes requirements. He also said that the inspection was merely a formality and was ordered by his mortgage lender. I also knew that my own financial situation was getting worse, and that I really needed to close on this house. I was in a tight spot. I told the buyer that I would allow the builder/inspector to do the home inspection and that I would be present. I also told him to let the inspector know that if there were any false claims or opinions given in a formal report, I would sue him.

On the day of the inspection, I greeted the inspector and told him that if he needed my assistance, I would be present. He remained cool and agreeable as he entered the house. For the most part, he kept his hands in his pockets as he walked from room to room. He looked up at the lighting and down to the magnificent hardwoods. He pointed to the crown and complimented it. The inspection took him less than five minutes. He shook my hand, thanked me for my time, and complimented my work. His subsequent, yet short report to the buyer was 100% positive. So what are you thinking at this point? I hope that you see the grave injustice the inspector did to his customers (the lender and the buyer). Remember that I was promised that the inspector would be objective and fair. In the end, he was neither. Further, he was paid $500 for a four-minute stroll through the house. How well did he serve his customer? He didn't check a single outlet for power or proper grounding. He didn't look at the HVAC systems. He didn't try a single faucet. He never asked for inspection tags issued by the codes inspectors. He didn't flip a single light switch. I pride myself on doing every project correctly from start to finish, but this inspector didn't know my work or me personally. What if I had been a hack builder who never pulled a building permit? What if the crawlspace had become a lake? This happens often. In this case, the buyer gave me a million-dollar cashier's check based largely on the report that this inspector gave him.

In both of these examples, you can see where a home inspector potentially hurt buyers and sellers. That being said, I have also known many highly qualified home inspectors who do their jobs with integrity. These are true professionals who keep the welfare of their clients as a priority. This is also why they are successful at what they do. Make sure that the home inspector you hire has strong references, and is well known in the industry as having integrity and the ability to be objective. When reading a home inspection report, be thorough but do not be scared by anything in the report. Keep an open mind and a willingness to learn about each line item. A loose gutter, some moisture in the crawlspace, and a deadbolt that needs adjusting are poor reasons to reject an otherwise magnificent home. Keep in mind that an undetected pinhole in a roof shingle can have far worse consequences than an outlet that doesn't work. Home inspectors cannot see a pinhole in a shingle. Home inspections rarely include the condition of a chimney. Creosote build-up or cracked brick inside of the chimney are common causes of house fires. Home inspections rarely include mold or radon testing. It is a good idea to meet with a trusted general contractor or home expert to help you understand the home inspection report. An experienced general contractor can identify where a pressure washer has been used to remove mold or algae. He can tell if a pressure washer has been used to clean a driveway, thus fracturing the integrity of the concrete's protective top layer. This is important because a new driveway can become compromised and begin to fail in a short amount of time without its protective top layer. He can also identify if the gutter size and downspout placement are adequate, given the pitch of a roof. He will also be able to tell you if water is a problem at the property. In other words, is there a mold, algae, flooding, pooling, or drainage issue? Evidence of such issues can be remedied short-term using pressure washers, pavers, and paint. An experienced general contractor is difficult to fool. You see, the home inspection report is time-stamped and dated. That report only takes into account a point in time and not the past or future of, and at, the property. You need to know what you are buying today, but also what the house will require long after you leave the closing table.

There is another inspection report that you must perform prior to purchasing a house. Did you drive by the property at night or over the weekend? Did you drive from the property to your job one morning? Did you see if you were able to back out of the driveway at rush hour? Have you taken a walk on that street or jogged it? Have you met the neighbors? Have you seen the house at night? Did you check the crime map to see how safe the neighborhood is? Do you know who lives next door? You see, most home searches take place on quiet and sunny Sunday afternoons when all conditions are ideal. Rarely do people house shop on dark and rainy days or during rush hour. Spending thirty minutes at a property in perfect conditions is a poor way to sample what life will be like after this expensive purchase. This is where your personal home inspection should take place. Nobody but you knows how you will feel about traffic, neighbors, noises, smells, crime events, and night lighting at that property.

In closing, keep in mind that there is so much more to learn about a property than what is found in a home inspection report. Since you have connected with this particular home, your decision is largely emotional. Take time to get to know the house, yard, and neighborhood prior to making an offer. If you are in a hurry to purchase a property and in a seller's market, you may not have the time to do the due diligence. This means that you may be in a hurry, and could make a very serious and expensive mistake. A seasoned and quality realtor will represent your best interests here and give you every possible "out" prior to making a formal offer on a property. Prior to going to contract with a buyer's agent, make sure to ask him what measures he will take to protect you in a seller's market.

## CHAPTER 8

# Your House: A Home or An Investment?

Is your house an investment? It can be. Your property can be a great financial or personal investment, made with the intention of pay-offs that are both financial and personal. There are many people who have made fortunes in real estate. Some of these people (and corporations) did so with their own houses, while others did it by investing in property. And the more you know about real estate, the more likely you will profit as a real estate investor.

If you purchased your house with the primary goal of finan-cial returns via increased value (equity), I assume you purchased the property at or near a wholesale price, and that you have the knowledge and means to improve the property to increase its value. There are those who purchase houses in areas that are predicted to experience handsome increases in value over a relatively short span of time. Buying a house strictly for the returns is fine with me, but before closing, make certain to calculate the expenses you will incur during ownership. These expenses will significantly affect the financial return at the time you sell. You will have recurring expenses such as mortgage payments and mortgage insurance, property taxes, and homeowner's insurance. You will also have the expenses of normal upkeep, repairs, and improvements. These expenses are often overlooked at the time of purchase. When it comes time to sell, you will also experience closing costs. These costs might be real estate commissions, marketing expenses, improvements, and other closing costs. This figure is typically represented as a percentage of the sale price and can be as high as 10% (with 9% being a common amount). In this scenario, you are really acting as a small-time real estate investor and treating your house more as a business venture.

Another factor that is often miscalculated is the amount that the property will be worth at a particular time in the future. It is true that the majority of real estate value increases over time. It is also true that recessions happen. Neighborhoods and even small cities can experience long-term economic stagnation with plummeting real estate values. This happens in small towns that cannot attract strong businesses. It has also been experienced by sections of large cities (Detroit, Flint, Cleveland, Los Angeles, etc.) that fall into decay. There are quiet and settled neighborhoods that experience population increases for a multitude of reasons. Sadly, many older homes are torn down and replaced by new and larger houses. The reasons can be complex. Existing home values plummet since the properties become worth only the land value.

Consider how incredibly popular and valuable the properties in downtown Detroit were during the early 1900s. Detroit may be one of the greatest American success stories, but it is also one of the greatest embarrassments in our country's history. Over time, this booming industrial fortress grew to be one of the greatest manufacturing cities in history. Detroit and its manufacturing were the gold standard, and a shining example for all other manufacturers around the world. The city, its quality of life, and its real estate experienced the greatest increase in value since the advent of the train. Today, much of it has become what appears to be a war torn and bombed out city following World War II.

In contrast, East Nashville has become famous worldwide, and is considered the *coolest* urban renewal campaign in the country. Twenty years ago, an F-5 tornado ripped through the heart of Nashville. It came from the west, plowed through downtown, and marched straight into historic East Nashville. At that time, East Nashville had become home to violent gangs, drug addicts, and impoverished elderly residents. Property values decreased as houses and neighborhoods continued to decay. The tornado changed all of that by destroying a lot of houses and trees. Initially, there was no effort to rebuild the neighborhoods. Within 2 years, developers, builders, and confident amateurs began to purchase properties for next to nothing. They invested money and time into restoring East Nashville, one house at a time. People fell in love with the historic architecture, sense of community, and affordability of the restored houses. In 1998, a house in East Nashville might have cost $20,000. Today, you cannot purchase a house for less than $400,000. I bought mine for $155,000 and sold it for $600,000 many years ago.

Depending on where you live, you may experience only a minimal increase in the value of your property as time passes. In other places, homebuyers soon hit the jackpot. Timing is everything. The *golden rule* in purchasing property is "location, location, location." My golden rule is "location, timing, financial reserves."

If you purchase a house for $250,000 with the hope that you can sell in 5 years for $300,000, you plan to make $50,000 for doing nothing more than purchasing the house and living there. It certainly looks like a good return. But if I dig a little deeper, I estimate your closing costs will be approximately $27,000. If you spent $15,000 on the new bathroom, paint, flooring, and back deck, so far, you stand to profit $8,000. That is still a good return. Of course, that number is hypothetical and doesn't take into account increased property taxes, a recession whereby your property drops in value by 10%, and unexpected replacement costs for the HVAC system, the water heater, the roof, or windows. So much for success as a real estate investor...

Another factor that can greatly affect the value of a property is its exact location. According to the National Association of Realtors, house values can be adversely or positively affected by other nearby properties. Let's say that there are two identical houses and one is located next to the park while the other, two blocks away, is adjacent to a homeless shelter. The house near the shelter will have a lower property value than the house located next to the park. People would generally choose to live next to a park or state wildlife refuge than a homeless shelter or nightclub. People are generally willing to pay more for a property that is perceived as safer or is more likely to increase in value. This follows the simple rule of supply and demand.

If you purchased your house because it is where you want to live, then let's switch gears. The house purchase and subsequent expenses are certainly an investment, but this type of investment takes into account not only financial returns, but also the personal returns that are associated with quality of life. Most of the expenses (investments) you have in this house will be in an effort to keep it well-maintained and well cared for in order for it to serve you and your family. Even though the payback in this scenario is more of an intrinsic return on investment, there is also likely to be a financial reward at the time of sale. The decisions you make related to the time and effort you invest in the house will determine how this house pays you back. In other words, you are making the house an integral part of your overall quality of life, and it becomes *home*!

In many of the great American suburbs, steady increases in home values tend to remain predictable. It is not the place to get rich quickly. The suburbs can, however, be the place to make a great home based on quality of living in a quiet, safe, and affordable neighborhood. Schools tend to be rated higher in the suburbs, and it is more likely that you would live among people with similar interests and lifestyles. According to Forbes, the average American home in a suburb can double in value every 12-16 years.

Many of the choices you make can have a great impact on the value of your property. One of the most rewarding things about owning a home is that you can *make it your own*! You get to paint the walls with your favorite colors and decorate in a way that suits you. You get to decide where plants go or how short to cut the grass. Of course, depending on your neighborhood, there may be certain guidelines and rules set and enforced by Homeowner Associations (HOAs). Freedom also comes with responsibility. You have the freedom to do whatever you would like *only* until it encroaches on the freedoms of another.

Have you ever driven through a beautiful neighborhood and among the homes is a house painted in bright orange or turquoise blue? There are yards that are manicured, but perhaps you see a house where the lawn is overgrown and there is a broken down car in the front yard. The orange house, the trashed front yard, and a host of other eyesores are all the result of choices made by owners. Such choices not only impact the value of the orange house, but those of nearby properties as well. Call me crazy if you'd like, but I prefer to relax on my back deck and oversee my beautiful yard. as opposed to a view of Mr. Johnson's best attempt at a landfill.

When you have your house appraised, the appraiser is assigning a monetary value to the property and the improvement (house). His opinion of the property may begin long before he arrives. He likely knows the neighborhood, surrounding neighborhoods, and other properties nearby that are similar to the subject. He further formulates an opinion once he pulls into the driveway and sees the actual property. People often make deeply personal and sometimes *weird* choices when it comes to modifications to their homes. In most cases, it is their right to do so. If attempting to increase your property value, remember that the color purple is best left to clothing, tattoos, and movie titles - and not house color. If 98% of all homebuyers detest a purple house, that means that a very small percentage of prospective buyers would like one. The purple house has less value than the tan one. The appraisal will reflect this because lenders base their loans on the value of the property. The owner of the purple house will have to lower the sale price of the house. A buyer may then step up and buy the house with the intention of using some of the savings for new paint (and preferably not orange).

There is a beautiful home that sits among the others in the third wealthiest zip code in the country. The houses are old, large, and stately. Many of the owners are descendants of forbearers who lived there. The west side of the house serves as a canvas for the owner. A few times each year, he hires artists to cover the wall in designs and messages. Sometimes, the art is abstract, and sometimes the wall is covered in intentional graffiti. The choice in artwork by the homeowner is eccentric, to say the least. His choice in art appeals to very few, and subsequently, the value of the property next door is jeopardized.

In closing, I would like to address the investment subject one more time. Janice purchased her house for $300,000. Over an eight-year period, her property increased in value by $300,000 and is worth $600,000. If Janice sells the house, did she profit $300,000? In this case, Janice has had many expenses over the eight years she has lived there. She paid a lot of mortgage interest over the eight-year term, but fortunately was able to write that off on her taxes (the laws have changed recently). Janice had the yard mowed for $30 per week (during the growing season). Her mowing expenses over the eight years total $5,700. She also replaced bulbs, built a deck, had a bathroom remodeled, and added granite, paint, and new cabinets to the kitchen. She even had HVAC repairs and bought a new water heater and windows. She paid property taxes and insurance. These things cost her $64,000 over the span of eight years. Janice had closing costs of $43,000. This means that she is not profiting $300,000. So far, it appears that she will profit around $187,000. There is more to it. Janice has to account for her time spent on the house and assign a value to it. If she has invested 2,000 hours of time in upkeep, chores, and routine maintenance, and assigns a value of $40/hour to her labor, then her time investment equals $80,000. That means her true return is more in the range of $107,000. That is just over 35% of what she claims to have profited. She will need to use that toward a down payment on the next house she buys. Hey, the return is handsome! Don't get me wrong. But it is important to add what it costs to own the property in order to get an accurate return on your "house" investment over the course of living there. Also keep in mind that many houses around the country do not double in value every eight years!

Next door, Jimmy reads about this huge profit that has fallen into Janice's lap. He wants in on the action! It would be hard to blame him. Jimmy is an excellent mechanic, but rarely works because he likes whiskey and sleeping in. He hasn't spent time or money for maintenance on his house. The roof leaks, the shutters have rotted, and many have fallen off. His windows are old and drafty, and the inside is a disaster. Jimmy is a positive man, however. He goes to the store and buys a For Sale by Owner sign (and a lottery ticket) and puts the sign in his front yard. He doesn't want to pass up the opportunity to get rich! He was unable to secure a realtor to list his house for $600,000. There are a few who offer to buy his house for $200,000 with the intention of restoring and selling the house for $600,000. Jimmy decides to drink more whiskey and just *hold out* for now.

If the payout for owning your house is merely a hard number, then you must also take into account what you paid for the house, closing costs, upgrades you have made, maintenance expenses, your time, and selling costs. However, if you take into account your experience and the positive effects on the quality of life while you have been there, you may have profited in many more ways than just financially.

# CHAPTER 9
# Return On Investment (ROI)

The first time I hosted a radio show, it was broadcast from a historically significant radio station. My show blasted across the airwaves to most states east of the Mississippi River, and was dedicated to remodeling with the emphasis on the return on investment that it could bring. Someone in Ohio wanted to know the increased property value by adding a garage, while another in Atlanta questioned the increased property value of adding a new kitchen. Though I tried to keep the show light and humorous, what listeners didn't know was that I stayed buried in statistics about the subject. I could have gone on the air and simply recited the statistics and trends, but that would have been as entertaining as listening to an auto mechanic recite wrench and bolt sizes. What the listeners and I discovered, in pretty short order, was that each of their situations were unique to them. A new kitchen for a single male in the northeast differed significantly in price and design from the installation of a new kitchen in the southeast for a large family. The Internet often fails to take into account regional differences such as lifestyles, cultures, construction costs, and societal trends. These things are ever changing, but once an Internet article is published, it is locked in time (for the most part) as the original contribution. And if the information is untrue or outdated, the contribution is rarely taken down or corrected/updated. The Internet also doesn't address, in real time, the unique needs from person to person. A bathroom for a severely handicapped person will require items that differ significantly from those needed by a professional baseball player.

There was a time when home elements that facilitated the needs of a handicapped person carried little value to the average homebuyer. Strange vanity or countertop heights, toilet heights, ramps, or rudimentary automation were seen as weird. The masses wanted modern and *cool*. Today, houses that offer ADA (American Disabilities Act) elements such as differing countertop heights, walk-in showers, grab bars, or ramps can now carry value that non-ADA compliant properties lack. Our aging Baby Boomer population is the one with all of the money. They are also the ones who now undergo hip and knee replacements. These folks would like a house with wide hallways and grab bars in showers. Baby Boomers are now experiencing the onset of dementia and Alzheimer's at an increasing rate. Wheelchair ramps are a value to this segment of our large and aging population.

Owning a house can bring with it a set of perils and unforgiving, steep learning curves. It makes sense to spend money and time to make the house fit you and your lifestyle, thereby adding to your quality of life, resulting in an intrinsic payoff. Unlike the negative impact of painting your house purple to personalize it, many of the choices you make can also bring value to a future buyer/occupant at your property. Owning a house can be one of the greatest experiences you will ever have. Making the most of your investment will bring returns both now and in the future.

As a consultant, I am presented with situations that require an objective approach. Such situations are related to a great variety of choices homeowners need or want to make. Most of these situations are also inspired by homeowners in search of some increase in the quality of their lives. In order for me to have a meaningful impact on their respective goals, I ask a lot of questions to find out what an increased quality of life really means to them. I cannot give them the answer in most cases. We simply have to arrive there together. I act as a facilitator. In one case, I visited a couple that wanted a new kitchen and asked for help in the design and budgeting. I like the idea of kitchen remodels. They can really increase the quality of life for the homeowner, and also add a nice return on investment. Remodeling a kitchen will almost always increase the value of a house and make it sell faster. To most of us, being told that someone wants a new kitchen seems simple enough, but notice that this couple used the words *new, design,* and *budget*. To me, *new* means that the entire existing kitchen is going in the trash. In other words, nothing about the existing kitchen works for them. To me, *help with the design* means that they are unclear of exactly how the finished product will look and act. To me, the word *budget* means that they likely have a limit on how much they can allocate towards a new kitchen. A new kitchen can range in price from $8,000 to $120,000. All three words are huge, and can mean so many different things depending on the person. I ask the homeowners what these words mean to them personally. Within the hour, I am able to formulate a plan and begin to budget. What we discovered was that they didn't need a new kitchen after all. They felt cramped when working in there together, which created tension between them. They also lacked storage, and as a result, the countertops became useless and cluttered. This meant that making meals was exhausting and time consuming. Kitchen remodels are usually the most expensive, disruptive, and challenging projects homeowners can face. Keep in mind that I wasn't there to close on a deal to contract with them to build a new kitchen; I was there to solve problems.

I sketched the room on graph paper with the existing footprint, cabinet, and appliance locations. I walked through the adjacent rooms as well. I showed them things about the kitchen that I would change to address their issues. The existing upper cabinets were fine. The bottom cabinets could be replaced with new cabinets that complemented the existing ones. The new bottom cabinets would double storage capacity. New large countertops in a lighter color and different material would offer more counter space, add light to the room, and appear to open it. The room behind a small kitchen wall was that of a larger and formal dining room. If we borrowed a 16 square ft. (4 ft. by 4ft.) section of that room, we could build a large pantry for food, cleaning products, and general storage. In the dining room, we could install built-in shelving on either side of the pantry protrusion with recessed lights and glass shelves (since the pantry would need electricity for lighting). The last item would be to repaint the top cabinets a color to complement the color of the new bottom cabinets. We could also repaint the kitchen walls and add a complementing tile backsplash. The price tag for the proposed changes would be approximately $14,000. A brand new kitchen would have cost almost $25,000. In this case, the couple easily increased the value of their house by $14,000, giving them a 100% return on investment. It also eliminated the negative impact that the older kitchen elements had on the family's quality of life.

About eight years ago, a homeowner called to ask my opinion about a master bathroom remodel. The reason she cited for the change was that she loved the color blue, and that the blue would "make the space *fun*." She had already collected samples of colors in the form of paint chips, swatches, tiles, and countertop material. At this point, are we all thinking that the project should turn out nicely? First, strong primary colors (such as the color blue) can be tricky. There are huge differences from one blue to another. Whites and grey are far more forgiving. I listened to her and looked at the colors she wanted. I wondered if she might be color blind or shade blind. The tile floor sample was of an expensive and special order cobalt blue. The toilet was refurbished in the color of turquoise. The sink and countertop were designer-grade, and in differing shades of navy blue. The expensive backsplash material (metal) and light fixture were different shades of powder blue. Yes, this is a true story. So far, can you and I agree that we are headed for disaster? I priced her project at around $12,000. When presented with my forecasted costs, she was mortified. I asked her why she had such affection for the color blue. She told me that she loves the color blue and that it makes her feel happy. I asked her why. She told me that her dad had a blue bathroom, and she grew up using his bathroom to get ready for school. "I just love the color, and I spend a lot of time in my bathroom." To boot, her mother, a retired interior designer, was moving in with her. The mother had not yet seen the color choices. What an emotional fiasco this could turn into. This was a tough one because for me to help her create a lasting, affordable, and valuable space, I was going to have to tangle with some very deep-seated emotions. I asked her if she could give the project a little time so she and I could think of ways to reduce the costs. She agreed. About a month later, we met at her house. I showed her some ideas that incorporated only the navy and the light blue. I also showed her how white walls, sink, toilet, and bath could really bring out the blue accents. The navy and the powder blue were approximately the same color, differing only in depth/shade. I convinced her to hang artwork or towels that were composed of the other blue colors that I believe clashed. This way, the atrocious blue could easily be removed or changed out at little to no cost. In other words, they were temporary. Down the road, if she realized her mistakes and began to hate the color blue, she could simply remove those elements. Changing out countertops, toilets, backsplashes, and flooring is expensive. The change in plans reduced the budget from $12,000 to $7,000. It also increased the value of her house. Doing it her way would have decreased the value of her house and diminished her quality of life. Over time, she would have probably grown to detest the bathroom. For her to have done nothing to that particular room would have appraised higher than a bathroom left to her design. Her deeply emotional choices were unlikely to appeal to anyone else (unless that person had grown fond of a Turkish prison... Please see <u>Midnight Express</u>). Allowing your emotional and "twelve year old" inner child to make critical decisions as an adult rarely ends well. Her need for a new bathroom had nothing to do with the bathroom. Her need was based on trying to emotionally capture a time in her past and closeness to her father, now gone.

Several years ago, I had a neighbor who was living as a renter. At the time, we were in a neighborhood that was on a fast track to experience soaring home values. She had an opportunity to purchase a house a couple of blocks away at a great wholesale price. As a favor, I visited the prospective house to help her decide if the purchase was a wise one. She bought the house and began to make it her own. I visited a few times and our relationship drifted apart. Years later, I saw her in a home improvement store. We greeted each other, but she seemed distant. I asked about the house. She must have been saving up her anger for a long time because she told me that the house was terrible. She told me that she regretted buying a house, and that she would never do it again. Her tone and words were fueled by her anger, and it was clearly directed at me. I calculated that she must have experienced at least $400,000 in increased equity since we last saw one another. I set my pride aside and asked why her experience had been so poor. I learned something very important as she answered. Her primary complaint was that the house required maintenance and that the utility bills were awful. Things were always in need of repair. The house was freezing in the winter and sweltering in the summer. Her dogs were muddy all of the time. It dawned on me that some people are better left to be perpetual renters. That is not a bad thing. There are 43,000,000 rental properties in America, and millions of renters experience an excellent quality of life in those homes. I suppose at the time, I encouraged her to purchase because I only saw the benefit of her experiencing an anticipated and handsome return on investment. What I failed to take into account when urging her to purchase was that she had no skill set, money, time, or desire to repair, restore, and maintain a property. Thus, owning a house caused her quality of life to plummet. Further, she felt chained to the house. It is terrible that her life had been miserable because of the house. As I look back now, I believe that she suffered from manic-depressive symptoms not related to homeownership. I doubt she will *ever* experience a rich, full, and healthy quality of life. The house was the focal point of whatever it was that troubled her. It was probably easy for her to blame the house and me. She did make the purchase as an adult.

What makes ROI (Return On Investment) even more dynamic is that it is a fluid number. It takes into account a project and added value to your home, but neglects to do so with an extra element called "time." If you're getting your house ready for market and believe that a new kitchen is in order, you may be right. You may be able to sell your house at a higher price than you can with the older kitchen. The new kitchen costs $25,000. An appraisal at that time may show that the house has increased in value by $25,000. However, when you sell the house years later, you may discover that the kitchen carries an increased value of $50,000. That is a nice return on investment. Further, your house is likely to sell faster than other houses with older kitchens. But why would you build a new kitchen then sell the property merely to just get the kitchen investment money back? In other words, get a new kitchen for you and enjoy it while you are there! Make sure the choices you make in finishes will appeal to buyers down the road as well. If your new kitchen is appealing and done correctly, you will get an immediate return on investment in physical and emotional value, as well as a financial return at the time of sale. Had you left the older kitchen in place, your home may not sell at the higher pric,e nor would you get the payoff of a new kitchen while there. The appraiser report would show that the existing kitchen had no meaningful impact on the selling value of the property. In these examples, the new kitchen would bring increased financial returns on investment and increased quality of life.

When we make investments, we do so with the expectation that there will be a positive return in some form. The return could be in the form of money or emotional benefits. Often, it is a combination of the two. In the end, what we seek as people is *comfort*. How each of us defines *comfort* is unique.

When it comes to home improvements, try to identify *what* impact the project will have on you and your quality of life. Identify *how* the finished project will do so. Make sure to identify the impact that the project will have on others living in the home as well. Are you a team, or is this all about you in particular? An open forum and discussions are a must prior to embarking on any new investments that impact people and their quality of life in this sacred place we all call *home*.

## CHAPTER 10
# Trends in Housing

Have you heard the term "raining cats and dogs?" It is rumored that this term comes from early European dwellers. Homes then were built into the side of a hill or mountain. These dwellings were largely made out of mud and logs. The roofs were composed of clay and vegetation. Since heat rises, dogs and cats would sleep on rooftops to keep warm. When it rained heavily, the rooftops would become slippery, and the animals would fall off. Therefore, when it rained hard, the event was described as "raining cats and dogs."

Changing cultures are invariably accompanied by changing lifestyles. Changing lifestyles means new desires and needs for Americans. The types of homes we desire reflect our changing culture and lifestyles. It has been this way since the birth of our country. Let's look at American housing in the 1600s. Houses then were built of mud and logs for the most part. European settlers would construct as close to a hill as possible to insulate against inclement weather. Later, as communities (small cities) arose, houses were made largely of wood (including the roofs). The masses lived in houses with one large central room. Corners of the large room served different functions. One corner was for food preparation near the fireplace, while another is where everyone slept. Not many of these houses still exist. They were not built to stand the test of time. The primary function was to provide shelter and safety. There was no reason to preserve them. There are, however, many areas that might have preserved these houses so that we could learn from them. Any larger, more stately houses from this time would be preserved on the National Historic Register.

Now, let's compare that style house to that of a home built in the early 1900s. The early 1900s witnessed unrivaled population increases in large cities all over America. This was another result of the industrial revolution. Other events that shaped America's population include: WWI, WWII, the Great Depression, and the birth of the Greatest Generation, then their children, the Baby Boomers. Those events not only shaped who we are as a society today, but also dictate the type of housing that would best serve the people of that time. Houses built during this time differed greatly from houses built in 1750. In single-family homes, people still used wood burning fireplaces as a heat source (but not the main source). Burning wood in a fireplace was replaced by coal burning heaters. Soon after, electrical heaters provided became common. Today, we use electricity or natural gas as a means of generating heat.

Similar to housing in the 1700s, functionality was still at the core of the average American house. Craftsman, Victorian, and early Ranch style homes were basic in construction. And though architecturally, these homes differed from one style to the next on the outside, they were all simple in design and similar on the inside, offering bedrooms for privacy, a bathroom, a kitchen, and a common room or parlor (later called a *living room*). Prior to this time, house exteriors were constructed of wood or stone. The early 1900s saw exterior home construction that began to include brick as a new standard. Homes in the southwest had exteriors of stone or stucco. They still do, given the climate and performance of stucco and other stone based products. And in the early 1900s, brick became more affordable to the masses. It was sturdier and more attractive than wood. Brick also offered better insulation than wood siding.

Many of the brick houses of the mid 1900s are still standing and occupied. Across America, these homes still serve us well. Most Craftsman, Bungalow, and Victorian style houses are commonly found in the inner city and just outside of downtown. These neighborhoods, by and large, fell into ruin in the mid 1900s during the great urban exodus, when new neighborhoods and houses popped up across the nation as young soldiers from WWII were coming back to marry and have children. Those WWII homeowners are now referred to as the Greatest Generation. These folks opted for yards, vehicles, pets, and parks for the kids. As the urban exodus continued, the older houses in the city fell into decline. These neighborhoods became the hotbeds for crime and drugs. The only folks moving in were drug dealers, drug addicts, and gang members. The remaining residents were the poor elderly who couldn't afford the new suburban houses, or who refused to accept that their neighborhoods were no longer the magical places found in memories.

Today, there is a nationwide push to reclaim and restore these neighborhoods called *urban renewal*. Builders and first time homebuyers are willing to purchase devalued property in order to restore it. By investing in these neighborhoods, they increase the value of the properties. Building new houses and restoring old ones makes the neighborhoods more attractive to new homebuyers. This causes property values to increase, forcing out the "bad element." The buyers in these areas appreciate the historic residential architecture, sense of community, price tag, and short commute to work. And though most of these inner city gems are dilapidated at the time of purchase, buyers allocate time and money toward restoring the houses. Spec builders purchase these houses, restore, then sell them for significant profits.

During the urban exodus, real estate developers in the center of cities stood to lose a great deal of money if residents moved to the suburbs. Local businesses would lose their customers and be left unable to pay their lease payments. In the 1950s and 60s, developers often bought land in the middle of downtown. They designed and constructed large apartment buildings that were intended to attract and retain an otherwise fleeing population. Because amenities downtown were sparse, the developers constructed restaurants, clubs, and theaters inside the apartment buildings. By the 1960s, developers installed swimming pools to increase tenant rates. The upsides were that residents had short commutes to work and usually had great views of the city. There was no lawn to mow. The downside was that it was hard to compete with raising a family in the safe and quiet homes of the suburbs. Today, many of these structures are targets for investors who want to own them - and are willing to finance the removal and replacement or restoration.

In the late 1900s, houses still offered functionality, but for the first time, began to reflect the personalities and tastes of the owners. Not only was there the modern kitchen with full appliance packages, the appliances were wildly colored in flamingo pink, avocado green, and black. Instead of choosing between white or off white trim color packages on the exterior, these owners would opt for turquoise, red, and even pink. Floors were no longer wood, tile, or concrete. Owners elected to clothe the floors with carpeting, and I mean wall to wall. Carpet was, for the first time, a flooring material that was soft to the feet. Carpet had color, dimension, and became available in almost any style - from short orange shag to tight, green, and fake grass! It was during this period that heat from coal was replaced by mechanical units fueled by electricity or natural gas. Units that could provide both heating and cooling were catching on for families that could afford it. Prior to then, houses were cooled by open windows, tall ceilings, and above-door transom windows that allowed warm air to escape. Formal dining rooms became common-place, and grew to be the heart of the home where families would gather almost ritualistically as a means to be together, maintain unanimity, and enjoy a fresh cooked meal. Dinner was served at a specific time and remained sacred until the 1990s.

Let's compare that home design and function to that which today's buyer demands. These days, the heart of the home is the kitchen. Kitchen design is returning to simplistic and functional. Cooking used to be a necessary part of life. Today's buyer opts to buy prepared meals or goes out to eat. Families are becoming smaller because more couples are electing to remain childless. That may explain why the traditional dining room of our grandparents' has largely become a thing of the past. Today's homeowner would rather sit at a kitchen island or in front of a TV at mealtime. There is no set time, unlike generations prior. Today, people eat when they are hungry (and often alone). As a result, square footage once dedicated to dining rooms is now allocated toward media space, closet space, or larger common areas.

Today's homeowner wants to live in maintenance-free surroundings. They are far less likely to know how to repair something around the house than their ancestors. Today's front and back yards are smaller and require less upkeep. Construction of the larger *McMansions* of the 1990s are becoming a thing of the past as well. Hey, cultures change and that is a fact. To further illustrate, let's consider my great-grandmother's mother. She never considered a string trimmer, Mr. Coffee, telephone, or Mac. These things didn't exist then. She might have been more familiar with how to ward off a bear, cook the best cherry cobbler in the world, or cure poison ivy. Let's then consider my grandmother. She never used WiFi, prepared a meal on a granite countertop, talked on a cell phone, or used YouTube because these things were new and unproven during her life. She did however, have a talent for packing TNT into the warheads of bombs for a B-25 Mitchell. She also knew how to get to a strange location without the use of Google Maps. She also knew how to drive a stick shift car and change the oil in it.

In 100 years, the Millennials will all be gone and their great, great grandchildren will be purchasing or renting homes that come with elements and things that the Millennials might have never considered. Each generation's lives will differ from those who lived in previous times - and those who follow them. Their needs will be different because their lives and societies will differ. I assume that home design in 100 years will be similar to simple white orbs. Decorations, furniture, and friends will be extravagant holograms.

# CHAPTER 11
# Necessity Is The Mother of All Invention

If a tree falls in the forest and no one is there, does it make a sound? Remember that one? I wonder if a tree falls in the forest if no one is there in the first place. For most of history, there would have been no way to prove or disprove the theory... But with all of the HD cameras that can catch footage of anything anywhere, I bet the answer has been found by now.

In college, my first economics professor started the semester with the words, "There is no invention or product that you can think of that hasn't already been created or thought of before." I believed he thought he had a stronghold on the statement with an easy out if anyone challenged him. His out was that he finished the sentence with the words, "...or thought of." It was a grand statement and quite a way to begin the class. I believe he purposely went silent for a minute or so as he looked over his young audience. I tried to think of products or services that I was certain I created, and that no one else possibly could have. I wanted to challenge his statement and still do. Looking back, I doubt he cared if it was a true statement or not. I think it was designed to energize our minds. If I could go back in time, I would have raised my hand and said, "Dr.

Smith, I missed that. Any chance you could group text it... Like... Real quick? My bad. Facebook photos keep coming in, and I was tweeting about a new app I am developing." My point is that new ideas become tangible products as technology demands and allows. When I was in college, there was no real Internet. How could some-one have thought that a surgeon in Japan would be able to perform surgery on a patient in Uganda, all through the use of the Internet and sophisticated software? Dr. Smith was a great and provocative teacher. He kept it interesting and I did well because of it. He was often late to class when his horse drawn buggy needed repairs.

For years now, there have been repair service companies that specialize in foundations and basement walls. Though the industry started off small, it has grown quickly and massively. Foundations built from the late 19th century through the mid-20th century were constructed and designed not to fail. Further, builders and developers took their time in deciding where to construct, taking into consideration soil, rock, landscape, and water. In America, and since the mid-20th century, builders and developers have stopped considering soil types. New foundations crack and fail at a much higher rate today than they did 70 years ago. Failing or cracked foundations generally have little to do with the quality of construc-tion, and more so with soil conditions, poor drainage, and under-ground water sources. Many of today's builders don't include a line item in their budgets for soil testing. Foundation repair is, therefore, quickly becoming one of the fastest growing home-related services in the country, with new companies popping up every year. The work is lucrative, and is often performed because of the threat of losing homeowner's insurance.

Replacing the water supply line to your house has always been a business opportunity for plumbers. However, over the last fifteen to twenty years, it has become an increasing stream of revenue for them. Houses that were built before the mid 1900s had water lines made of galvanized metal. This continued through the 1960s. As galvanized pipe began to wear out in the 1980s, the lines were dug up and replaced with water supply lines made of copper. In the late 1990s, the price of copper skyrocketed. Plumbers had to find a pipe made from a cheaper material. There is a type of water pipe that had been used to carry heated water under tile and concrete floors to keep the floors warm year round. This flexible, plastic piping had proven its durability and reliability. The piping came in different sizes and is a cross-linked polyethylene known by its acronym, PEX. It doesn't corrode, costs 30% less than copper, and is easier to work with. The only downside is when the pipe is exposed to sunlight for extended periods of time, the integrity of the pipe is weakened. Can you imagine how many thousands of miles of PEX sat in plumbing yards or in the back of plumbers' pickup trucks before this little fact was known?

In the mid 1990s, mold became the #1 public enemy for homebuyers, who were taught to be terrified at the mere mention of this horrible word. Not being a mold expert, I would venture that mold has been around longer than we have. We probably ingest and inhale more mold than we will ever see.

So, be wary when it comes to the latest and greatest, but also keep in mind that houses are made of parts and parts wear out. If you notice houses on your streets that are contracting to get new water supply lines installed, just know that you may be next!

# CHAPTER 12
# Laws of Nature and Consequences

"Remember, how you handle *you* may have more to do with the outcome than anything else."

—Wes Taylor, *The Home Stretch*

If I go in a different direction, please trust that I am a good driver and am getting us to a safe place while using a few back roads. I would like to share a concept related to homes, our contractors, and us. It is at this juncture that I will put on my "dad" hat for the first time with you. If you are older than I am, this is a chance for you to feel young again. I am neither a scientist nor a philosopher, though I did play a mad scientist in a sixth grade theatrical production, so that will have to do for now.

The elderly among us made it this far as a result of good genetics, luck, and wise decisions along the way. Most have mastered the laws of nature. There are many laws of nature, but I shall refer to only two: the physical laws of nature and the temporal laws of nature. Both are very important to understand and master. They have everything to do with our decisions and the results of those decisions. The better our decisions, the better our quality of life tends to be.

I believe that we have become a victim society. So much of what happens in our lives has more to do with our decisions than anything or anyone else. I understand that bad things happen to people through no choice of their own. Losing your house to a tornado, for example, is happenstance, as you happen to be a great guy who makes smart decisions. Losing your house to a fire because your meth lab exploded, however, is because of your bad decision. I still think you are a great guy... Just not very smart. There are those who fail to learn and continue to make poor decisions no matter how good their options are, and their subsequent life events tend to end poorly. Because of the victim mentality in America today, it is so much easier to blame others for our own circumstances and claim victim status than to identify and change that in us which leads to poor decisions and behaviors. A great quote from Eleanor Roosevelt reads, "In the long run, we shape our lives, and we shape ourselves. The process never ends until we die." I believe that simple fact has been neglected in homes and schools. I also like the quote, "chicken gonna' learn or chicken gonna' die..."

## The Physical Laws of Nature:

Janice recently sold her house for $600,000, pocketed a bunch of cash, and decided that she wanted to take the money and live a little. Given her perceived windfall at the time of sale, she made a list of things she has always wanted to do. At the top of the list she wrote, "skydiving." Within a month, she found herself on an airplane. She left Lansing at 7:00 a.m. bound for Phoenix! There is a stop and plane change in Colorado Springs. The airplane used in the second leg of the journey was a new Bombardier regional jet. Upon touch-down at Sky Harbor, Janice took an Uber to the skydiving facility where she paid the class fee. For a week, she carefully listened to the instructors. During practice, she performed the motions flawlessly. The instructor believed that Janice was ready for her first jump. The group assembled just outside the hangar with equipment in tow. The old twin-engine cargo plane pulled up, and the door opened. The students prepared for the jump. One at a time, the instructor guided them to the open door, and they each jumped out. On the way down, Janice experienced a wonderful ride and landed correctly. She was successful because she respected and followed the physical laws of nature. In this case, the laws are related to gravity, density of a human body, specific equipment, meteorological conditions, and a distance of nine thousand feet. Her good decisions will better ensure that she can jump again someday.

Meanwhile, Janice had a white trash neighbor named Redneck Jimmy who got wind of her skydiving adventure. This news inspired Redneck Jimmy. He decided to go skydiving as well. He wasn't able to sell his house because it was trashed, but he was able to sell some tire rims that had been in his backyard. He spent the money on a plane ticket, since he believed that to be the first step to any successful skydiving adventure. Ironically, just as Janice's flight left Colorado Springs, Jimmy's plane left Lansing, bound for Miami. As Janice's plane touched down at Sky Harbor, somewhere over Kentucky, Jimmy made his way to the emergency exit door. He grabbed and pulled the door handle. The door opened, and Jimmy jumped gleefully into the sky! This was his first attempt at sky-diving! In the end, Jimmy was successful in fulfilling his goal to skydive. His landing on the ground is where he will learn the negative impact of making a poor decision (maybe). There are negative consequences for his actions. The same physical laws of nature are at play in these two scenarios (minus one detail). But the results are strikingly different. Why?

The physical laws of nature are factors related to actions and their associated reactions. We refer to these reactions as consequences. In the case of the human being, most actions are the results of decisions we make. The consequences, sometimes positive and sometimes negative, typically reveal themselves in a relatively short span of time. The consequence of Jimmy's poor decision was not immediate. The penalty for his bad decision took a lengthy one minute to play out. That is still a short span of time in relation to the length of the average human lifespan. In all, physical laws of nature and consequences happen in pretty short order.

## The Temporal Laws of Nature

Most of our decisions and behaviors have consequences. Physical laws of nature tend to reveal rather immediate consequences. But as humans, we believe that consequences *delayed* are consequences *avoided*. Enter the temporal laws of nature! Trying to outrun a state trooper may seem like a good idea at the time. Our thinking is that if we can just outrun him, then we can hide until the dust settles and go back home later! This is an exercise in tempting the temporal laws of nature. There is a chance that you will indeed be able to hide until the dust settles and go back to living a wonderful and fulfilling life uninterrupted by prison time. The problem is that a camera or the State Trooper himself was able to record your license plate number. You may have avoided immediate consequences of your poor decision to outrun the Trooper, but within a day or so, you will likely be sitting handcuffed in the back seat of the very cruiser you attempted to evade the day before. Ironically, in the set up of this example, there is another possible option that has nothing to do with escaping or getting caught. Here is where we can possibly reintroduce the physical laws of nature smack dab in the middle of messing around with the temporal laws of nature! This is fun! During the chase, you lose control of your car, hitting a bridge post at 120 mph... Lights out! In these examples, there are consequences. Some are physical and immediate, while the other is delayed. Believing in our minds that we can outrun or outsmart the consequences of our decisions and actions is a lesson in futility. If you have a conscience, then stealing could bring the consequence of feeling remorse or guilt. If you give charitably and anonymously, you may experience the consequence of feeling either regret or pride. All actions have a reaction. It is science, fact, and unstoppable.

During the course of our lives, we interact and form relationships with others. At almost every point along the way, we will make decisions and take actions related to these people. The laws of nature are present and never changing. Life is tough. John Wayne said, "Life is hard. It's even harder when you're stupid." Even making decisions with the best intentions can reveal poor outcomes (please see marriage/divorce). Developing a healthy respect for the laws of nature can, at least, guide us and give us a fighting chance of living healthier and more fulfilling lives.

The laws of nature apply to the choices we make related to our homes. Remember that our home is composed of wooden studs, a roofing system, family members, celebrations, and so many more things. If you choose to turn a blind eye to the tiniest water spot on the ceiling, you are tempting the physical laws of nature. The marriage of water, gravity, and drywall rarely ends well for the drywall and floor below. Had you addressed the tiny water spot immediately, you would have discovered a tiny hole in the vent stack boot directly above the upstairs bathroom. The immediate fix would have been a dab of silicone on the boot, since the rubber boot keeps water from running down a vent stack (pipe) and into the house. The long-term solution would be for a handyman to replace the worn boot: a $50 paint touch up, $10 boot, and $75 labor charge. Obeying the physical laws of nature... PRICELESS!

Sadly, a long delay in your decision to address the water spot resulted in drywall tear out ($500), the addition of two 2x8x8' ceiling joists ($1,500), installation and finish for new drywall ($1,000), and priming and painting the new ceiling ($800). The price for ignoring the physical laws of nature: $3,800.

The temporal laws of nature can come into play when you interact or go to contract with those who can help you repair and maintain your property. You must be honest, thorough, and upfront with these people. You must pay them in a timely fashion for work that has been performed correctly. You must make reasonable promises and abide by reasonable contracts. The consequences of not doing so will eventually come to pass, although some may be delayed. Good contractors have mastered both the physical and temporal laws of nature. Let's take the example of a new roof project. The eye of an average homeowner may not be as discriminating as mine when it comes to a roof. A homeowner may not notice any difference between two brand new and seemingly identical roofs. Over a year's time, a neighbor might notice that a few shingles have gone missing. The owner might notice a watermark on the ceiling. Had I seen the two roofs at the time of installation, I would have known that Roof A, which cost $7,000, would experience several failures in short order. I would have also predicted that Roof B, which cost $9,000, would stand up to the manufacturer's warranty, given that it was installed correctly. In this example, the installer of Roof A ignored the physical and temporal laws of nature. He knew that his starter row, fastening schedule, compressor PSI, and roof sheeting replacement were incorrect. He also knew that he could get paid faster and quickly move on to the next roof to make more money. By doing so, he has robbed the trusting homeowner and disregarded the potential consequences. He may get away with it. I see it all the time. Then again, the homeowner may call another roofer to repair the failing roof. While the new roofer is walking across the roof, he falls through where plywood sheeting was removed but never replaced (under the shingles). The new roofer is severely injured. The homeowner and roof contractor may then decide to sue the first roofer, and likely win. These are consequences, though delayed.

In this example, the installer of Roof B followed the physical and temporal laws of nature. He was paid for the quality of the roof and materials he installed correctly. The consequences are that he is getting more quality business from referrals by the owner of House B. The installer of roof A sits in jail. How well did the owner of Roof A do by saving $2,000? Over a period of 20 years, 1,000 heavy downpours, 60 heavy snowfalls, and hailstorms, I would say the money for roof B was well spent.

# CHAPTER 13
# Your Home, Your Responsibility

*"Liberty is the prevention of control by others."*

—John Acton

One hundred years ago, contracting and the mortgage business as we know them now didn't exist *en masse*. There were entities that built houses and sold them, but as a general rule, a person would buy property with money saved and family help. Homeowners maintained and repaired their properties themselves. Homebuyers purchased or built based predominantly on location as with today's buyers, but unlike today, buyers demanded impeccable quality and could recognize it when they saw it. They could identify that which was lacking in quality and why. Quality was vital, as buyers would be responsible for doing the repairs and maintenance for the rest of their lives. All of them had tools and knew how to use them. Today, most homeowners don't know the first thing about maintaining or repairing a house. What happened that caused such a difference between homeowners then and now? Buyers back then grew up on or near farms. They learned repairs and how to handle tools at an early age. They lived in their houses for a lifetime. They worked at the same business for 30-40 years then retired. Again, it is likely that they paid cash for their houses with saved and borrowed family money since mortgage products may not have existed. I would guess that the majority of today's homeowners never grew up on a farm or even visited one. Today, people buy a house, live there for a few years, then move to a different house. This behavior is in response to a larger, more connected, and technologically driven economy. Creative mortgage products also allow buyers to buy quickly and with little required cash.

I believe that homeowners prior to the 1960s took care of their houses out of necessity, but also out of pride. This type was that of the Greatest Generation and generations before them. Most of our WWII soldiers were teenagers. Millions of them went straight from their family farms onto the battlefields in Europe and Asia. Following the war, these young men came home but did not return to the farms across the country. Instead, they chose to marry, rent, and then purchase small houses. Builders referred to these small houses as "baby makers." Some of them chose to rent apartments closer to the big cities in order to get good jobs and live near their offices. As they became more stable, they opted for larger houses in the suburbs where many of them live today. Keep in mind that many of these houses were constructed 80 years ago and remain in excellent condition.

This generation raised families with hopes that their children would grow to become smarter, wealthier, healthier, and more comfortable than themselves. These parents encouraged excellence in education, as few of them had the opportunity or financial ability to afford college. These parents encouraged their children to participate in sports as a means to achieve excellent health while learning about leadership and teamwork. Their efforts paid off, for the most part. Those children grew up. Their lives became centered on comfort, earning more money, living in the biggest houses and in the best neighborhoods. Their evenings would be spent watching TV and the evening news. Their free time was spent pursuing activities that brought pleasure and relaxation. Having a college education was the norm. It was during this time that homeowners opted to pay someone else to repair and maintain their houses for them. They also had enough money for entertainment and vacations. They had the resources to choose a tan and a well-sealed door threshold simultaneously.

The people of my generation (Boomer and Gen X) adopted a lifestyle with more dependence on contractors to identify problems and address them. Since we have become a reactionary society (as opposed to proactive), issues that could have been avoided in the first place become larger problems later that require experienced contractors. If we happen to notice something that looks a little odd in the corner, we just call someone to come and take care of it.

The newest generation of homeowners, the Millennials, desire a habitat that is virtually maintenance-free. Statistics tell us that the percentage of this group that prefers to rent is larger than any other generational group (35-45%). According to the *Wall Street Journal*, 70% of millennials who purchased a house regret doing so. I read the story over coffee at the kitchen table one morning and slumped in my chair. I find this tragic, but again, changing cultures means changing lifestyles. Owning real property has always been a key tenet to experiencing the American dream, wealth, and financial stability. Ahem…

When a component of your roof wears out and a subsequent hole occurs, water can get in and cause destruction. Whose responsibility was it to make sure that the roof was in proper working order? Was it the responsibility of the roofer who installed it? Since you may have no idea who installed the roof or even how old it is, perhaps you should call a roofer and have him come to repair the thing. If the roof leaks again, whose responsibility is it to repair? Surprisingly, many will agree that the new roofer is responsible. After all, he was the last one to work on it. Right? I mean, it worked fine prior to him working on it. Side note: I wouldn't be a car mechanic for anything. When a windowsill becomes rotted, do we blame the man who installed the windows? The installation was fifty years ago. I doubt he is available. The important question is whether or not you have maintained the sills and kept them sealed and painted correctly. If your key doesn't open the back door deadbolt, should you blame the lock manufacturer? My first guess is that you haven't kept the internal parts well lubricated with white lithium grease or Dry-Lube. If you notice a large yellow section of drywall on your first floor ceiling just below the tile shower, do you blame the contractor who built the shower pan in 1962? The answer to all of these questions is that pieces and parts wear out. Houses age like we do. Every square inch of your house matters and must be maintained as we do our bodies. Unfortunately, there are tens of thousands of contractors who seem unable to identify potential threats to your house that become larger problems later because they are not in your house every day. You are! Also, successful contractors are not interested in a tiny yellow spot on the ceiling or a saggy gutter. They are making real money somewhere else.

Why is it that when we hire a painter and notice paint peeling within two years that we blame the painter? It makes a lot of sense. But did you hire the painter based on bid/price? Did you check references? Perhaps your paint contractor was the best in town. Have you inspected and kept up with the exterior of the house since he left? Did you check the joints for caulk integrity every few months? Have direct sun exposure and temperature variances caused material to separate from the silicone or caulk? The exterior of a house can be a very hostile place. A paint contractor cannot control temperature or the sun. Did your contract include labor charges for him to come back and check exterior joints every quarter? Did you address the issues you were having with the paint contractor as they were discovered during your scheduled inspections? A new paint job can last for years if it is done correctly. There are also tasks that homeowners must do to ensure that the house exterior and paint are keeping up with hostile weather and sunlight (that have nothing to do with the quality of paint and paint job). Few protective stains can stand up to the sun when trying to protect a cedar-shingled dormer. This material can require annual treatments. Raw lumber, though seemingly dry at the time of primer and paint application, can retain moisture. As the lumber dries, it can shrink, opening joints. Rain gets behind the joint and re-soaks the material causing paint to peel. It is the homeowner's responsibility to inspect his house and property for naturally occurring changes. Good paint contractors are loyal to their customers, and are usually willing to help with touch ups, routine inspections, and solid advice on how to maintain and identify threats to a paint job. But in the end, it is up to you.

Did you thoroughly inspect your house prior to purchasing it? In other words, given that your house is composed of many systems and materials, did you inspect every single one of them? Did you know what you were looking for? The obvious answer is that you had it done by a home inspector prior to the purchase. But understand that most home inspectors do not inspect water pressure, gas leaks, chimney systems, roofs, foundations, soil types, ventilation systems, framing, ductwork blockage, or concrete. They don't test for radon, mold, carbon monoxide, sinkholes, or roof leaks. In your defense, how could you have known that these things were critically important? How would you have known what to look for or what you were seeing? After all, you are a dentist or teacher. But you are not off the hook!

In most cases, nobody ever told us these things. How on earth are we to know? Did your home inspector give you an inspection schedule and set of instructions? Did your realtor? She made a nice commission for her expertise... No? Since your mortgage lender has a huge stake in the condition of your property, I assume he gave you the inspection schedule and set of instructions. Did any of these people give you a monthly and annual inspection line item list? I know our parents didn't. My dad has never even been to my new house. Nobody educated us about these things. This causes an ever-growing gap between our homes and us. Maintaining and repairing your property can be expensive and time consuming. But in the end, this house belongs to you. It is your responsibility from soil to the chimney top.

I find it fascinating that we purchase a house based on location and assumptions with almost complete disregard for the actual product we are buying. Much of that might be because we have now evolved into a completely disposable society. Most of the junk we buy is made by slave labor in third world countries and is not intended to last. While on that subject, why can't an American company make a lawn sprinkler that actually works and continues to work? In a disposable society, we simply replace cheap items when they break with new cheap items. But can we apply having a disposable mindset when spending $500,000 on a house? The answer is, "maybe." After all, we will use the house for a few years then sell it. It doesn't need to last and serve us for the rest of our lives. Gone are the days of the classic cars of the 1950s and 1960s. As with their homes, these buyers knew quality. They also performed maintenance and repairs on their own vehicles, by and large. Disposable cars hit the market in the early 1970s. Honda and Datsun (now Nissan) made these small and cheap cars. They were good on gas, which was important given the gas crunch at the time. They were inexpensive. Americans took pride that their Chevys or Fords lasted over 100,000 miles. That was a gold standard benchmark. The cheap Japanese cars didn't last a fraction of that. Ironic that now, all manufacturers are making cars that seemingly last forever. Manufacturer warranties can last for 100,000 miles. I believe that most Americans don't know anything about auto repair. And as with the average homeowner, those who cannot repair are forced to either learn how to do it or pay someone else. Hiring someone to maintain or repair your car or house means that you will have to learn how to interact with these people. We will do that together.

Part of living in a disposable society means that we have less patience and more desire for immediate gratification than our parents and grandparents. We are consumed with being rich, famous, younger looking, and finding excitement at every turn. Drama enters our personal lives through friends, work, TV shows, YouTube, social media, and politics. Who has time to spend a Saturday in the crawlspace and attic?

I have a young friend who is funny, smart, good looking, and dynamic. She comes from a good midwestern family and has high personal standards. Her life, however, is comprised of successive dramas. If she isn't hearing about one, she is creating one. I happen to prefer peace and quiet because I am under pressure and in noise all day, every day. Our conversations are meaningful and important up until the point that she brings Jeff's sister's boyfriend's father into the mix with how depressed he is, and the other day he this and that. His wife had a nephew that said this and that... One night, I became overwhelmed. I sipped my beer, set it down, and put up the "time out" hand gesture. I said, "Stop... Just... Stop. These people are important... And great... I'm sure. But I don't want them in my house tonight. I have set aside time for you." I pointed my finger to the northeast and said, "Just 6 miles away, there are four hospitals. There is a child being held by his mother for the very last time. There is a man who has just been told he will have to lose his legs. There is a teen being wheeled in with several bullet holes. Jeff's mother's sister's boyfriend's pet rabbit is NOT a problem." I pointed again to the northeast and said, "THAT... Is a problem." All this is to say that there are real problems that we are handed almost every day, then there are self-induced problems that result from our poor choices (don't forget Janice and Redneck Jimmy). Problems we face in our 20s pale in comparison to those we face in our 40s. Problems we face in our 60s pale to the problems we face in our 80s. Mastering your choices early will help you to more easily overcome, if not avoid altogether, the problems that present themselves later. This same principle applies to your house. Life is so much easier if we spend five minutes caulking a drip edge, instead of replacing it because it has rotted from neglect. We may grow scared of a yellow stain on the ceiling and therefore put it out of our minds. This only ends poorly later. How you handle issues early and head on will determine the degree of severity. Of course, you may ignore the spot. Later you will be blessed with all the drama you'd like! It is your choice.

When I was younger, I thought that being wealthy would mean having fewer problems. I agree that a huge check can solve a lot of problems, but problems become more complex and vexing with age and success. Having more money and assets results in a need for increased poise, responsibility, and wisdom. If you don't have these traits, you end up like a pro athlete who is paid millions of dollars and ends up broke in a few years. An ingredient in maturing is learning to successfully deal with problems. You must develop the ability to prioritize the relative importance of your problems (and dramas). We can eliminate many of our future problems by changing our choices, associations, and thoughts. It is best to address the problems that we face as quickly as they occur, rather than letting them fester. Problems related to your house rarely fix themselves. They grow into bigger problems. The other aspect with problems is to remember that many problems are self-induced. We invite or allow them in. Part of problem solving is to recognize what to own and what not to own. It is often helpful to identify whose problem it is. Sometimes I say, "I didn't cause it. I cannot solve it. I cannot make it better. I am not the Messiah. Sorry, but I can't help."

Being responsible for maintaining your house may seem like a mountain to climb, but it really isn't. You need to learn a few basics and commit to trying. You will be surprised at how your approach to these things changes once you get comfortable with a tape measure, caulking gun, and ladder. Confidence leads to increased confidence.

Reading this book is a great start. If you take time to soak in what you read, you will learn just about everything you will need to know about your home.

I attest that most homes built after 1985 are junk compared to those built earlier. This may explain why contracting is so lucrative. As with your body or car: if you maintain it, it will be healthier. If you know what to look for at home, you can maintain your house and make repairs - or hire it out for a fraction of what it will cost if neglected. When I build a house, I do walkthroughs with my buyers. I educate them on all the extra measures that were taken during construction to ensure a long lasting and quality structure. I believe that most homebuyers can see that a stairway is elegant or that a plumbing fixture is cool. I want my buyers to understand roof pitch, gutters, what to look for on the outside in the way of deterioration, and water egress (from rain). I also point out the things that will require their attention and tell them when to perform inspections. I give them remedies if common problems arise. But most of us do not buy houses from empathetic builders and developers. We buy them from sellers and their realtors. Many realtors know a lot about contracts and the rules of representing a buyer or seller. They, however, are not seasoned contractors. Your lender is interested only in being paid every 30 days. Your neighbor might lend advice, but his true working knowledge may be from limited experience or folklore.

When you undergo surgery, the doctor will ordinarily give you specific instructions on how to heal, and tell you what will be required of you in order to ensure a strong comeback and healthy result. He cannot do it for you. If you are smart and you care, you will follow his instructions to the letter, even if it is uncomfortable or disruptive. If you fail to follow his instructions, you are asking for trouble in the way of infection, repeated surgery, ongoing therapy, loss of a limb, or worse. Maintaining a house is similar. It will cost a little money along the way, be disruptive, and may even cause you physical discomfort. But if you follow my advice related to your house, you will fare much better than if you don't. If not, you'd better start saving money for extensive repairs, for when you get ripped off, get injured, or get sued. This is a good time for you to ask yourself if you should close this book, sell the house, and rent. Renting certainly has its place. But if you close the book, you will miss out on all the fun.

Aside from mechanical failures related to water heaters and HVAC systems, most of the maintenance will have to do with the naturally occurring and atmospheric wear and tear on the exterior of your house. When contractors are called for repairs, it usually has something to do with water. Let's consider how destructive water can be, how much of your house comes into contact with water, and how often. Let's start at the chimney and flue. Let's move down to the roof and the flashing where the roof meets dormers, brick, and siding. Water comes into contact with gutters, downspouts, and splash blocks at the bottom. Water comes into contact with vent pipes and vent boots, electrical wires and the riser conduit, fascia, soffits, siding or bricks and mortar, drip edges and windows, window hardware and sills, door ledges, door hardware, door glass, caulk, silicone, trim, paint, concrete, the foundation or slab, fence, yard, and the mailbox. Humidity exists virtually everywhere. The exterior of your house is in a battle against water and is constantly playing defense. Let's go inside. Water comes in contact with every faucet, sink, under counter pipes and valves, countertops, cabinetry, floor, base trim, tubs, drywall, lighting, insulation, framing, refrigerators, dishwashers, laundry machines, garage floors, carpets, HVAC units, and water heaters.

The damage water can do to a house is usually the result of exposure for a long period of time. It can come from a breach in the exterior of the house or from inside the house. Most of the time, we do not notice a water-related issue until it becomes a problem. The right thing to do is to try and discover the source of the water. It might be a hole in the roof. It might be under a cabinet or appliance. If it is coming through the roof, a roofer can typically make the repair for a reasonable price. It is probably a simple fix if the water is minimal. Ignoring a water issue could end up costing thousands over a period of a few months. It is your home and your responsibility. You can make it easy or difficult, depending on the choices you make early on.

I thought you would like to know that Redneck Jimmy actually survived the jump (haystack).

# CHAPTER 14
# What Is A Contractor?
# The Answer Might Surprise You

When we close our eyes and picture a stockbroker, what comes to mind? I bet that most of us have a similar vision. I picture a young professional male with hair slicked back and wearing a suit. I imagine him on the phone making a sales pitch or at lunch handing out his card. I picture a lawyer much the same. Of course, if the weather is cold, he has his hands in his own pockets. When you picture an ex-ray technician, what comes to mind? I picture a younger female wearing scrubs and in a hurry. When you envision the average mechanic, what comes to mind? Now I ask you to picture a contractor. I sure wish I could read your minds. I would venture to say that we have different visions depending on what kind of contractor he or she is. We picture the builder in khaki pants and boots wearing a golf shirt (warm weather) or state-of-the-art coat (cold weather). I picture the plumber in dirty clothes. I picture the roofer in dirty clothes, driving a large, very dirty, and beat up truck. It is human nature to categorize people and assign predictions about their looks and behaviors based on their line of work. Our minds assign certain attributes both inaccurately and accurately. They are based on our perceptions.

Having a functioning brain is to have the ability to discriminate. In order to survive, we have to be able to make conscious and unconscious decisions that lead us to the choices we make. I would rather walk through a dog park than a rattlesnake infested cave bottom. In other words, I discriminate against rattlesnakes. That may sound like an extreme example but we make many of these choices every day. I would bet that we discriminate a hundred times each day. I prefer to cross a street when there is no traffic. I do not like being hit by cars. That doesn't mean I hate cars. It means I like legs that work. I prefer vanilla ice cream to carrot cake. I do not like bullies and prefer to spend time with intelligent people. When we discriminate against other people, we are labeled as hate-filled. There are laws related to discriminating against other people based on ethnicity, age, and a host of other factors. And even though these laws exist, it is human to make judgments in our minds about others based on attributes we assign to them, whether we know them or not. A tall man may be attracted to tall women and that is his right - but if he refuses to hire short women, that is against the law. In other words, we cannot help but see others and things as more or less attractive in our minds, and assign them more or less in value based on the way we perceive them. Our perceptions come from our experiences and what we, personally, have learned along the way. That being said, simply hating people based on their religion, skin color, sexual orientation, or physical attributes may be more harmful to the hater than the hated. Discrimination and hate are two different things entirely. Discrimination might well be the result of a strong internal opinion about someone else. But discrimination isn't always bred of hate. Discrimination may well be the result of love. A married man might discriminate against intimacy with women other than his wife. He doesn't spend intimate time with other women and finds them less attractive than his wife, if at all. He is not exhibiting hate through his discrimination. He is exercising his learned ability to discriminate against other women, in certain ways, because he loves one woman in particular. In my social circle, you will find people of differing socioeconomic classes, races, sizes, and genders. We tend to all want success and happiness for each other. We are honest. We are generous toward, and protective of each other. The reason I bring up this topic is that we tend to assign attributes and values to others based on our deeply held beliefs. Sometimes, our perceptions are negative and completely without reason. At other times, we tend to elevate others based simply on something other than what is real. Perhaps you wouldn't invite a homeless bum to dinner. He probably smells terrible, is drunk, and has been in and out of the system several times… Or at least that is a perception. What if that bum is actually the victim of several life traumas that included the tragic loss of a family and everything he owned? Perhaps he also lost his career due to illness. He may have spent his fortune on cancer treatment. He could be highly educated and someday, regain his life and happiness. Many of us would enjoy having the top leader of our political party over for dinner! He is powerful, dynamic, a great father and husband, and believes as we do! What a fascinating dinner that would be… Or at least that is our perception of that person. He may be the most corrupt person on the planet.

I also believe that we as a society assign values to people based on their professions. We look down on auto mechanics and look up to physicians. Ironically, one of my best friends is an aircraft mechanic. One of the most vile and dishonest people I have ever met is a retired urologist. The most insecure jerk on the planet, in my opinion, is a famous actor adored by millions who never had to spend time with him! We tend to elevate ourselves above workers in the business of housing. The plumber is dirty. The electrician is a weirdo. The general contractor is going to try and get away with our money. The HVAC technician is going to try to sell us a new unit. These are stereotypes that are also inaccurate. I know plumbers who are highly successful. My land guy (bulldozers) put his college kids through two of the most prestigious universities in the world and lives in a million dollar home. I have known more plumbers who are multi-gazillionaires than lawyers. These contractors have a keen sense about finances, the law, taxes, and real estate. They are successful parents and neighbors. They are extremely capable of interacting with people from all walks of life. They can have highly effective conversations with successful bankers, then hang up and call the least educated among their workers. In order to earn a good living, contractors must master finance, social skills, and run an honest business. Initially, I may have perceived that an uneducated bumpkin stepped out of the dirty pickup truck. I was wrong. This kind of man is my friend. My dad had a friend who was much older, and old enough to be my grandfather. He was always in dirty overalls and drove a beat up van. He was a plumber. He never said much and always had a cigarette hanging from his lips. When he passed away, he left three hundred million dollars to the cancer society (one billion in today's money). He owned most of what is known as Aurora, Colorado. He knew how to buy land correctly. Just sayin'...

The contractor's office can be in the bitter cold or the searing heat. He may find himself in a pristine symphony hall or in a carcass-laden attic. He may be hanging 300 feet off the ground or moving explosives a mile under the earth's surface. He has mastered the abilities to effectively communicate with homeowners and lenders. He has mastered the planning and execution of an elaborate project. The contractor is a successful manager of people and time. He knows billing and tax software. He wakes at 4:30 every morning and closes the books at 9:00 every night. And when he walks in to the box store to buy lumber and arrives at the checkout register, he greets the cashier with a smile and the question, "How are you today?" The usual reply and gum snapping by the cashier is "I'm tired. It's cold in here." The contractor thinks of something uplifting and shares it with the cashier as he smiles and says, "Have a nice day." He then pushes his heavy lumber cart across the icy parking lot and loads the heavy lumber into the bed of his truck.

Picture yourself at your place of work. How many hours per day do you work? How much of that time are you producing at 100%? Are you firing on all cylinders while at your job? If you overlook a few details or put off some things that can wait until tomorrow, what is the result? Do you ever send social text messages or emails to a friend? Do you sip on a beverage or take a personal call? Contractors, for the most part, have none of these luxuries. Time doesn't allow for it. In many cases, if the general contractor misses a few details or leaves something unfinished, someone could be injured or killed. It's not to say that contractors are perfect or flawless. They are flawed like us. It is to give you a glimpse of what work is like for the successful contractor. It is to convey how dangerous any construction project can be. A construction site is one of the most dangerous places you will ever visit. Broken bones, lacerations, and electrocution are common hazards. When service technicians or contractors are at your house, how much of their time do they spend sending personal text messages, sending personal emails, looking at Facebook, sipping coffee, or sitting comfortably in the air conditioning? Chances are, the answer is "zero." It is difficult, wasteful, and dangerous to do these things while on a ladder, under a house on your back, or carrying materials. Contractors are not paid to be there. They are not on the clock. They are paid for accomplishing and keeping safety as priority #1 during the project and after they finish. Good contractors have a firm handle on their work sites 100% of the time, whether they are present or not.

There are many types and categories of contractors. Typically, homeowners will interact with either general contractors or subcontractors (tradesmen). The title of general contractor (GC) refers to a professional who is licensed and insured to go to contract with the general public. That contract reflects the amount of money the homeowner agrees to pay him in exchange for providing services to the homeowner. Those services are outlined in the contract. He is not necessarily an electrician, HVAC technician, or roofer. He may have an extensive understanding of each of these, but is more likely to hire a subcontractor to perform the actual electrical, HVAC, or roof work. The GC has an understanding of all phases of construction and what will be required to successfully begin and complete that project or task. Some general contractors prefer to work with homeowners (residential construction) while other contractors prefer to work with businesses or in the commercial arena (commercial construction/development). Some general contractors opt to work in both the residential and commercial settings.

The term "tradesman" refers to contractors who are licensed to work only in a specific trade such as plumbing, HVAC, or electrical. When these tradesmen work for, and report directly to the general contractor, they are called, "subcontractors." When they report directly to the home or business owner, they are referred to as "tradesmen." If you call a plumber to install a new kitchen faucet, he reports directly to you and you pay him directly. When you call a general contractor because you need a new kitchen faucet installed, he will visit your home, examine the scope of work, contract with you, and hire his best plumber for the job. That plumber may have little or no personal interaction with you. You might wonder why you would call a general contractor if you could bypass him and hire a plumber yourself. This is more common than not.

When you call a tradesman, you are going to pay retail price and rely solely on his representations and experience/skill level. A general contractor can typically procure the services of a tradesman at a fraction of retail price. A plumber might charge you $300 for a new faucet installation. The general contractor might charge you the same amount and pay his plumber from a portion of the $300. In this scenario, you paid the same amount. But remember, by adding the expertise of a general contractor into the mix, you would be paying for professional oversight and accountability. Also, you enjoy the greater likelihood that the plumber will be capable of handling your needs, and that he has insurance, which offers priceless peace of mind. A plumber may come and install the new faucet and disregard water damage to the base cabinet and tile floor. He is not a carpenter by trade. A general contractor would consider the entire scope of work that needs to be done to repair that which has been damaged by the original leaking faucet. The faucet replacement, tile floor, and damaged cabinetry are items that must be addressed in a certain order and in a timely fashion. The lone plumber is not typically set up for this. A general contractor is.

One of the worst things you can ask a general contractor is for the name of a good plumber (or roofer, or painter, etc.). You might be asking him for a referral because you don't want to get ripped off. Perhaps you believe that the GC will know a good tradesman. How the GC may interpret your question is, "I have little respect for what you do for a living. I don't care that you have probably paid dearly over the course of your career to find the good ones. I don't want to pay you for your experience or knowledge, so hand over the information." I ask you, what is the value of knowing that you will be in good hands, charged correctly, and that the job will be done correctly? If that really carries no value, then Google the name of a plumber and hire him. The question is similar to calling a lawyer for the name of a good paralegal who can write a legally worded letter for you. It is similar to calling a local auto repair shop and asking for the cell phone number of his best mechanic. Again, the GC can usually retain the services of a tradesman at a fraction of what the tradesman would charge you directly. If the GC places a dollar amount on top of the bill that the plumber charges him, you end up paying approximately the same. The advantage is that you can be assured that the GC will not send a terrible plumber who is going to rip you off. Remember, the plumber reports to the GC. The GC reports to you.

In most municipalities in America, people wishing to obtain a general contractor's license are required to attend classes and pass exams administered by his state. If the candidate passes the exams, he must be audited by a licensed CPA. This is to prove the amount of his assets and discover his net worth. The candidate's net worth is a vital ingredient in determining the cost of structures he is permitted to build.

There are different types of exams at the GC level. Typically, one exam is for residential/small commercial projects (houses or small offices). The other exam is for industrial and large commercial construction (factories and skyscrapers). The amount of liability insurance a GC is required to carry depends on the type of license he obtains and the nature of his contracts (size and value of the projects). It was during the Great Recession of 2008 that many developers/contractors lost most of their assets. Consequently, they lost the GC licenses as well. It would take years, if ever, to attain large savings accounts, significant home equity, or sufficient credit to purchase vehicles and equipment and a new GC license. Many great contractors and subcontractors were removed from the world of contracting and are now in different lines of work. The third test that a general contracting applicant must pass is a lengthy law exam. This exam is to ensure that he knows the laws related to contracting, construction, and development in his state.

As I mentioned, general contractors are required to carry liability insurance. This policy is intended to protect him, his workers and subcontractors, and the general public. The liability amount that the GC carries is typically many times that of a subcontractor/tradesman. A roofer might be required by the state to carry a minimum of a one million dollar policy. The same thing might apply to the painter or the window installer. If something goes wrong during a general contractor's project and nobody knows about it until fire breaks out at a property, it is likely that the homeowner, lawyers, insurance company, and mortgage lender are going to want to know the identity of the GC. Those lenders and lawyers may not try to track down some electrician or laborer. The GC will be held responsible. Since the GC's liability insurance policy will provide blanket coverage for other workers (subcontractors and laborers), the GC will typically pay far more for his policy. A plumber's liability insurance may cost $650 per year. The GC's insurance could cost him $21,000 per year. The commercial rates are much higher.

There are more subcategories of general contractors. Some GCs prefer to work with homeowners and remodel kitchens and bathrooms. Others might prefer to build custom houses. My experience and preference is one of real estate development. I enjoy purchasing and preparing land. I like designing and building single-family homes. My title would be that of "spec builder" (meaning speculative). It is a risky path for the general contractor, and carries tremendous liability and innate exposure. In other words, money from a homeowner or small business isn't coming my way as I complete various tasks. I spend or borrow funds to acquire the land and build the houses. My goal is to sell the house before (or soon after) construction ends. I typically make a larger profit per project than custom builders do. I fund the project (not a homeowner) and I assume all the risk.

I would like to address again the liability that GCs face when housing, credit, or lending industries falter in the economy. I briefly touched on the impact that the recession had on the contracting industry in order to drive home another point. Many Americans today do not really understand the widespread devastation that happened during the Great Recession that started in 2008. Those in the housing industry (builders, lenders, realtors, insurers) lost their homes, assets, jobs, life savings, retirements, cars, licenses, and even lives. Keep in mind, this occurred only a decade ago. Those of you who are recently out of college weren't even teenagers. And this wasn't a matter of a few thousand people being hurt. This was a matter of hundreds of thousands of lives that were ruined while millions of people were severely hurt. Suicide rates were the highest they had been since the Great Depression of the 1929. Many of those whose lives were ruined were great business minds and leaders, highly intelligent and caring professionals, and extremely skilled at their respective trades. Many of these people are responsible for creating many of the places you visit or live every day. Sadly, even today, so much talent and experience remains sidelined and unable to fully participate in today's economy as licensed and insured professionals. I believe it is right to hire experts who are licensed and insured, but I have also hired many along the way who will never be able to reestablish their licenses. I broke my own rule and did so because I would rather hire someone who is the best at what he or she does than contract with another who isn't. Of course, I have experience that most of you do not when it comes to hiring workers. Just know that work ethic, experience, and honesty cannot be guaranteed by a license. Further, some of the biggest con artists in the business of house and home are licensed, wealthy, hire unskilled third-world laborers, and keep attorneys on retainer.

It is important for you to know how to identify a con artist contractor. I believe the common trait found among almost all con artists is to focus too much on getting your money. Like thieves, they take more money than what you get in return in the way of product or service. Sometimes you get nothing. Other times you get something, but it is not nearly the value of what you paid for it. These con men typically get as much of your money as possible on the front end - before work begins. I am not referring to good contractors who are trusted, licensed, insured, and came with strong referrals. I refer to the storm chasing roofers who ask for $6,000 up front and never return. I refer to contractors who perform some of the work then ask for a large sum of money and never return to finish. Some con men will start and finish a job and leave once paid. Their work was terrible and the new kitchen or roof begins to fail immediately. You can never reach this con man by phone. Con men aren't good at delivering follow-up and customer service - they are too busy conning the next homeowner. Con artists do not want to have their signatures on any formal document or contract. They cannot provide a business or contractor's license. They have no proof of liability insurance. They cannot provide references. If they do, the references will be few and likely the phone number of a friend or a girlfriend (who are also con artists).

When asking for proof of insurance, get the name of the insurance company, policy number, and expiration date of that policy. Call the insurance company to ensure that the contractor is in good standing. When checking references, ask for the names of, and contact information for, previous customers going back five years. Ask for the scope of work the contractor provided for these customers. This is important because a storm chaser will give you a reference of your neighbor who hired him a few days earlier to install a new roof following a hailstorm. Not enough time has passed for your neighbor to discover that he has been conned. In other words, a real con man will turn and walk away from you because he knows he will be found out by your thoroughness. He doesn't want to go to jail. Good contractors are glad to provide you with all the information you need. He is proud that he has a license, references, and past customers who trust him.

In closing, a few years ago, I gave a speech to a real estate entity, and in that speech, defined the role of the general contractor when he is at work. There are many parallels between the duties of the symphony conductor and a general contractor. Both have an excellent working knowledge of the players (musicians/tradesmen). Both understand the tools that are used (violins and trumpets/circular saws and nail guns). They both understand the larger picture and nature of the event (the performance/the actual construction). They are both the most skilled at leading their respective events from one minute to the next (timing of the music and players/timing of the phases of construction/critical path). The symphony conductor may not be the best cellist. He doesn't need to be. He needs only to recognize, hire, and direct the best cellist. The general contractor may not be the best framer. He doesn't need to be. He needs only to recognize, hire, and direct the best framers. The failure or success of the symphony performance lies at the feet of the symphony conductor (as she stands in her tuxedo). Success or failure of a project lies at the feet of the general contractor (as he stands in his khakis and fleece jacket).

Knowing the difference in contractors will help you to understand who does what, when, where, how, and why.

# CHAPTER 15
# Interacting With Contractors

*"If you think hiring a professional is expensive, imagine how costly it will be to hire someone who isn't."*

—Chris Cianciolo, Carbonek

The quote is profound and accurate. It was made by a friend of mine. He charges a premium for his work and delivers the best possible result that a homeowner can attain. Relentlessly, he approaches each project detail with total focus and dedication. He is protective of his customers and their lives, does everything by the book, is fully licensed and insured, and warrants everything he does. It is no surprise to me that he is the busiest and most successful contractor I have ever known.

Who is performing the work at your house? Certainly you understand that most workers at a project are not contractors and are not licensed. They might be employees of a contractor. Many times, they are not employees but are hourly, and sometimes, temporary laborers. Contractors often save money by paying lower wages to their workers, passing that savings along to you in the form of a lower bid. Do you recall how sacred your home is? Remember the laws related to privacy, safety, and the fact that your home is your castle? Should you be concerned if complete strangers have access to every room in your castle during projects? These workers will be tearing it apart and disrupting your life. They will have extremely loud and dangerous equipment and tools, and will perform various surgeries on your house. How important are your belongings? How important is your jewelry or your medications? How important is the mental and physical safety of your 13-year-old daughter? Many of these workers are foreigners who are on the run from law enforcement officials in other countries. I know this to be true, and have interacted with many of these workers. Officials have no idea that they are in this country. They will be close to your valuables and possibly children as you are at work or on vacation. Not all of these people have ill intentions, but let's face it, anyone can be a thief. If something goes missing or terribly wrong, will you have recourse if you don't know the identity of the people in your castle? You may be saving $1,000 on the cheaper bid for the new interior paint job, but would the extra $1,000 of the higher bid have been worth your safety and peace of mind?

As in any industry, the world of contracting is full of highly conscientious contractors who themselves own beautiful homes and are raising wonderful families. But it can also be an industry ripe with con men and the least desirable among us. Make sure to get to know your contractors and their workers prior to signing contracts with them. Checking references is critical. Good contractors will gladly share them with you.

Given our perceptions of others based on their respective jobs, I find it tragic that police, as a group, can be seen in such a negative light. These people chose a career that involves putting their lives at risk in order to serve and protect us. It is ironic that we miss them so badly when things get dangerous in our lives. We tend to look down on the average mechanic. We cannot believe he would charge $85 per hour, while not scoffing at the $5,000 retainer and billing at $300 per hour from the lawyer. Have you ever wondered what the world would look like without mechanics? I suppose we would still be riding horses to get to our daily destinations. Do you know how much money your doctor makes? Most of us have no idea. I would bet that an excellent general contractor knows your house as well as your physician knows your body. Given that last sentence, I wonder if you think that I am here to defend the contractors over those who pay them. Hang in there because in a while, I am going to jump back over on your side of the fence. For now, I would like to expand your mind. Allowing me to do so will benefit you.

It is common for us to call a contractor, explain a situation to him, and ask if he can come over to take a look at an issue we are having at home. He will come over, make a diagnosis, and we might ask him for a bid. Is this what you do with a mechanic, physician, or lawyer? The contractor has a specific vehicle that carries him from client to client. His primary means of communication is with a smartphone and tablet. In his vehicle, he carries his professional license, proof of liability insurance, a few thousand dollars' worth of tools, and is dressed as if ready to take on your account the moment he arrives. He is prepared. What enabled him to acquire the tools and knowledge and licensing? You asked him to come over. He drove 45 minutes to get to your house. He will spend an hour with you, listening and diagnosing. At his truck, he will spend another 15 minutes drawing up the critical path (tasks that your project will entail and the timeline for completion), and formulate a price for you. He leaves knowing that he has another 45 minutes to get to the next client. So far, he has invested almost 3 hours into your account, identified your problem, given you the answer on how to solve it, and an estimated cost for the remedy. How much did he get paid for his vast experience, knowledge, fuel, wear and tear on the truck, his time, and the risk he assumed on that ladder while with you? Does your doctor spend 3 hours at your house properly diagnosing your illness? Does he bring his testing equipment and respective tools of the trade? If so, does he do so for free? Consider your line of work. Can you spend 3-6 hours per day working and not getting paid? If so, how many days per week can you work without getting paid? Many of you may be thinking that the contractor wasn't really working. Instead, he was just looking. Tell that to your doctor or lawyer after he spends 3 hours listening to you. When consulting with an attorney, he may listen to you for an hour and ask questions. I suppose during that time, he is not actually working. Right? After all, the lawyer isn't thundering away at a defendant. He isn't carrying heavy books and files up courthouse stairs. He isn't buried deep in research or deposing anyone at the time. When you visit your doctor and explain to him about your terrible pain, would you consider that he is working? After all, he isn't lifting a heavy body, scheduling your surgery with support staff, or cutting into anyone. He is merely listening and diagnosing, therefore he must not be actually working. Right? In that case, you should not be charged a fee of any kind. You are free to leave his office. In truth, it is likely that he has tremendous expenses in tools, staff, insurance, software, and office equipment. He has also studied for, and passed, extremely difficult exams and paid a fortune for his education. So now I ask you again: when the contractor came to your house, was he working? If not, then why did you call him and ask for his knowledge, expertise, and diagnosis that also required his tools, insurance, license, workman's comp, personal tax on his equipment, CPA fees, and personal and professional liability while hanging 23' in the air on a ladder? As a society, we have learned to expect that a contractor should work for free in order to get your business later. If he does this twice a day, then he works for free half of the time. Can you afford to do this at your job?

Let's say that you and this particular contractor have chemistry. He seems to really know his stuff. You invite him to tighten his numbers and plan, and schedule a time to get started on your project. In order to formulate an extremely accurate price for you, he will need to make several calls to secure and schedule labor and materials. This will take him a cumulative 6 hours if he is smart. So far, he has worked two days to solve your issue and not been paid a dime. If, prior to the start of your project, a neighbor gives you the name of a different contractor who is cheaper, will you engage with the cheaper contractor to see if you can get a better deal? If you stick with the original contractor, it is likely that his price includes his time and expenses in formulating your price and critical path. If you do not hire him, and opt for the cheaper contractor, then he has lost valuable time and income, and regrets ever answering the phone when you originally called him.

Would you call the original contractor back and tell him that his price was too high? On what grounds would you base your assumption? Have you ever walked out of your doctor's office following his diagnosis and cost to remedy your problem, telling him that his price is too high and that you want a cheaper doctor? Keep in mind that it is not a contractor's job to diagnose and repair your property. That responsibility belongs to you. If doing either is beyond your pay grade, then you need to hire a contractor who can price it correctly and complete the job safely and on time. To do so requires tremendous skill and experience on the part of the contractor. It is likely that he didn't learn it on YouTube prior to meeting you. Please review the quote at the beginning of this chapter.

## The Bid Process

There is a famous moment in NASA history that occurred in the final seconds of the violent countdown to blast off of one of the Mercury rockets. It has been told that John Glenn or Alan Shepard looked at the other and said, "How does it feel to be sitting on top of $200 million of low bid?" I understand that the average homeowner has no idea of how much it costs to fix broken pipes, repair a deeply scratched hardwood floor, or replace old windows. We have learned that we can call a contractor and that he will shoot us a price. How will we know if that price is accurate and fair? $8,000 sure seems like a lot of money. Perhaps you call a different contractor and his price comes back at $10,000. Now the original eight thousand dollars does not seem so bad. It is human nature to find the lower price more desirable. Over time, people have learned to rely more on the bid than anything else. To choose a contractor this way is to choose peril. Do you recall the game show *Let's Make a Deal?* As a kid, I would watch it. It was entertaining and full of frustrating pitfalls. Here was Janice from Lansing, Michigan. She just won a trip to Vegas, a trip to Jamaica, *his and her* mountain bikes, a new grill, and $500 in cash. Then the dreaded, "or you can have what's behind door #2." I thought, "Janice... Janice listen to me. Take the bird in the hand. Walk away from the fake garage door and Monty Hall. Don't look him in the eye... Back away. Get on that plane back to

Lansing and pack for Vegas and Jamaica! Grill with a new tan, ride the bike and lose the double chin. Waaaalk Awaaaaay. Who needs a donkey?"

If you are lucky enough to cross paths with a professional and qualified contractor who comes with excellent references, confidently proceed with him.

Picking contractors based on price is natural. We like to keep as much of our money as possible. But the most underrated word in the world of contracting and homeownership should is "value." The psychology of the bid process is that it may be the only aspect of any project where homeowners actually feel they have control. Once the project has started, walls get knocked down, electrical and plumbing lines are cut, and bathrooms are gutted. Homeowners sit in the dust and noise with absolutely no knowledge or control of what is happening or about to happen. Successful contractors and homeowners know that the bidding process is best left to government contracts and desperate and ignorant homeowners. Contractors must profit in exchange for lending their time, skill, and knowledge in order to increase your quality of life. I hope my mechanic profits so that when my car breaks down, he is still in business to repair it. I hope my attorney profits so that when I am sued, she will be in business to defend me. I hope that my contractor profits so that when my heat goes out on a cold winter night, he will be in business to repair it. My doctor, mechanic, and lawyer are able to afford their vehicles and mortgage payments. I hope they make enough profit to buy food as well. It should be no different for contractors.

How do we find a good contractor? How do we know how much they will charge? First of all, if you want the cheapest, it should be easy to find. The neighbor boy is available this weekend. But as with any professional trade, you will get what you pay for. And the shocker is that when you broadcast your need and ask contractors to submit their bids, you inadvertently seek the most expensive price! That's right. When you ask a contractor for a bid, he knows that you likely have little experience or knowledge related to the issue you need him to solve. You have exposed your weakness. He knows that you have no idea how much the issue should cost to address and repair. It is natural for him to submit an inflated price to you. Another reason his price will be high is that he has experience in dealing with homeowners who pick contractors based on price. These homeowners tend to be bossy, controlling, and opt to cheap out at every turn. Materials such as cheap tile, cheap plumbing, or junky lighting fixtures can make his job more difficult. Cheap materials often require more time to work with because they easily break, are missing parts, or get installed only to be removed and replaced. This type of situation is exhausting to contractors and the work conditions can be stressful and grueling. These home-owners are also more likely to skip out on the final payment than homeowners who are strong partners and seek value. Asking for bids almost always assures poor results. You will end up with lesser contractors, higher prices, and the relationship between you and contractors will be strained from start to finish.

The best way to find good contractors is by word of mouth. Your friends, family, neighbors, and local trade supply store clerks should have information on strong contractors who will treat you professionally and fairly. Beware of choosing doctors, lawyers, and contractors by data found on the Internet. The Internet is large and complicated. It can be terribly deceptive. Google ratings can like-wise be deceptive. These sources can insulate the homeowner from pairing with excellent contractors while delivering incompetent workers to your home. We might find an excellent review on a local handyman that was written by his girlfriend. Likewise, we may read a terrible review about a contractor who failed miserably at every turn that was written by his competitor. There are contractor-locating sites that claim to flush out the best and worst contractors in your area. Some of the claims at locator sites may be false. There are business-rating services in most metropolitan areas that assign the highest ratings to the highest paying donors. In addition, there are many large contracting firms with huge advertising budgets. They also have in-house attorneys to fight you when work they perform is of poor quality. My advice is to stay in familiar waters. Word of mouth is strong because contractors who have proven themselves to your friends could be of great value to you.

I suggest forming relationships with contractors and service providers before you need them. Many HVAC contractors offer annual maintenance service and checkups for a small fee. This marketing approach helps to increase your loyalty, and certainly places them to the front of the line when your system fails. If outside temperatures plummet, you and your neighbors may experience HVAC system failure. It should give you peace of mind that by being a preferred customer of an HVAC contractor, you will be placed ahead of those who don't have a relationship with him. It is a great idea to meet and get to know a plumber. Small and medium sized plumbing outfits are in the business of repair and maintenance. Larger outfits can be in the business of selling appliances and equipment. The same truth can apply to larger HVAC companies. You can locate good service technicians by asking experienced salespeople at plumbing fixture outlets or plumbing supply outfits. Most of these supply houses have a city counter to serve average homeowners. These city count-ers usually have card racks where dependable service professions will leave their business cards. City counters have knowledgeable staff that can point you toward great service technicians or steer you away from the bad ones. Service technicians spend their days in dark crawlspaces, on their backs, getting yelled at, or in the searing heat. Getting a random call from an energetic and positive home-owner just to say "Hello" and "Have a nice day" can mean quite a bit to the weary technician! Invite him in for cold water or hot coffee when he is in the neighborhood.

If you are in the market for a new deck or fence, drive through the nicer neighborhoods in your part of the city. New decks and fences are easy to spot. Don't be afraid to visit the homeowner. Knock on the door and introduce yourself. Compliment the owner on the new fence and share the fact that you want to explore having one installed at your house. Most homeowners are more than happy to see you. First, since you are a local, they will want to be helpful. Further, it is at this time that they get to boast about how great their contractor was and be proud of his/her decision to hire him. This could also be a great opportunity for the new fence owner to let off some steam about how crappy the contractor and his work was, citing that the workers were sloppy, the gate doesn't close right, and he won't return calls. In you, that homeowner has found an ally. In exchange, you could gain valuable information contrary to what you may have read about a contractor on the Internet.

How do we know how much the new kitchen is going to cost? It is good that you are asking that question at this point. That means you are learning that it is your job to price the new kitchen since it is your house. You will spend your time, your calculator battery energy, and your gas to price the new kitchen for your home. Not long ago, the average homeowner did all his own repairs and improvements. These folks didn't have the Internet, YouTube, or box stores. You do. They had knowledge, books, and tools. You also have neighbors who have undergone various house surgeries. I would ask that you get a pencil and piece of paper. Go into the room or space that you want to change. Close your eyes and envision the finished product. Let's say you envision a new kitchen. As you picture a refrigerator, backsplash, tile floor, and cabinetry, open your eyes and write these items down. Be as specific as you can be. When you picture the cabinets, you should be able to envision the pull knobs. Write how many you will need for the drawers and doors. You may picture all new appliances and a stainless steel countertop. Write it down. Now sketch a mock up (rough) drawing of what element should go where. The sink should be here and the dishwasher there. I picture the fridge there and the island here. With your tape measure, find out how much wall space there is for the upper cabinets. Do the same thing for the base cabinets. Measure the approximate distance from here to there for the future countertops. Measure how much finished flooring you think there will be. Now add line items for the faucet, sink, disposal, and paint. The next step is to find average costs for these items on the Internet. You should also visit a cabinet shop, tile store, stainless steel fabrication shop, and box store. The goal is to get a rough price for these items. Along the way, you might even discover labor costs for the installation of the items. If the rough number you come up with is $15,000, then you have a starting point in your pricing. You will also have tear out, labor, and general contractor fees. You can go it alone, as many try to do. Acting as the project manager means that you will become the general contractor and responsible for ordering correct materials, scheduling subcontractors, accounting, payroll, site preparedness, and clean up, all without making any mistakes. Material that arrives a day late means that you could lose the subcontractor for an indefinite period of time to another job. Missing several material delivery deadlines could easily cost you months. If you are a dentist or teacher, it might be best to hire a general contractor to manage the chaos, drive the ship, and mine for savings along the way. This will also better ensure that the project finishes on time. Living in a construction site can gravely affect quality of life for those who are living there. If you agree, then we are beginning to see things the same way.

Your contractor is going to be paid for his knowledge and time. His livelihood is dependent on getting customers, but it also relies on the quality he delivers and the skill level and cost of his subcontractors that will handle specific parts of the project. Typically, the general contractor is not paid for his physical labor. He is a professional who is paid for his extensive working knowledge of systems and the people on his team. Keep in mind that a kitchen remodel is complicated. If a contractor prices a project as detailed as a kitchen, then he has invested in you. Chances are good that part of his decision to invest in you was based on the fact that you had done your homework. You had a good idea of what the pieces and parts should cost. You took the time to envision the finished product and sketch it. You were able to articulate that vision to him. In you, he found a homeowner who cares and is willing to communicate and roll up your sleeves. He believes you will be a good customer and partner. Do not expect him to hand over an exact price until you two have agreed on everything else. Then you can go to contract and he will solidify the final price. He may also have a clause in the contract that protects him in case the cost of materials increases during the building process. He cannot predict the future or problems lurking behind walls or under floors.

I believe references are every bit as important as a contractor's license. Municipalities, lawyers, insurance agents, EPA officials, and colleagues might disagree, but just like contracts, the printing on the document is only as good as the people behind the document. All the insurance in the world is not going to pay you for chasing down a lazy contractor who knocked down the walls, collected a check, then never showed up to finish a project. There are contractors who will do just the minimum in order to get paid. If he leaves you with a shoddy finished product, how much is it going to cost you in legal fees and court costs to sue him? You may end up with a negative judgment because of a poorly worded or weak contract. You may end up having to hire a good contractor to undo, then redo, the entire project. These scenarios are common. Having strong personal references is a critical ingredient to your success.

The contractors and workers you invite into your home better understand the critical nature of the relationship between you and your home. He needs to have a healthy respect for your quality of life. Will he treat your home as lovingly as you do? This has similarities to the relationship between a surgeon and your child. You may have a knack for reading people upon meeting them. You might not. Pay attention to red flags that pop up when meeting contractors that come to your house. The right surgeon will not walk in to your child's surgery room with a cigarette hanging out of his mouth, telling off color jokes, yelling at his nurse, and asking you for money, only to leave the room a mess as you hand him your insurance card. He will not leave fast food garbage in the waiting room and burp.

The surgeon will not park in a space that blocks everyone else from leaving or coming. If so, then you may have chosen this surgeon based on the price he gave you during the bid process. Folklore that leads people to the bid process is kept alive by others who relied on it, and got only what they paid for. Who created the bid process? Mr. Grumpy down the street is a terrible source for reliable information about how to secure good contractors. "Let's see now, as I learned it back in 19 and 71, we would get three bids. That's your magic number! First we would toss out the lowest bid. Then we would throw out the highest bid. Right there you will find your surgeon. Yessirree Bob... A bonafide surgeon!"

Contractors take into account the pricing and planning, tear out and disposal, materials delivery or acquisition, framing, plumbing, HVAC, electrical rough-in, materials and costs, drywall and drywall finishing, paint, cabinetry and associated cabinet ergonomics, countertop material, flooring hardware, codes permits and inspections, trim out, finishing duties, weather, and the people they will need to do a project correctly from start to finish. He is taking into account hundreds of things that must be addressed on the front end. If he did this for every single job in order to submit a bid, he would work half the year for free. If, in the end, his hourly rate seems a little higher than your hourly rate at your job, keep this in mind. There is a lot more to being a successful contractor than getting the job because he is the cheapest. Choose your contractors and service providers based on referrals and form open, honest, and lasting relationships with them.

## Our Emotions

The human being has an amazing mind. Not even the greatest computers to date can match the power of the human mind. What makes us superior to the manufactured computer is our emotions, discerning souls, and the ability to make our own decisions. These things cannot be built like a computer, tire, or beer can. There are animals that appear to express emotion. For example, mother elephants have been witnessed being distraught at the death of their calves. Dolphins can appear to be happy and excited. In many instances, we attribute and assign emotions to animal behavior. We believe that our cats are happy or that our goldfish are lonely. But what makes us superior to animals is that we have discerning souls. This means that we have the ability to make critical and conscious decisions based on probabilities and outcomes, and good and evil. We also experience a wide array of deep emotions that are sometimes based on fact, while at other times, on our perceptions only. These things qualify us as being superior beings to all other animals (oh yeah... And that opposable thumb thing). The impact that emotions have on our lives is remarkable. Much of what we believe can fuel our emotions and subsequent behaviors. An emotion can be the ingredient that drives us harder than the next guy in pursuit of that Olympic gold medal. It can also drive us to kill another person. What you see or believe at any given stage during a home construction project is often the result of your perception of what is happening at that time. Sometimes your perception will be accurate, while at other times it won't be. To add to the trouble, it is in our nature to generally believe our perceptions and arrive at conclusions. Contractors deal primarily in facts and science. During a project, homeowners deal primarily in hope, the future, and guessing. When homeowners feel that something may not be right related to a project, they can begin to react emotionally. Lack of knowledge can be a disaster cocktail in the making. For example, near the end of a project, suppose a customer walked through the construction site after working hours. In the silence, he began to notice many items that had not been done. He felt angry that the project was taking so long to finish. He forgot that the material delivery was a month late due to unusually heavy rain. He forgot that he was $8,000 behind in paying the contractor a recent draw (portion of full payment). The following morning, the homeowner approaches the general contractor and tells him that he will not pay another dime until the project is completely finished. The home-owner points to all of the items that need to be addressed. The contractor reminds him of the rain, the delayed materials delivery, and that he is behind $8,000 in payments.

Husbands and wives will visit their home projects after hours when all of the workers have gone home. The projects may be far from finished. Since neither husband nor wife truly understands the things they are seeing, they begin to question why something is this way or other things are that way. They begin to worry and fuel each other's worries to the point of leading themselves into victim status, or that they are shortchanged somehow. They drum up unlikely possibilities that are in contrast to the finished product. Finally, in bed with the moonlight shining on them, they are the perfect emotional team to keep each other company all night, fueling the despair.

I had a customer who was a young physician. He and his wife were fine people and had no experience interacting with contractors. The large and beautiful home was their first. The project was pretty simple, and consisted of removing carpeting from the expansive living room and replacing it with pre-finished hardwoods. My guys made terrific progress that first day, and had more than half of the floor installed by closing time. That evening, I noticed my phone showing a recent voicemail that had been left for me. I listened to the voicemail and it was from the young doctor. His voice was faint and unconfident. He simply asked me to call him as soon as possible. I immediately returned the call in case it happened to be an emergency. He greeted me, then nervously told me that our cables got black oil all over the floor. Quickly, I dissected his statement. I heard, "cables, black oil, and floor." He added his wife's substantiation that she witnessed cables strewn across the floor, and that the cables had to belong to us since we were the only people there that day. I told him that no cables were, or are, ever used when installing hardwoods. She is probably referring to the pneumatic air hoses that run from the compressors to the nail guns. No oil is used during the installation of hardwoods and those air hoses are kept clean from oil and adhesives. If the air hoses were oily, we couldn't handle the material or the heavy nail guns.

For a brief moment, my emotions almost got the better of me. I perceived that there was a possibility that the doctor was looking for a way to avoid paying us for materials and labor. Calmly, I told the doctor that we would be there first thing in the morning and get to the bottom of the problem. I assured him that there was an answer and that it would be handled. I told him where he could find a roll of blue masking tape in a large red tool bag. I asked him to place a piece of that tape near any spot that appears to be black oil. He agreed and we hung up. Immediately, I called a close friend and told her what happened. I couldn't wrap my mind around what the doctor and his wife saw. As we spoke, she walked through her house to the foyer where she and I had installed a similar floor. She laughed and said, "I know what it is. You got black oil all over my floor too. You refer to it as *wood grain*." The following morning I arrived at the doctor's house to find hundreds of pieces of blue tape across the entire floor. The doctor and his wife never lived in a house with hardwood flooring. Hardwoods were something they simply never noticed when they were in the homes of other people. They thought that hardwood meant white and flawless like a baseball bat or basketball court floor. They opted for new hardwood flooring because they read that it would increase the value of their home and reduce pet dander. I waited until after lunch to call the doctor on his cell phone. When he answered, I explained what he and his wife thought was oil was actually the beautiful grain in the oak. I told him that I was finished, and would lock up. He was quiet for a second then said, "You guys did a great job. Your check is in the top left kitchen drawer."

Having knowledge and keeping a cool head prior to formulating what we believe to be fact can mean the difference between success and failure of a project. A few days after that job was complete, I received a text from my friend with the matching floor. My dog Sox was staying with her and her daughter for a couple days. It read, "We have a huge problem with Sox over here." I called her immediately. She said that Sox was covered in black oil. Sox was a black dog.

# CHAPTER 16
# Good Contractors Are Picky

If you are new to owning your own property, you will interact with neighbors as it becomes your home. But as society evolves, we interact less frequently with neighbors. I find that sad. Some of my best memories are the result of deep and lasting relationships with neighbors along the way. This goes back to my childhood. I pride myself on those relationships. My 200 lb. English Mastiff, Doc Holliday, was the mayor of our street for a while. At least that is what he told me. Some speculate that the demise of close neighbor relations is the fault of modern day air conditioning. That makes sense. Before air conditioning, families would eat dinner as a unit and retire to the front porch for fresh and cool air. Children would leap from their front porches to play with the other children. Parents would wave to other parents and visit in the front yards. I wonder if, on every street in America, there is that one bad egg. You know… That one neighbor whose path every other neighbor works so hard to never cross. Most of us know that bad neighbor. Mr. Angry and Mrs. Miserable could live right next door or down the street. Their children are bullies. Their dogs bark at everyone who passes by. Know that they have the same needs for contractors that the rest of us do. They experience HVAC system failures, broken water pipes, and roof leaks. You may have the luxury of avoiding interaction with these bad neighbors, but someone has to work for them.

Let me offer you a few scenarios related to this subject. The following is based on a true story. There are writer embellishments and certain liberties taken in order to drive the point home.

Scenario A:

You have read enough of my book and are confident about taking on a project to see how much you have learned so far! You believe it is time to paint the upstairs interior of your house. Junior is due to arrive in a couple of months and his baby room should be blue to match the curtains that your mother-in law made for him. You and wife decide to call and invite me over for advice, and to possibly even take the account as a project. The following morning, you call me and we schedule a time to meet.

When I arrive, I notice that the lawn has been mowed and the house is beautiful. You greet me at the door. I look inside to find a clean and well-decorated living room. You are both happy and well groomed. I notice the little league baseball trophy on the fireplace mantle that was awarded to your seven-year-old future Chicago Cub. You offer me a cup of coffee and ask if I would consider doing a project for you. Your friends, Janice and Steve, (yes, the Janice from *Let's Make a Deal*) referred me and offered a positive review. We walk the upstairs then sit in the den to discuss our thoughts related to prospective wall colors, paint brands, and general costs. I extend my contractors' paint discount pricing to you as a house-warming gift. It is then that you inform me that your child is to be named Wes, not Junior. Our relationship is off to a great start and all it took was a little courtesy, professionalism, ethics, and a baby.

Scenario B:

You are reading this book and think, "We need to get something done about this damned place. Junior is about to pop out of mama in no time, she looks like she's gettin' a beer gut, and the walls are trashed. Maybe we should call Wes. He'd probably paint it cheap." Just then, you lean forward and yell out, "Loreen, where'z my beer at? I thought I told you to git my beer ten minutes ago?" Loreen makes her way from the back room and up the hall, stumbling over the empties, a toolbox, a trash bag, and broken toys. She throws a beer bottle toward you before realizing that you have passed out on the couch. The following morning, you take some aspirin and a little hair of the dog that bit ya'. You call me and say, "We gotta get a room ready on the 'count of a young'un. I gotta' find someone to paint it cheap cuz mama over here is a bit lazy and we're runnin' outta' time." I reluctantly agree to meet you, but if I were any less of a man, I would tell you that I am too covered up at this time. But since I am writing this book, I am going to meet dude and Loreen.

When I arrive, I see many repairs that the house desperately needs. One window is covered in foil. Another is broken. The shutters are rotted and the front yard is full of dead patches, weeds, and a post and chain where you keep your pit bull. Trash lines the fence. I make my way to the door and notice that the doorbell is hanging loose. You open the door, burp, scratch your chest, run your hand through greasy hair, and extend it for me to shake. I can see inside the living room, but it is dark and smells bad. I also notice a stack of utility bills piled up on the fireplace mantle next to the empty coke bottle serving as a tobacco spitter. We step in and you yell, "Loreen, Wes is here. Get your butt out here. Don't leave the man awaitin'. He's a busy man." Just then, Loreen can be heard down the hall as she yells, "You didn't say nothin' about no handyman comin' over. I've had it with you and the crap you pull. You're no different than my cousin Janice." Frustrated, you leave the house slamming the door behind you. You get in the truck and leave.

Just then, Loreen appears in the living room. She pushes the dishes aside on the couch, sits down, pats the open seat next to hers and says, "Well it's good to have a real man around here for a change. Have a seat. Now what are you gonna' fix?" I look at my watch and tell Loreen that the time has really gotten away, we need to reschedule, and that I will call. Appointments are appointments. I get up, let myself out, and quickly walk to my truck. I get in, start it, rev the motor to 5,000 RPM, and drop the tranny. I pull a Ricky Bobby and… Poof… I'm gone! After all, *if you ain't first, you're last*!

So while on the subject of that one neighbor… C'mon, you know the one I'm referring to. She is nosey or mean-spirited, cheap, and is often nasty to children. She hates dogs and makes sure you know it. She may be married. These couples fight and everyone can hear them. Everything is a drama and all about them. At some point, contractors are going to have to work for these people. These people have the same needs you do. But good contractors are picky about their customers. They are more discriminating about homeowners than the other way around. They are experienced and have antenna that can identify trouble customers a mile away. In fact, experienced contractors can begin to formulate opinions about prospective customers based solely on a simple phone call. And I promise that no matter how lean times may get or how bad a recession, good contractors avoid them like the plague. These bad neighbors are the way they are because they lack intellect, are narcissists, are greedy, are petty, or simply don't care. I will address the subject of bad neighbors later. And because of how rotten these people are, their projects tend to turn out poorly and at the hands of lesser or desperate contractors.

There are customers who, once the project starts, will hover over their contractors and engage in topics related to money. They will give Grammy award winning performances about how tough times are and how many expenses they have. A few years ago, I visited a friend as he worked at the home of an extremely wealthy elderly woman. She joined us as we were talking on the back porch. She appeared to fight back a crocodile tear as she said, "It is so hard being on a fixed income. So many people just don't understand." Meanwhile, her $75,000 Mercedes was parked in the driveway of her 5,000 square foot house that had been paid off years ago. When a potential customer brings up the subject of his or her financial state, the experienced contractor becomes wary and will avoid going to contract with him or her. The only reasons for a prospective customer to bring up their personal state of finances is because they are either broke, fishing for the lowest possible price, or place money as the fulcrum of the contractor/client relationship.

Good contractors don't place money at the center of a project. They strive to be that way and remain in good business practice. A good contractor will avoid potentially bad customers. They know that the product they deliver will be superior if they have a respect and liking for their customers (and the other way around). For example, do you work for someone who doesn't respect or like you, talks about the poor financial state of the company, doesn't trust you, or actively searches for ways to pay you less and engages your help in doing so? It makes for a terrible work environment. Contractors have the choice of either going to contract with these types of customers or not. If they do, like you, they will soon search for other ways to pay their bills. If a contractor has an opportunity to profit $2,000 to pour a new concrete driveway for Mr. Grumpy and is offered another opportunity to profit $1,500 by pouring a driveway for a great customer, which account do you think the contractor would choose? The answer is that a good contractor will choose the better account for less money. By doing so, he stands a much better chance of being paid for the work. In addition, he will enjoy his work environment and likely experience strong referrals.

The relationship between contractor and owner can be simple and mutually beneficial. It is up to both of you to find each other and maintain respect, civility, honesty, and relational stability. Your home is important to you and good contractors will treat it that way. The contractor's livelihood is every bit as important to him as yours is to you. Good customers will treat it that way.

Interaction: I have worked for almost every personality type there is. I have ventured into the unknown and come out victorious or beaten to death. Many homeowners will cite the same about their experiences with contractors. Having been entrenched in both camps, I have a deep understanding of the dynamics when the two worlds collide. Sometimes, when the two meet for the first time, little cartoon hearts flutter all over the place as they shake hands and high five over and over. Other times, the two drown in selfish pride, trying to outsmart or outwit each other. Homeowners can be very knowledgeable or very lacking in knowledge about their homes. They can be fair and reasonable or cheap and petty. Some contractors can be highly knowledgeable and competent, while other contractors can be lacking in knowledge and guessing their way through a project. Other contractors are hacks and rip-off artists. Some contractors are on time, tireless, committed to a correct finish, and bill their customers accurately. In contrast, there are plenty of contractors who are chronically late, sloppy, and send inflated invoices.

There are homeowners who haven't a clue related to the systems of which their houses are composed. Some seek professional help when things go wrong. Some homeowners ignore problems. In contrast, there are homeowners who are hands on and have a strong working knowledge of their houses. Of these, many do not have the time or tools to perform the work themselves. Some homeowners are extremely controlling while having little working knowledge about other houses. These are the guys who hover over workers' shoulders and say, "Looks good. You're doing a great job. Excuse me, but why does that not look right to me?" When facing this person and this question, I might reply, "It would take too long to explain. Let me make a little progress here and I will tell you later. The project has a ways to go yet. Keep in mind that you are witnessing sausage getting made." These owners are usually the ones who hire based on the lowest bid. Subsequently, their contractors end up working for $4 per hour by the time drawn out projects get finished. These contractors end up not making enough to warranty their work. This type of contractor is worth only what he gets paid. A real professional will be required to undo then redo the lesser contractor's work.

Warning: the following sentence may be the longest question in literary history… Isn't it interesting that when a loved one needs surgery, you are placed in one room as he is carted off to another room where a team of people will cut open your loved one's body, drop surgical instruments, bruise organs, dodge blood as it spurts across the O.R., with the "ping" monitor flat-lining from time to time, and then your loved one is sewn, stapled, and glued back together into something recognizable, cleaned up while the surgeon changes into clean scrubs and calmly walks into the waiting room to update you, smiling as he says in an airline captain's voice, "He did very well and you should be able to see him in his room within the hour." (?)

Realize that when a contractor does surgery on your house, you get to see the tools when dropped, the tile when cracked, the blood as it drips from a worker's elbow. You see workers cut, sand, break, bang, shred, and fall. I ponder the implications of anaesthetizing a property owner and carting him off to another room until the project is finished. As he regains consciousness, the freshly showered contractor appears in a pressed business suit and sits down in a chair next to the homeowner. The contractor smiles, and in his calm and confident voice, says, "Morning sleepy! I'm pleased to tell you that the project is finished. It went very well and you should be able to go in there within the hour. We are cleaning it up as we speak. As for me, I'm headed to the club to play the back nine."

# CHAPTER 17
# Speed, Quality, Price: Pick Two

If you read only one of my writings, let it be this one. In any industry, there is insider knowledge or rules of thumb that are specific to each industry. The world of contracting is no different. I will often approach subjects in general terms so that it will apply to as many of you as possible. This chapter is about a very specific rule that few contractors, and fewer homeowners, take into consideration. The rule is cited in the title of this chapter. It applies to almost every service-related purchase you will make. Speed, quality, and price: pick only two!

In every service industry or contracting situation I have witnessed, heard of, or experienced, I have found it impossible for a contractor to deliver high speed, exceptional quality, and low price simultaneously. It can happen only on TV or in slave encampments. Any advertisement that claims to deliver all three is false and misleading. Knowing this rule will help you to better understand the process of hiring contractors and managing your expectations.

When you hire contractors and service personnel, you are given three potential options. They are speed, quality, and price. Of these three, you get to pick two. You may elect to choose speed and quality, or quality and price, or speed and price. You may demand all three, and be promised all three, but you will not receive all three. In the planning phase of a project or repair, you have to decide which two are the most important to you. You will have to ask yourself if speed is important. If you are in no specific hurry, speed may not be paramount. If you demand high quality, then quality is a vital choice. If you are on a tight budget, price is critical.

If you want speed and quality, it will cost more. By choosing speed and price, you forfeit quality. If you want quality and low price, you may be placed in the back of the line and have to wait a while. I will provide a few examples in order to illustrate how this works: Janice wants to have the exterior of her house painted. The time of year is autumn. There is only a small window of time before the weather will become too cold and unpredictable for painting. Janice realizes that she is going to have to hire someone who can get the job done quickly. She interviews paint contractors and learns that the licensed and insured contractors who come highly recommended are expensive ($10,000). Wanting to avoid mistakes, short cuts, injuries, and shoddy work, she comes to the conclusion that quality is important to her. In this example, Janice has chosen speed and quality. Low price isn't possible.

Prior to choosing her paint contractor, Janice has a change of heart. Being placed in the front of the line and getting great quality costs more than she has budgeted, and she doesn't want to dig into her retirement funds. On her way out of the grocery store, Janice notices a business card pinned to the community bulletin board. The printing on the card reads, "Redneck Jimmy's Quality Paint Jobs." Janice calls Redneck Jimmy and invites him over to get a bid. She is also conscious of the fact that the clock is ticking and winter will soon be knocking at the door. Jimmy shows up, walks the property, and returns to his truck to formulate a price for Janice. When he returns, he reveals his price of $6,000 to paint the exterior of Janice's house. This price is within Janice's budget. This will afford Janice the opportunity to fly to Los Angeles over the holidays for an upcoming taping of the popular television game show *Let's Make a Deal*. Unfortunately, when Janice calls Jimmy's references, nobody returns her voicemails. Janice becomes frustrated but suddenly remembers that the neighbor boy was handing out flyers about his budding handyman business. Janice walks down the street and rings the doorbell where Junior lives. She tells Junior about the opportunity and he is all too willing to take on the paint job! His price is $2,000 and he can start immediately. In this scenario, Janice has chosen speed and price. In short order, Janice will soon discover that she has mistakenly forfeited quality.

Within a couple of days, the boy begins to paint her house. Meanwhile, Janice's brother texts to her a video link titled "Painting a House." The short video is about the process of house painting. In this video, it first shows a crew of workers washing, then scraping and sanding the exterior of a house. The second segment shows those same workers filling cracks and joints with caulk, silicone, and patching compound. The third segment showed those same workers covering windows and doors with paper and masking tape before applying paint to the house using high tech airless sprayers. The workers in the video were wearing protective breathing masks and eyewear. Just then, she remembered reading something about hiring the right contractors in a great book, *Bridging the Gap Between Homeowners and Their Homes*. She decides to go outside and talk to Junior. Janice walks out front, then to the side of the house. She finds Junior's wooden ladder but no Junior. She then notices that a lot of paint has been spilled onto the brick wall just below the siding. Being in the direct sunlight, some of the paint has already dried. The empty bucket rests on the mulch. Janice places a call to Junior's house and asks Junior's mother if Junior is there. The mother tells Janice that Junior is in his room watching YouTube videos related to paint removal from brick surfaces. Janice asks her to tell Junior to come to the house as soon as possible. Janice returns home and tries to rinse the paint off of the brick. It doesn't work. By this time, Junior appears with a gallon container of muriatic acid and a wire brush. Janice tells Junior that part of a paintjob is to prepare the surface by cleaning, removing loose paint, roughing the existing surface, and applying primer to bare surfaces. Junior looks at Janice as if she were speaking a different language. They both look at the spilled paint. Junior apologizes and promises to try to handle it as soon as he gets back from soccer practice. The following afternoon, as Junior is scraping the old paint, a paint chip falls into his eye. Junior rubs his eye, causing the paint chip to lacerate the eyeball. With a hand over his eye, Junior makes his way home where his mother can try to rinse the chip out. Sadly, Junior's dad is a fierce attorney. The money Janice saved on the paint job will now go toward legal fees and medical bills. Remember, Janice chose speed and price while sacrificing quality.

I have a great friend who bought a beautiful new home in a very nice part of town. He wanted a remodeled kitchen and master bathroom prior to actually moving in. He had a deadline in mind. I agreed to help him procure the right contractor for the job as well as build the budget. We chose a top contractor and asked to be placed to the front of the line. The contractor agreed, and said he would need to hire extra labor to satisfy our ambitious and rigid schedule.

In this scenario, my friend chose speed and quality while forfeiting price. This project cost 15% more because my friend had a deadline. Money was not an issue in this case.

The following is a true story.

A young couple hired a contractor to tear out a wall and existing bathtub in order to build a new walk-in shower. The contractor was a friend of a friend of theirs. He agreed to do the project knowing that their budget was small and unrealistic. He did it as a favor to this nice young couple. The contractor met with them on several occasions to go over materials costs and offered some great ways to save money on materials, tile, and fixtures. The contractor's fee was a set amount, and he would be paid on a schedule that reflected amount of work completed. The project was contracted at a total price of $7,500. This meant that the contractor would be paid $2,500 twice based on work completed, and $2,500 at the conclusion of the project. Prior to the project starting, the couple became increasingly needy of the contractor's time, asking for meetings at tile showrooms, bath fixture houses, and box stores. So that their requests wouldn't get out of hand, the contractor told them that each consultative visit would be charged at $75 per hour in addition to the $7,500 project price. The requests for meetings stopped. The couple had no respect for the contractor's time and knowledge. The young husband called the contractor to tell him that they were ready for the project to start.

The first day at the job site was loud and dirty. The wife asked the contractor for the time he planned on finishing that day as she had guests coming over at 2:00. He told her that he would accommodate her and left by 2:00. This robbed the contractor of four good working hours. Upon arriving at the house that next morning, the wife asked the contractor if she could show him something. He agreed and followed her into a bedroom, where she pointed out several places on the walls that looked damaged. She said these things were not there prior to him starting the work the day before. He told her that they are unrelated to his work and that the nail pops are nails that back out of their holes. This phenomenon is caused by poor framing at the time of construction, and happens with changing outside temperatures. By the end of the week, the contractor was due his first payment (draw) that represented the tear out, framing, drywall installation, and a shower pan (floor). The couple fought with the contractor over the dollar amount (which was agreed to in the contract). He showed the couple the original contract and budget. Somehow, the couple ignored the money saving strategies offered to them by the contractor when they purchased materials. They had spent almost their entire budget on extravagant high-end tile, fixtures, lighting, and shower hardware. The couple reluctantly paid the contractor his draw. In other words, the couple blew their money on designer finishes and believed that the expenses could just be taken out of the contractor's fee (which was already ridiculously low). The following day, the husband approached the contractor with a new pattern of how the wife wanted the tile to be set (installed). The contractor told him that it would require purchasing 25% more tile due to waste. It would also cost an increase of $300 in labor given how tedious and time-consuming the cuts would be. The following day, the wife refused to speak to the contractor. The husband approached the contractor and said, "We really need to get this project finished. We are headed out of town." The contractor said, "But I have another full week to be finished and the project completion should be right on time." The husband held firm. The contractor loaded his tools into his truck and left for good. Within the week, rumors about the contractor's poor quality and bad attitude began to infiltrate their social circle. This expert contractor's decision to try and help this petty and narcissistic couple was a poor one. He lost money on the materials he purchased for the couple. He lost money and time by not charging for his consultations and expertise in framing, shower pans, and tile setting. I know this couple, believe the young wife has serious mental issues, and think that this marriage will not last long. In this scenario, the couple initially wanted quality and price. In quick order, they demanded speed as well. Nobody won.

I felt it important to further explain the price, quality, and speed maxim by using these examples. It can be applied to so many jobs at your home. Jobs or repairs around your house will be ranked as critical, somewhat critical, and not all that critical. I define critical as that which requires immediate attention. Critical items might be related to flood damage, a tree falling on your roof, electrical issues, HVAC failure, and anything that poses a threat to your safety. I suggest that you always choose speed and quality when addressing critical items. It might cost more to be fixed, but your life and immediate safety are worth it. Items that are somewhat critical could be a small roof leak, an exterior door that doesn't open and close correctly, or a damaged handrail. When addressing these things, you could choose quality and price. Somewhat critical items can be addressed over a period of a week to a month and they do need to be fixed immediately. Items that are not all that critical are items that you could live without by making a few personal changes. Such items might be a failing oven, filtered water dispenser, disposal, electric garage door opener, or peeling wallpaper. You can choose to ignore these repairs or have them addressed later. Speed is not important. Price may or may not be a factor. Quality is important because nothing is more expensive than doing it twice.

When it comes to lawn service or house sitting, you may choose any criteria you would like. I like hiring neighbor kids to mow the lawn or dog sit. I once hired a neighbor's son to be my ground guy, filling the insulation blower with cellulose insulation while I was in the attic with the hose blowing insulation in between the ceiling joists. Speed, quality, and price did not come into the equation.

Speed, quality, and price: you get only two. To change your decision once work has begun at your home is unreasonable, unfair, and unrealistic. Proceed!

# CHAPTER 18
# Exterminators

Did you ever see the Alfred Hitchcock movie *The Birds*? I suppose the same thought crossed Alfred's mind as it did mine about groups of animals and how easily they could take over a population and destroy it as we could (and do) destroy theirs. In that movie, birds decide to gang up and destroy a town and its residents. I consider how tough animals have to be in order to survive the outdoors. Sometimes people will come across a baby squirrel with the intention of turning it into a cute little pet. Cartoons prove that it can be done, but I suggest that you not try it. In cartoons, a squirrel wears aviator goggles and speaks English. In real life, squirrels can cause amazing destruction and injuries to human fingers. Cute or not, squirrels, like most animals, are genetically programmed to grow up and sharpen their survival skills. Animals that are natural prey will stop at nothing to survive a threat. Cute and young squirrels turn into adult squirrels that view the human hand as much a threat as a dog or snake.

In the animal world, humans included, there is safety in numbers. Almost all animals and insects operate in groups in order to minimize their chances of being killed. Humans have few natural predators. When you consider how outnumbered humans are by insects, it is amazing that they haven't wiped us out. They could do so very easily. But most animals and insects are genetically programmed to avoid contact with humans (excluding polar bears, mosquitoes, and tigers. Polar bears, mosquitoes, and tigers *will* kill you). It is usually only when they are threatened or injured that they harm us. Though the mosquito isn't really considered an animal, it kills more humans than any animal in history. Surprisingly, the ranch cow and hippopotamus rank at the top when it comes to deadly attacks on humans. But these deaths are usually the fault of the victim.

As humans, we are not concerned about being exterminated by animals or pests. And closer to home, we avoid being stung by wasps, bitten by spiders, and invaded by mice. Spray repellants and mousetraps are big industries. So is the business of professional extermination. And just as with any industry, there are good ones and bad ones.

Exterminators have been around for years. The industry is necessary. It is our responsibility to maintain and protect our homes. Knowledge of pest behavior and how to rid our lives of them requires expertise. Insects, spiders and varmints will often interact (or try to) with your home. Your home is where pests find food, shelter, safety, and a dark place to breed. Only occasionally will you interact with your crawlspace, roof, or attic. It is normal for critters to make these places their homes. Since they are attracted to your food, trash, heat, pets, shade, and your bed, you will ultimately interact with pests. There are instances when you will have to take matters into your own hands. I have introduced Mr. Spider to Mr. Shoe. I allow my dog to introduce himself to Mr. Mole. After all, who are we to be unsocial?

Pest extermination can be tricky and as complicated as your HVAC or roof systems. This means that you can easily become a target of a con man. I recall the first time I interacted with an extermination company. I had just finished remodeling my 1870s Victorian home (and no... I did not buy it when it was new!). My home was beautiful and healthy. I decided to sign a yearly contract with a company, largely because their office was less than a mile away from my home. The exterminator was a nice guy and seemed knowledgeable about pests and home insurance policies. Given that this was my first home purchase, I had little experience with exterminators. I didn't know about scheduled inspections, costs, and what inspections involved. For an annual fee, the company would send an inspector to look for evidence of pests such as termites, wood-dwelling insects, fire ants, and the list went on. I wrote him a check and our relationship began. Every month, a representative would come to the property and walk the outside of the house exterior. He went under the house to look in the cellar. He would emerge, tell me that everything looked good, and leave. I lived happily ever after until it became time to sell the place. Termites, ants, and mice were all over the place and lurking in the cellar. The termites had caused quite a bit of damage to the floor joists. There was also a large patch of black mold that was due to pooling of water in one corner (that was difficult to see or get to). Naturally, I addressed the issues, made the repairs, and took care of any problems found by the buyer's home inspector. It turns out that the inspections performed by the exterminators were not adequate inspections. Standing in a position at the base of the cellar stairs and looking for problems with a flashlight does not equate to a thorough inspection. Just before closing on the sale, I contacted the original exterminator representative to tell him what happened. He came and I showed him termite carcasses and dead ants. He told me that the termites were not actually termites. He admitted to never seeing mold or a problem with water under the house. He also told me that I should have called to tell them when there was a problem with mice. I replied, "What? You didn't see these things during your inspections?" In other words, he was off the hook since it would be hard for me to prove my claims in court and that he was a phony. I knew so little about termites. We pick our battles. I chalked it up to experience and was very careful the next time I contracted with an exterminator.

Prior to hiring an exterminator and signing an inspection contract, you must have, in writing, all of the pests that they will be responsible for managing, killing, and any means they will enlist for eradication if necessary. That list might include termites only. It might include every common bug specific to your home's location. Methods of eradication are things you need to know. If they use chemicals, you should know what those specific chemicals are and the effects they have on humans and pets. Ask what critters are common to your location. The exterminator should know if there are problems in your neighborhood with snakes, mice, rats, possums, cats, raccoons, bears, deer, mountain lions, or alligators. You might find that an exterminator deals in insects only, while another exterminator includes wildlife such as mice or poisonous snakes. It must be spelled out in the contract. Keep in mind that the broader the spectrum of pests they contract to control, the more expensive the contract will be.

Next, walk the property with the exterminator and ask him to physically show you exactly how each inspection will be performed.

If his inspection includes just a stroll around the yard, thank him for his time and let him know that you will call him if you need him. If his inspection includes spraying the inside of your house, treating the perimeter of the house exterior, treating the basement (or crawlspace), and treating the attic, then he is thorough. If his monthly inspection includes the floor system under the house and roof system in the attic, he is very thorough. Having a description of the actual geographical locations of his inspections outside and inside of the home must be spelled out in the contract. Inspecting the crawlspace from a single location is NOT a thorough inspection. He must spell out that he will inspect all floor joists, the bottom framing plates that rest on the foundation (including up to 6" above those plates), even if it means crawling on his stomach through dirt. Remember, he is charging you for this. If you can afford his contract, he is likely your guy. Remember to make sure this is in writing before signing anything or paying anyone. If these things are spelled out in the contract and he neglects to honor any part of the contract, point it out quickly. You should always address problems early. He might scoff, but he is a legal agent and representative for the extermination company. They must honor their contracts. Further, they don't want any trouble or bad publicity.

What do exterminators look for and how do they find it? How will they treat a found issue? Some exterminators show up, spray chemicals along the base of your interior walls, check the termite repellants in the ground, and leave. Other exterminators take a conscientious visual inspection of everything. Some exterminators will include termite control around your swimming pool. Termites can destroy a pool liner quickly. Exterminators are looking for bugs and critters that can cause damage to your house or cause physical harm to you. Spiders are difficult to treat. You may not see dangerous brown recluse spiders unless you go into the attic once in a while or tear the siding off your house exterior. Black widows like cool and dark places. They live in your water meter in the front yard. They live in brick piles and in basements. To get rid of spiders, you have to remove their food sources (other bugs). I never poison mice or rats. They crawl inside a wall and die. Their deaths are miserable and their smelly decomposing bodies are worse. I choose to capture and release or use traps that kill instantly. If you have dogs and cats, traps might not be a good idea. Paws have nerves. Raccoons and possums are best captured and released. Of course, they don't become pests unless your garbage or pet food is accessible to them. Growing up in the Rockies, I witnessed larger pests at my house. We had bears, elk, giant squirrels, and an 8' mountain lion in the yard/property at any given time. If you live in their natural habitats, you assume the risk of having them as daily visitors. There are serious laws related to interacting with or killing them. The same thing applies to poisonous snakes and birds of prey.

You may recall that when you purchased your house, a termite letter was required by the lender prior to closing. Your lender needed the assurance that a licensed and qualified exterminator inspected and/or treated the house for termites. The lender doesn't visit your house prior to lending you the money. They have to rely on public records, the deed, the appraisal report, and the exterminator's letter. They don't want to lend $250,000 for something that is about to fall over. Termites can destroy a house frame faster than water damage can. It is difficult for the untrained eye to find and identify termites and subsequent termite damage until the damage is excessive. Over the counter bug spray may kill termites, but does not treat for termite colonies. Complicated chemicals applied by experienced exterminators are the best way to handle these bugs. Part of hiring a good exterminator is you being proactive, as opposed to being reactive. Because the contracted price from one exterminator to the next will not differ significantly, check references and the Better Business Bureau prior to signing an exterminator's contract.

By the way, did you know that snakes often live in your fireplaces and attics?

# CHAPTER 19
# DIY (Do It Yourself)

For some homeowners, the most rewarding experiences are doing home projects themselves. Working on a house as a team (partners and family) is a great way to bond, learn, teach, and accomplish. Some people love yard work and gardening. Others like to paint. Decorating can be fun. I encourage homeowners to increase quality of life by doing home improvements that further make a house a home. It can be highly rewarding both spiritually and even financially. Increasing the value of your home while simultaneously increasing your quality of life is a great idea. However, I encourage homeowners to place maintenance and repairs above elective projects. *Needs* should always be placed in front of *wants*. If repairs and maintenance are things you can afford to hire someone else to do, then hire away and immerse yourselves in the fun stuff.

There is another camp among homeowners that wants absolutely nothing to do with working on or around the house. These people tend to live in apartments, townhouses, or condominiums. Their lifestyles might place golf, fitness, or social activities above mowing and painting. To each their own. Many of these people choose to rent rather than buy a home. Most residential lease contracts will include strong wording related to property improvements made by renters. Property owners don't want amateur renters making structural or material changes for obvious reasons. Renters might choose to paint the walls in deeply personal colors such as pink or red, leaving the rental property less desirable to the next potential renter. I have clients who allow renters to make changes or improvements as long as the changes are agreed to in writing prior to the renter making them.

As a former TV guy, I learned a lot about home genre programming. Shows about houses and homes rank high among the most popular TV programs. Advertisers love them because of the target audience (homeowners) and the broad spectrum of products marketed provides a financial boon to them. Travel and food related programming ratings have declined recently. These networks began to broadcast shows that weren't about food or travel at all. The idea was to capture a larger audience. Home programming might broadcast shows with varying subject matter, but they are all home based. Although these home related shows are entertaining and informative, it is important to keep in mind that most of what you see on television is scripted and planned. This includes reality shows as well. Not everything you see is true, real, or practical.

In college, I studied psychology and had a particular interest in consumer psychology. I was interested in why people bought the things they did. Understanding why we buy food is a no brainer. But why do we choose one food over the other? From the 1970s through the 1980s, there was a lot of controversy about egg consumption and cholesterol. Some health gurus told us that eggs were deadly because of the cholesterol and warned of imminent heart attacks. This coincided with university scientists (and hired scientists, both paid through huge grants) scaring the world population that the earth was facing global cooling and we would all freeze to death if we used certain products. The public became convinced that the egg was the culprit responsible for heart attacks, while disregarding smoking, high fat diets, and a disdain for exercise. In a brilliant marketing move, Jiff peanut butter created a new label for their jars. It read, "Jiff Creamy Peanut Butter Contains No Cholesterol!" Jiff shot to the top of the public's peanut butter preferences. To date, no other peanut butter manufacturer has equaled Jiff's massive market share. Chevy Nova sales were a dismal failure south of the American border. What General Motors failed to take into account was that, in Spanish, "no va" means "no go." It really can be all about the marketing. I cite these examples because as marketers spend billions of dollars on research, testing, and product placement, they do so knowing that the public is hungry for new and exciting additions to their lives that promise to increase happiness, wellness, and comfort.

We watch television to escape our respective "days in the life." A lot of research goes into the making of what you see on television. The more interesting a show is to you, the greater the likelihood that you will watch it and the accompanying TV commercials. At night, we escape the daily grind by opening a beer, plopping down into the easy chair, and being carried far away from the office, classroom, or factory. The easiest way to do it is to invest our minds into *Who Sings Like Taylor, Dancing with Elephants, Watch the Cops*, or *Where is Bob Ross*. Long before television, C.S. Lewis wrote, "We read to know we are not alone." I believe that is true today. I also believe we use social media, watch TV, listen to radio, and spend time on the Internet to know that we are not alone. We have far more, and far more attractive, real life diversions than ever before.

We listen to music that calms us or takes us back in time to a much better place. We tune into political talk shows and get all fired up! We become glued to the reality stars or the dancing walking dead or whatever the networks can deliver that commands our attention for a few hours.

Home related TV shows are similarly designed to get your attention. Viewers are highly entertained by programs that relate to homes and quality of life. These shows offer more than entertainment. I love *This Old House*. Shows of this type are designed to show you what's possible and how to achieve it. The problem with many other shows is that they often depict highly complicated and dangerous projects and deliver them in a way designed to make viewers think they can achieve the same thing. A complete remodeling project is planned, executed, and finished in less than 40 minutes of broadcast time. I am amazed at how many amateurs are trying to get into the business of house flipping. They cite a television show they watched and want to get in on the profits! They like picking out wall colors and feel they have a real knack for choosing tile! They are led to believe that they can repeat what they have seen on TV, when in reality they haven't the skill or aptitude to be on a construction site cleaning crew.

My approach may seem mean-spirited. The opposite is true. What do you do for a living? You may be a mechanic, software designer, receptionist, property manager, accountant, teacher, or linguist. I am amazed at how many tools I have taken to a job site to accomplish the simplest task. I think of how many muscles and motions the human body will enlist to perform the simplest task. Some of these tools are very heavy and dangerous. Many of the motions are dangerous. On television, producers, set directors, and actors make the motions appear to be easy and natural. But tools and materials are already in place. What tools do you use at your job? What tools are specific to your industry? What is physically required of you to successfully perform your duties? I bet that most of you will answer these questions with items such as telephones, cars, your voices, computers, and chairs. Some tools are unique to certain professions. Most of us do not rely on complex navigation equipment. Pilots do. Most of us don't use micro soldering irons. Computer repairmen do. Most of us don't use expensive camera equipment and lighting sets. News anchors do. Most people don't use, or own, tape measures, levels, compound miter saws, compressors, pneumatic tools, 40-foot ladders, wrecking bars, or mud knives to make a living. How strong are the muscles in your body? If you work out a lot, then your answer might be impressive. How long can you hold a twenty-pound worm drive saw over your head? How long can you bend over while on your knees to set a cumulative 1,000 lbs. of tile and mortar mix?

There are thousands of examples of homeowners attempting to emulate something they have seen on TV, only to find themselves broke, injured, and living long periods of time in a disaster. It is during these times that relationships are severely and negatively impacted. During one of my broadcasts, I went over the statistics related to the subject of home projects and the impact these projects have on marriages. In my research, I found a study that revealed almost all relationships were negatively impacted by a home project. Sadly, 8% of marriages fail because of a home project. Only 14% cited no change in the relationship as a result of a home project. I imagine they were in Jamaica during construction! I know women who are attracted to men that are good with tools and know their way around the world of construction. One such woman is a neighbor of mine. She is a self-proclaimed do-it-yourselfer! The problem is, she doesn't have many tools and has less working knowledge about construction and house systems. Consequently, she dates handymen. One such talented handyman is also a neighbor of ours. Their relationship blossomed quickly. She soon discovered that he liked tackling new projects. The hard part is that he does so prior to finishing the previous ones. They live in a perpetual work site. So much for increasing quality of life.

Doing home projects yourself can be highly rewarding. It is very possible for you to learn how to accomplish almost anything at your house. It usually doesn't happen as a result of watching YouTube or television. If you get the chance, look up the statistics of causes for emergency room visits. Broken bones, electrocution, severed limbs, blindness, and burns are highly common reasons for emergency visits, and the majority of those injuries are sustained in the home or at construction sites. I have personally known highly experienced construction professionals who have been injured while engaged in a construction project (including myself). I have also known many amateurs who have been injured or killed during a project. One such death was a friend of the family. He was cutting a large dead branch from a tree in his yard. Sadly, there was a rope around the branch and the other end was tied around his hand. Once the large branch was cut, he backed down the ladder. As the branch broke free, it made its way to the earth. He was immediately pulled skyward and went head first into another large branch. He died instantly. Having the right tools, clothing, knowledge, safety gear, physical strength, time, and health insurance is critical to successfully tackling any project at your home.

The most common DIY project is house painting. If you do it correctly and use the right colors, it can offer a 100% return on investment! Do you know what primer is? Do you know the difference in primers and when to use them? Do you know the differences between paint brands, purposes, and sheens? Do you know what colors compliment others? Do you know how to neutralize existing wall colors and why that might be needed? Do you know the difference between man-made versus natural bristle brushes, or why you should never use a disposable roller cover? What is a 2" cutty? A good paint job will require you to have these answers.

Landscaping is another common DIY project that can really compliment the house and yard. It can also create a wonderful outdoor living area while increasing the appraisal value of your property. Drawbacks include making the wrong choices in plant type or plant location. Don't begin landscape projects unless you are physically able to complete them. In your neighborhood, you may have seen landscape workers. These workers have amazing musculatures. Rarely are they overweight. They are strong and flexible. Their backs are strong and limber. One of these workers can accomplish more in a single day than most of us can in a week. Depending on the scope of work, you can really benefit from engaging in landscaping activities. Gardening, planting, and mulch spreading are a lot safer than laying rocks or pavers or planting larger trees. Laying pavers can require quite a bit of preparation in the form of digging, spreading sand or gravel, and even operating small heavy equipment. Planting trees requires a lot of digging and awkwardly moving the tree prior to placing it in the hole. If your back goes out, it may be a long time until you are able to work outside again. Unless your muscles can support your joints (bone, connective tissue, and tendons), it is best to keep to the lighter activities.

I suggest that homeowners invest time, money, and sweat equity into their properties. The idea is to understand and become one with your home. The better you understand your home and know how to work on it, the stronger your relationship with your home will be. I also suggest leaving the complicated and heavy work to the professionals. If you are seriously injured, you will have a terrible quality of life no matter where you live.

# CHAPTER 20
# The Perfect Tool Kit

The perfect tool kit for you may not be the perfect tool kit for your neighbor. You two have different lifestyles, skill sets, and knowledge. My dad never had tools that could repair electronics or computers. Most Millennials do not own a lathe or circular saw. But there are some tools that I believe all homeowners should have. Not everyone needs woodworking tools or circuit board soldering equipment, but everybody should own a screwdriver.

I plan to identify a set of common tools that you will likely need as a homeowner. I have a very close friend who is a member of the Rock and Roll Hall of Fame. He also happens to be the handiest homeowner I have ever known (including myself). That he grew up on a farm in the Ozarks may have had a lot to do with it. He is now my dad's age. He also has more tools than I do and knows how to use every one of them. I have another close friend who lives in a condominium. She had only a flat head screwdriver and a hammer that looks like something a cobbler might use. She told me that she borrowed the hammer from a friend to kill spiders. Over the years, she has collected more tools and knows how to use them.

Tool storage is very important. Most tools or tool groups should be kept together. Keeping them organized with easy access is important. Making dangerous tools hard to access is important. A child can pull on a power cord and bring a heavy saw down on his/her face. All tools should be kept in a dry area with moderate temperatures. Even tools that are for outdoor use need to be protected. A shovel left outside over the winter is a useless shovel in the spring. They are difficult to use with rotted or broken handles. Exterior conditions tend to rot, erode, and rust metal, wood, and plastic.

## Your Brain

Tools can pose a physical threat if abused or not used correctly. You should know how to use a tool correctly prior to trying. Something as simple as a box cutter can lead to disaster. At a minimum, it can quickly sever a tendon in the hand or artery in the leg. It can bring down an airliner. I realize it would be a challenge to fit your brain into a tool bag, but let us agree that the most important and powerful tool you have is your brain. As with any tool, it works much better if used correctly. This tool can do more than all the other tools combined. Your brain is a tool that if left behind, will lead you to injury, disappointment, regret, frustration, and even death. Your brain can keep you safe while directing all the other tools and body parts. No matter which task you choose, your brain must be there and alert 100% of the time. It will remind you to wear gloves when handling dangerous materials. Your brain will defend your eyesight. It will keep safety front and center. Use this tool all of the time. I just re-read this paragraph aloud. I am sitting at my office desk. I sound eerily like one of those flight instructors from the 1940s news reels.

## Eye Protection

It takes less than a second to change your life for the worse... Forever. It can take less than a second to become paralyzed, disabled, or blind for the rest of your life. A small object can turn out to be a cause of great pain. One Saturday afternoon, a tiny paint chip fell into my eye (and I was wearing glasses). It cut my eye and festered for the rest of the weekend. A neighbor, who is an ophthalmologist, got it out late Sunday night. I recall one beautiful fall day when I was in my driveway cutting trim. Yelling to my buddy on the ladder, I accidentally lowered my circular saw onto my right hand and cut off my thumb. Fortunately there was a surgeon at the "Doc in a Box" a block away. A friend of ours was very talented at building racecars and engines. He had over 40 years of experience. One afternoon, he sprayed a cleaner on a part. The problem is that the discharge hole was pointed directly at his eyes. He is now permanently blind. These things happened in a flash, and to very experienced and competent people. It used to be that eye protection looked goofy. These days, eye protection is very stylish. Besides, it is better to see yourself as a bit goofy than to never see yourself again. Since life-altering injuries can happen to anyone, it is best to use tools when there are no distractions. You must be able to think through every move you make. You must perform to purposely avoid a bad outcome. Again, I sound eerily like one of those flight instructors from the 1940s news reels.

## Ear Protection

Our hearing ability is usually the first of our natural senses to decline. Losing hearing is an occurrence that creeps up on many of us slowly and over the course of our lives. Damage to our hearing is a cumulative thing. One loud airplane engine is not going to make us deaf. Hearing that same engine many times a day over twenty years can make us deaf. It is proven that exposure to loud noises does have a negative impact on our hearing. People who have worked in loud areas without ear protection suffer hearing loss at a much higher rate than an office receptionist. Recently, a prominent doctor on TV cited that younger people who frequently use ear buds are experiencing permanent hearing loss at very early ages and at alarming rates. This is sad because these people aren't required to wear the ear buds as a means of making a living. Ear protection comes in many forms and is available at any box store. Earplugs are very inexpensive and easy to use. I use the disposable kind. They are little pieces of foam that you squeeze between your fingers and install in the ear. As they expand back into shape, they form to your ear and block loud noise. When finished, you take them out and throw them away. I use them when around loud tools or when shooting at the range.

**Hand Protection**

It wasn't until I was well into my building career that I began to protect my hands. I just got tired of splinters, cuts, abrasions, and dry skin. I will admit to never getting a splinter that didn't eventually come out. The irritation and pain of carrying it around under the skin gets old quickly. Splinters from metal and pressure treated wood hurt worse. We take our fingers for granted. It is amazing to discover which part of each finger is responsible for what action. It is easy to find out the answers once that finger or part of a finger is injured. Using clippers, scissors, a fork, opening a doorknob, turning a key, and so many other things can seem impossible with even the tiniest splinter or cut. If you don't wear gloves, you will find out what I mean. I have been bitten by black widow and brown recluse spiders. I prefer gloves.

## Toe and Forehead Protection (Flashlights)

I am surprised at the numbers of homeowners who do not own a flashlight, or have one that doesn't work. In the old days, good flashlights were big and heavy. The battery life was relatively short. Today, we have small yet powerful LED flashlights. They have longer lasting batteries and emit far more light than their predecessors. They cost less than old style flashlights. Flashlights are extremely important. Head, foot, and toe injuries are common as we make our way through dark homes. Losing power to our homes is common. Electricity is another thing we take for granted. We sure miss it when it goes out. It is imperative to have working flashlights in the house. Notice that I wrote, "flashlights"…Plural. They are affordable and often come in multi-pack sets. Crawlspaces and attics rarely offer adequate lighting. You should keep a flashlight in the attic and another at the crawlspace opening. Flashlights are valuable to have when looking for roof leaks. Not only can it help you find the water, it can lead you to where water ran across roof rafters and plywood as you search for the source of the leak. The older flashlights were heavier and larger, but could serve as a great home defense weapon. Police still carry them. The LED (Light Emitting Diode) was another great NASA invention (the microwave was the best).

## Fire Protection

I will write about home safety in another chapter, and will cover the subject of fire extinguishers in depth. I believe in the importance of having fire extinguishers in your home. Before you buy your first piece of furniture, you should buy an extinguisher. The reason to have it is obvious, but still, this purchase usually falls to the bottom of the list. Fire extinguishers are a lot less expensive than house fires. I would rather come home to a large timber rattler or bear in my house than a fire. Simple stove fires, electrical fires, candles, or faulty venting systems are just waiting to consume your entire home and kill your family. Having working and tested fire extinguishers generally means that you stand a reasonable chance to win against a fire. Owning a fire extinguisher is only part of your responsibility. You need to have it serviced periodically to ensure that it is ready when you need it. I had to use a fire extinguisher in my kitchen once. The stovetop caught fire and for a second, I didn't know what to do and my mind raced. I thought of soaking a hand towel in order to smother it. I realized that there was an extinguisher about 10 feet away in a hall closet. I pulled the pin and began to spray. It worked almost instantly. Whew.

## 20-Foot Tape Measure

Most homeowners engage in the occasional home project. Having a tape measure offers freedom. It can measure rooms for furniture and kitchens for appliances. If you want to feel good about your space, you need to know what will fit and where it should go. Furniture can be expensive and moving it is a pain. Measure rooms and furniture and place it once! Having artwork helps to make any space your own. Hanging art in the wrong space or at the wrong height can detract from its intended purpose. Hanging art is a simple task. Filling nail holes, sanding, then matching paint can be a chore. I carry a 30' tape measure because I work in large areas with lengthy materials and large dimensions. A 20' tape measure is good for the average homeowner since most rooms are 20' or less in width and length. Ceiling heights are generally 8', 10', or 12'. You might guess that I buy expensive tools. I prefer to say that I buy high quality tools. It is no different with my tape measure. Mine can stand up to constant use while maintaining its strength and accuracy. My tape measures cost approximately $30. You shouldn't need one that is this expensive, but you should avoid buying the cheapest one. You will need it to work many times.

**Electrical Tester**

There are many tools and devices that measure or detect electricity. I have a few voltmeters that detect both the presence and the amount of electricity. I also have a simple tester that detects if there is active current running through a wire. Every homeowner should have one. These simple testers come in a few shapes and sizes. The most common testers look like a very fat pen and are the length of your hand. They have an on/off switch, a flat end, and a pointed end. When the device is on, you aim the pointed end toward an outlet or wire and touch it with the tester. If the tester beeps and you see a corresponding LED light, there is live current at that outlet or in that wire. In your time as a homeowner, it is likely that you will come across an outlet or light that doesn't work. You may find loose wires or some other errant wire that looks out of place. Wouldn't it be nice to know if the power is off prior to touching the wires? Not knowing and touching the wire is akin to Russian

Roulette. These simple testers don't cost much and are worth every penny. By the way, it is becoming more common for cheap light bulbs to break when you try to unscrew them from their sockets. How on earth do you get the bulb base out of the socket with no bulb? How do you do it without being electrocuted? There are great Internet videos related to the subject. Before attempting to remove a bulb base, the first thing is to unplug the lamp. If the bulb is in a wired fixture such as a ceiling fan, turn off the switch and turn off the breaker that goes to that fixture. Hopefully the electrical panel is labeled on the inside of the panel door. Once you have turned off the power, you will use your tester to make sure the electricity is dead. Put the pointed end of the tester into the bulb base. If the tester beeps, it is still hot. If it doesn't beep, try the tester on an outlet or electrical switch in another part of the house. If it still doesn't beep, the batteries in the tester may need replacing.

## Pliers

Pliers come in many shapes, sizes, and quality grades. Some pliers are intended for large metal pipes, while others are made for specific car parts. Pliers are a must at your house. You may end up using pliers more than any other tool you own. It can tighten nuts and bolts. It can unscrew a screw head that has stripped. It can bend cans and twist wires. They can be used on cars, bikes, furniture fasteners, hot grill parts, walnuts, and even crab legs (yes... I did). I opt for the pliers with the rubber handles. This helps to insulate your hand from electricity. It also makes the tool easier to hold if the pliers have been sitting in the hot sun or stored in freezing temperatures.

## Needle Nose Pliers

Unlike the pliers in the previous segment, needle nose pliers are more for grabbing than for compressive strength. They have long thin jaws. They can get into tight places that bulky pliers cannot. These pliers are good for removing washers and gaskets from inside faucet assemblies, small nuts and bolts, and pulling wires through small holes. I build and fly high-speed remote control airplanes. I use mine weekly and keep them with me.

## Hammer

Everyone should own a hammer. House framers use large, heavy, and balanced hammers that weigh 21-28 ounces. The face of the framing hammer has a textured waffle pattern. This is so that the face of the hammer will grab and direct a nail into material without the hammer ricocheting off the nail head. There are mid-sized hammers. These hammers are what we think of when thinking of hammers! The technical name for this type of hammer is "finish hammer." This is not because they were invented in Finland, but because finish carpenters use finish hammers. A finish carpenter is the guy who installs interior trim and makes light repairs around the house. The nails he drives into material are smaller than framing nails. Further, if he misses hitting the nail head, the flat face on the finish hammer stands less of a chance of damaging the trim than the jagged waffle face on the framing hammer. You can use a finish hammer to drive finish nails for hanging artwork, light projects such as bird houses, trim repair, drywall nails, when repairing a large hole in the wall, and crab legs (outside... Not that I would know). Contractors who use hammers do not need a rubber grip on the hammer handle. Their hand and wrist strength is enough to manage the tool. I suggest that homeowners get a hammer that comes with a rubber grip. Again, Mr. Hammer is good at killing Mr. Spider (though I in no way suggest you to do the same).

**Crescent Wrench**

There are hundreds of types and sizes of wrenches. I own many of these. Common types include socket, crescent, and oil wrenches. Socket sets are super tools. They are designed to give the user speed and strength. But if I were stuck on an island, I would choose to have a crescent wrench (and crab legs). The common crescent wrench is comprised of a handle with adjustable jaws for sizing at the end. There is a metal gear that allows your thumb to move it back and forth to adjust the jaw size. It is one of the most useful tools you will ever own. I suggest buying a quality crescent wrench that has a rubber grip. Also, I am not really sure why someone would even need a wrench if stuck on an island...

**Screwdrivers**

I believe that all homeowners should own screwdrivers. Years ago, there were only two types of screwdrivers. One was called a flat head, and the other a Phillips head. The Phillips head has a tip at the end in the shape of a cross. The flat head has a tip that is the shape of a single flat line. Years ago, bolts and screws could be hand-driven into material or a threaded slot. A flat head screwdriver tip was the only tool that fit the slot at the top of the bolt or screw. Years later, the Phillips head was introduced. Engineers discovered that a flat head touched the groove in the screw in two places only. The Phillips head touched the cross-shaped slot in four places, giving the screwdriver more torque, strength, and stability. These days, there are a dozen screw tips to address all of the screwdriver patterns in the top of screws and bolts. You never know what you are going to come across related to pattern or size. You might need a #3 star bit to drive or remove a deck screw. You might need a #2 hex head bit to drive a finish screw. Instead of locating screwdrivers for the different screw head patterns, my suggestion is to buy a packaged set of drivers and bits. The driver is the handle. The bits are the driver head that fits the screw. You can remove one bit from the end of the driver and replace it with a completely different bit in less than five seconds. This particular screwdriver package will save you a lot of time, money, and frustration. You will use this tool often.

## 2-foot Level

A level is used to determine if one side of something is higher or lower than the other side independent of the adjoining surfaces such as a floor, a door, walls, or the ceiling. If my floor isn't level, it may be because of the concrete floor below that isn't level. Had I been the original builder, I would have checked the level of the concrete surface prior to installing the floor. Had I discovered the flaw in the concrete slab, I would have taken measures to correct the level of the concrete slab. Such measures would have been to use a long level and find out how high one side of the concrete slab was over the other side. Prior to installing the floor, I would have built up the lower side of the slab until it was level with the rest of the slab. Once the supporting concrete and added leveling material was level, I could install the floor with the assurance that it too would be level. This would have been extremely important. Having a level floor helps to ensure that everything above it is level, such as cabinets, countertops, walls, doors, and windows. If these things aren't level, the homeowner will be miserable! Doors and windows will not operate correctly and cabinet doors will not stay closed. If, during the course of door installation, I came across a rough opening that was out of level and was not square, I certainly wouldn't attach the door to that rough opening. Instead, I would place the door in the opening, check for level and make adjustments by installing shims (small wooden wedges) between the doorjamb and the opening lumber until the door was perfectly level and square. With the shims firmly holding the door in place, I would gently screw the doorframe to the rough framing. When checking a concrete slab, I would probably use an 8 ft. level. I use a long level when checking slabs or the dirt at the house exterior. I want to make sure that water will drain away from the house. The 8 ft. level gives me a more accurate reading over a longer distance. When checking a door opening and doorframe, I would probably use a 4 ft. level. Around my home, I keep a 2 ft. level. This is great for hanging artwork, televisions, curtain rods, and shelves. Nothing looks worse than a TV or artwork that is out of level (there is the case of men wearing yoga pants…). Never drop a level. Levels are finely tuned instruments and that is why they are costly. If you drop a level, you may later discover that something you hung is out of whack, making it necessary to re-hang the item and repair nails holes in the wall.

Originally, levels were called "whiskey sticks." The liquid inside the level's glass tube must be able to withstand freezing temperatures and still be accurate. Back then, they filled the tube with whiskey since anti-freeze wouldn't be invented for a couple hundred more years.

## Utility Knife

All households must have a utility knife (also known as a box cutter). You may find yourself using this tool quite often. It is one of the most versatile tools in a home. We use them to cut and open packaging, boxes, crab legs, and electrical wires. Contractors use them to shave wood into shape, sharpen contractor pencils, strip electrical wire, cut open large bundles of material (lumber, conduit), and hole out doorjambs for proper striker plate placement. It is common to get cut with this tool, given its razor sharp blade and the physical strength we sometimes use when handling it. If you apply a lot of strength to try and cut with this knife, the knife may cut through the material and your body's momentum can cause your leg, arm, or hand to uncontrollably end up in the blade's path. Like any other tool, your mind and body must remain in full control of the tool and its direction. Losing full control of a tool will almost always end poorly.

There are pre-packaged tool kits at most box stores. I have researched them and am impressed. These tool kits contain most of the tools I have mentioned in this chapter. These tools are neither engineered nor intended for use by the average contractor. It is true that contractors use similar tools almost daily, but their tools are better in quality and subsequently, are more expensive. They must stand up to rigorous and everyday use.

There are other tools that you will likely need along the way. Given your needs, lifestyle, and skill level, you will buy tools unique to you. You may not have a large yard and never need a shovel. Your neighbor might have a riding mower for his large lawn. Another neighbor might have the hobby of building or restoring furniture.

He probably will own a table saw, heavy-duty clamps, and a biscuit joiner. The light gardener may think that a biscuit joiner is a southern term for peanut butter!

If I had to choose to own only one power tool, it would be a battery-powered drill/driver. Parents sometimes give an electric drill as a hand-me-down. The electric drill has its place. It is designed to do only one task and that is to drill holes. A battery-powered drill will come with different speed settings (slow or fast). The high speed is for drilling into wood, metal, or tile. The slow speed is for driving screws into material. It would be difficult to screw a deck together with a hand held screwdriver. The trigger allows you to control the speed of the bit.

Another tool I would elect to own is a quality ladder. These also come in many shapes and sizes. A-frame ladders are steady, and are usually used inside the house or on flat surfaces. People use them for painting, changing overhead light fixtures, cleaning windows, etc. Extension ladders consist of two ladder sections. When leaned against the house they allow you to extend one of the sections, virtually doubling the length of the ladder. Some ladders may extend from 4 feet to 8 feet. Other ladders may extend from 20 feet to 40 feet. Extension ladders are typically used outside for painting, changing floodlights, or accessing a roof. I own both types of ladders. Additionally, I own ladders that can act as both an A-frame and extension ladder. These ladders are very versatile, tend to be heavier, and cost more than other ladders. I prefer heavier ladders because they offer greater stability, especially if I am standing on one at 25 feet above the ground on a windy day. All ladders come with the risk of injury. It is when we are careless or push our limits that we can get injured. The kind of clothes you wear when you are on a ladder is important. Wearing sandals or no shoes at all is a bad idea. Your feet will hurt and the pain will last for a long time. Loose clothing is also a bad idea because it can get caught on something while you are climbing and using a ladder. It can also block your ability to see anything below your waistline. I will not hire a worker who wears baggy clothing for this reason. Also, loose cloth can get caught in tools or machines. Loose clothing and tools go together as well as sleeping pills and laxatives.

## The Belt Buckle Rule

As a BICSI certified cable installer, I have witnessed how dangerous it is to stretch out and lean away from a ladder. Once a ladder begins to move or slide out from under you, you will not be able to stop the ladder's motion. The Belt Buckle Rule means that you should never extend your upper body to the point where your belt buckle is outside the ladder frame. To help illustrate my next point, I would like to teach you a simple no-no when riding a horse. If, while in the saddle, you ever get caught in a position of leaning all the way back, the next few seconds will be miserable. Once you are in that position, you have lost 100% of your control of you and the animal. You are likely to end up on the ground, under the horse, being dragged, or knocked out by a tree or post. Having strong stomach muscles and balance means you will remain upright whether on a horse or ladder. When you ascend on the ladder, you will read the words, "not a step." If you disregard this helpful information, you are in a position of losing all control. Ladder movement, loss of footing or balance, wind, or experiencing light-headedness from a change in your blood pressure means you could be going down. The higher you stand on a ladder, the worse your center of gravity. To illustrate, try to balance a golf ball atop a straw while holding the straw at the bottom end. See how long you can balance the ball. When on a ladder, the lower step provides greater stability and a lowered center of gravity. I love the saying, "The fall doesn't hurt. It's the sudden stop at the bottom."

# CHAPTER 21
# Lending and Borrowing Tools

*My neighbor asked if he could use my lawn mower. I said "Sure, just don't leave my property with it."*

Don't you love that there is a chapter about this subject? It is like reading a table of contents and finding a chapter titled "Beer is Your Friend." There is a feeling that homeowners get when they buy their first house and move in. There is a tremendous sense of pride in ownership. You believe you have achieved a major milestone in your life, similar to celebrating your 16th or 21st birthday. In many ways, you have! You and the other successful neighbors get to become one big happy family and live out the American dream, and in multidimensional clarity and color!

It is a good idea to own an electric engraving tool. You can buy a good one for around $20. I believe that your name should be engraved on every important tool you own. Writing your name on a tool is only a temporary solution. Ink can be sanded or washed off in seconds. Ladders are common targets for thieves who can sell a ladder to a pawnshop for around $20 (enough for hit of crack). If the engraved name on a ladder doesn't match the thief's name, the thief will have a difficult time selling it. If your phone number is engraved as well, there is a good chance that you will get your ladder back. Pawnshop owners don't want to get arrested, and have pledged to never knowingly purchase stolen merchandise. Engraving also reminds tool borrowers that they are in possession of someone else's property.

As a builder who lives on the street, I must have a big sign on me that reads "Forego the tool rental shop. Just ask me!" I used to be generous with my tools and allowed neighbors to borrow whichever tools they wanted. That didn't last very long, and it engendered a sense of awkwardness between me and the borrowers. I have borrowed tools and lent tools. It works out well when the tool owner and borrower understand the rules. What on earth could possibly be wrong with borrowing a tool? I never borrow a tool that I cannot afford to repair or replace in the event that I break or lose the tool. This rule is essential for borrowers and lenders. The second unwritten rule is that the borrower must be experienced with any tool he borrows.

Years ago, I let people borrow my pickup truck. Today, I would never do that. It used to be that pickup trucks were primarily found on the streets and farms in rural areas. Borrowing or lending a truck was a normal practice. Trucks were industrial by nature and used for work. It wasn't surprising if a truck sustained a scratch or mud bath. It was during this time that drivers of trucks were looked down on as second-class citizens or common laborers. Sam Walton, the founder of Wal-Mart, stood out like a sore thumb when driving his old red pickup truck across the country from store to store. I believe he was "old school" for sure. But it also let the citizens of these rural towns know that he was one of them. At that time, Wal-Marts were built in rural towns to serve people who weren't geographically close to malls and shopping centers. He was one of the wealthiest people in the world at the time. Today, new pickup trucks cost more than most high-end luxury cars. Most of the pickup trucks you see today will never carry cargo, soil, or tools. These trucks will never pull heavy equipment or a trailer full of cattle or other livestock. If I lend my truck to ten different people, one of them is going to have to account for a dent in the tailgate door, a scratch down the side, or a bent bumper. How happy are you when you loan your BMW to a friend and it comes back with a long scratch down the rear quarter panel?

In many cases, people use trucks in order to make a living. It may serve as an office or lunchroom. A pickup truck is a valuable tool to a contractor. It is essential to his ability to feed his family, pay his bills, or make a good impression on a potential customer. Think about that. If two different contractors show up at your house to meet you, are you more likely to hire the contractor whose truck is clean and well cared for, or the contractor whose truck is filthy, dented, and leaking oil in your driveway? If someone asks to borrow my pickup truck, I reply, "no." We Americans often need a way to transport a sofa, a Christmas tree, or carry bags of yard debris. Others might buy mulch in bulk or need to transport bikes and *just* need my truck for *just* a few minutes and return it when *just*... *Just*... *Just*... If I lend my truck to a neighbor, will the neighbor remove the tree sap on the side of the bed, the mud in the bed of the truck, or have repaired the dent he caused? Most borrowers don't consider these things. The typical mindset is, "Oh well, it is *just* a truck." If someone wants to borrow my truck, it means he doesn't own one and is not practiced at driving one. He doesn't have a thorough understanding of how to handle this particular tool. You can remove the word, "truck" and replaced it with any one of your expensive possessions.

A neighbor asked if he could borrow my ladder. I asked a few questions related to his intended use of this tool. He told me that he needed it to unclog a gutter on the back of his house. I could see the gutter from my back yard. It was installed at a height of approximately 23 feet. I consider that height to be an altitude! To me and other experienced contractors, twenty-three feet is high but still doable if experienced. To the average homeowner, it is a *long way up there*. It sounds doable, but once the average person climbs a ladder, they tend to feel scared at about 10 to 12 feet. 23 feet is double that. Further, there is a height comfort level for each person uniquely. There is also a height we contractors refer to as *freeze altitude*. There are climbing/working heights that we achieve in comfort. But further up than that is where we could find a freeze altitude. We arrive at a height, then freeze up once we realize how potentially vulnerable we have become. It is human nature. It is also very dangerous, as it would be difficult to help or save you. I thought that if my neighbor were injured or killed while using my ladder, I might be held responsible in some way. If he were severely injured, not only would I feel terrible, but a lawyer would want to know who owned the ladder as well. In order to keep peace with the neighbor, I told him that my ladders were at a jobsite for a few more weeks. Eventually, he stopped asking.

I have another neighbor who frequently borrowed my tools. He is very handy, but would rarely return my tools. I would have to ask and ask in order to get my tools back. I stopped lending him my tools when I discovered that he was lending my tools to his friends! This was a significant problem. Do friends leave my power tools out in the rain? Do friends lend my tools to their friends? Nothing good came from lending my tools to him, so I simply stopped.

Another neighbor asked if she could borrow a large hammer from me. It was an unusual request. The only large hammers I own are a 28 oz. framing hammer and heavy sledgehammer. I told her that the framing hammer was for driving large nails into wood. The sledgehammer was overkill according to her. When she returned the framing hammer, it was ruined. I asked her what she did to my hammer. She told me that she used it to break bricks and mortar apart on an old outside planter. What she needed was a mason's hammer or a sledgehammer that she could wield. The waffle shaped head face of my hammer was ruined. I threw it away.

Another friend asked to borrow my truck so that he could round up bags of leaves that his son had filled in order to make money at neighbors' houses. I gave him the keys. An hour later, his son was driving the truck up and down the street.

People don't mind borrowing tools and freely ask to do so. They don't mind carrying expensive power tools around by the cord or cutting through nails with a new circular saw blade. I don't generally lend my tools anymore. The best policy is to *just say "no."* They are how I earn a living and are of excellent quality. Lending tools may benefit the borrower, but not the lender.

There are a lot of places to rent tools. Of course renting them can be a bit pricey. Then again, the tool rental store executives know how people treat tools that aren't their own. Rental shops take into account the wear and tear that their tools experience. That is why you can opt to purchase insurance for the tool in case it breaks while in your possession. I strongly suggest you buy the insurance if they offer it to you. You do not know how the previous renter cared for it. They also carry large insurance policies to cover those who rent tools and become injured.

If you decide to lend tools to others, you must find out the reason this person needs this particular tool. If the person asks to borrow your expensive compound miter saw (used to cut fine trim and crown molding) in order to cut cement fiber siding, then the answer is "no."

You must ask the borrower when he intends to use the tool. He might say that he needs to pick it up on Saturday, but since the rest of that day is full, he intends to actually use the tool on Sunday. Knowing when he will actually use the tool should be important to you since you may need that tool at the same time. You also do not want your tool to be sitting outside his house all day and night.

When a person borrows a tool, you accept liability and risk exposure. If your tool injures him or others, you could be named in a lawsuit.

You must ask a borrower how long he intends to use the tool. This will give you a good idea of when to expect its return. You must press this issue so that you are not left wondering whether he will return it. Ask for a specific day and time. This lets the borrower know that the return time is important to you. It also keeps it fresh in his mind that you expect it back at that time. If the tool is not returned at that time, it gives you fair cause to call that neighbor and ask for the tool. Tell him that you need it back. The reason why is not important.

I would let the borrower know the monetary value of the tool. Let him know that you must have it back in the same condition it is at the time he takes possession of it. Tell him that is important to you. If the tool carries little monetary value but instead carries sentimental value, then you should never loan this tool.

I realize the rules between borrowers and lenders may sound impractical to you. Based on experience, the rules are important and are not difficult to follow. Moreover, what I have described to you has more to do with the relationships between you and your neighbors. I would rather they have respect for you and your belongings than no respect because you are careless.

Here are a few examples of how your up front questions can benefit you and the neighbor later. A neighbor asked if she could borrow a shovel. I asked, "What kind of shovel?" She told me that she needed to dig an old tree root out of the ground. I knew that if she did this, the handle would break or crack internally, then break on me at a later time. I told her that what she needed was a pickaxe and digging bar. If the neighbor is smoking hot, lend her the pickaxe and digging bar, and maybe offer to help.

I witnessed another neighbor lend a tool and follow the lender rules correctly. I was the borrower. He was in the automotive business and his tools were of exceptional quality and condition. One evening I asked to borrow a heat gun. He asked how I intended to use it. He asked how long I would need to use it and the time that I could return it. He was satisfied with my answers. As he handed it to me, I noticed that his name and phone number were engraved in the tool. I used it and returned it. See how simple this is? After all, a heat gun can quickly start a house fire or burn the user.

Now, as for you borrowers, never borrow a tool that you don't know how to use. Never borrow tools that you cannot afford to repair or replace. Always expect a request to borrow a tool to be met with "no." The word "no" is a complete sentence. If you ask to borrow a tool and your request is declined, keep in mind that it has nothing to do with the personal relationship between you and your prospective tool lender. Do not let it affect your relationship. When borrowing a tool or truck, you assume risk. Imagine borrowing a friend's truck and upon returning it, he notices a dent in the bumper. You may be held responsible even though you didn't cause the dent.

Drug addicts know the value of your tools. Since you and your neighbors own nice things, they may be coming to your neighborhood to steal. They know that wrenches and paintbrushes are worthless on the open market. They know the sale of ladders, space heaters, and power tools can pay for their next high. Never leave your tools exposed or unattended.

Rarely will others take care of your things like you do. That is part of life. And even if 90% of people do take care of the tools they borrow, that leaves one out of ten who will not.

# CHAPTER 22
# Home Safety

There is no way I can address each of your individual safety needs. The needs of an apartment dweller can be very different than the needs of the mansion dweller. Please take my general advice and apply it to your life and home. I could write a 2,000-page book dedicated entirely to the subject of home safety, but that is not the purpose of this book. I am here to educate you and champion your efforts to become proactive homeowners and learn everything you can to increase your quality of life. That starts with safety. Taking my advice should lead you to doing further research on the Internet in order to address your unique and personal settings.

One hundred years ago, it was common for those venturing into the wilderness to be well armed with guns or knives in the event that they encountered bears, mountain lions, dog packs, or thieves. Today, we take a hike into God's country on foot or bike with little fear of potential dangers. That means the only thing standing between you, a bear, and death is a thin layer of spandex and a water bottle. We become victims. Later, if we survive attacks, we can make police reports and ask for more morphine resulting from the severed arm. We are forced to be reactive. It would be smart to study shark and jellyfish behavior if you spend time in the ocean. It would be smart to study mountain lion or elk behavior if you live in the Rockies. I love the University of Colorado Buffalos. I hate being chased by wild buffalos.

There is no teacher like experience. When it comes to disasters at your house, I hope you have little experience. That means you are vulnerable. Being a homeowner means being faced with situations that occur and bring with them extremely steep learning curves. It is your responsibility to lessen those curves by making good decisions before creating, or having to interact with, dangerous situations. In other words, having better control over threats means that you are living proactively at your home. Pursue knowledge that can offer you *alternatives* when faced with threats. Not doing so will force you into a reactionary state, and that is where we often find victims.

Americans are shocked, cut, burned, poisoned, drowned, suffocated, and experience broken bones at home. Over 18,000 Americans are killed each year as a result of an injury sustained at home. We visit hospitals and clinics from these injuries an estimated 21 million times per year at the cost of $220 billion. What is sad is that most home injuries and related deaths are avoidable.

Americans tend to live a reactionary existence. We become more so with each passing generation. Three hundred years ago, people lived a far more proactive life. In order to avoid starvation, they had to carefully prepare for their hunts. They would plan and execute every detail in order to maximize their chances of success. Far in advance of feeling hungry, they set out to kill an animal or cultivate that which they planted. When hungry today, we simply order a pizza.

Home safety can mean many things to varying degrees. Your decision to participate is to adopt a proactive approach in order to ensure a better outcome when faced with threats. You and your loved ones are worth the small investment of time that it will cost you. I do not consider myself a home safety expert. I do consider myself to be highly aware and proactive when it comes to my safety. If I can do it, you can do it.

When I was a child, my dad and I were on a road trip somewhere in the middle of Oklahoma and came upon a horrific car accident. Cell phones did not exist. Dad pulled over and we stepped out of the car. Moving toward the wreckage, I witnessed something that would have a lifelong and positive impact on me. On the hood of a car was the upper half of a woman's body. The other partially severed half remained inside of the car. She looked directly at us while trying to move her lower jaw up and down with her bloody hands. She murmured, "Oh my God... Oh my God..." After the ordeal, dad drove for miles in silence. Breaking the silence, he kept his eyes forward on the road and in his typically stoic way said, "That's why you wear your seat belt." I too kept my eyes on the road and didn't reply. I have never driven without my seat belt fastened properly. I don't know if a seat belt would have saved that woman's life, but physical laws of nature tell me that she would have experienced a better outcome. Her decision to buckle up would have only cost her two seconds. The decision to not buckle up cost her life. Again, I don't fasten my safety belt when I notice a drunk driver headed for me as he runs through a red light. I fasten my safety belt the instant I start my car.

Here are the most common causes of house fires: cooking, arson, appliances, HVAC, clothes dryer venting, combustible chemicals, electricity, fireworks, holiday decorations, fireplaces/chimneys, and smoking. Do any of these items apply to you and your lifestyle? One of my broadcasts dealt exclusively on this subject. My guest was a local fire chief. Listeners learned that almost every house fire is avoidable, if only a better decision is made just before the fire starts. In other words, if you experience a house fire, there is a good chance that you are to blame for it.

What is the most dangerous threat to your house? What is the second? The single greatest threat to your house is your chimney if you have a wood-burning fireplace. The second most dangerous is your dryer vent duct (flexible silver colored tube).

## Fireplace and Chimney

There is an industry that has become large and lucrative in recent years. It is the business of the chimney sweep. As children, we learned that a chimney sweep, a mythical character, looked like Abe Lincoln on crack and carried a tired broom from rooftop to rooftop. That may have been true a hundred years ago. Today's chimney sweep wears protective gear and his primary tool is an HD camera. Decades of fireplace use, along with a resurging popularity of the wood burning fireplace, requires a professional to inspect, maintain, and clean them. That professional is known as a *chimney sweep*.

Burning wood results in smoke that carries unburned gases up and out of the house through the chimney. These gases create creosote. Creosote is a foul, sticky, and highly combustible substance. Creosote builds up on the inside walls of the chimney or flue. When it comes into contact with sparks and cinders, it can catch fire and explode. These explosions crack the mortar and bricks inside the chimney, allowing for the flames to come into direct contact with the house. It is nearly impossible for a homeowner to extinguish, let alone become aware that the fire has started.

A licensed and certified chimney sweep will use a video camera to inspect the inside of your chimney. He will be able to determine if creosote is present, or if there has been any damage to the chimney from previous fires or explosions. He will offer you a price to clean, maintain, or repair your chimney and fireplace. If you do not have the money to clean or repair the chimney, you can elect to do so later. But now at least you have valuable information, and can make the wise choice to not use the fireplace until you have it cleaned and repaired.

## Fireplace Sparks

Wood burning fireplaces are far more appealing to homeowners than gas logs. They have become a part of our holidays, memories, and traditions as a magical source of peace, joy, and romance. When prospective buyers walk into a house, they typically enter through the front door and into the living room. Their eyes are first drawn to the fireplace. Remember how deeply subconscious and psychological the decision to purchase is? The fireplace is one of the first times a buyer will picture the house as their future home. They will picture themselves celebrating, napping, or opening Christmas gifts by a fireplace. I find that a roaring fireplace, college football game, and freezing cold adult sparkling beverages are a great way to spend a Saturday evening. Most modern fireplaces are actually gas fueled instead of wood burning. This is because chimneys are expensive to construct. Gas fireplaces are cleaner and far less expensive to operate. Wood burning requires wood, fire, and air. Flames cannot burn without air. That air comes from inside your home. Because heat rises, the heat from the fire will draw air from inside your house and exhaust it outside. The problem is that the air inside your home is already warm because of the HVAC system. This means that your HVAC system will have to work harder and burn more gas to maintain the thermostat temperature. Wood burning fireplaces cost a lot to use. Vent free gas fireplaces add heat to a room without exhausting existing warm air.

Fire investigators report that many house fires start by a spark that is shot from a burning log into a room. When you hear that *pop* and *snap* as the fire roars, small and flammable pieces of burning wood are shot out and away from the log. Usually they remain inside the firebox. At other times, they shoot out onto the living room floor. Carpet, newspapers, and furniture can be very flammable. Many metropolitan codes regulations require that all wood burning fireplaces must have a glass doors or a metal screen between the burning logs and the room. I researched the topic of injuries and gas log fireplaces. Hundreds of people are severely burned every year as a result of coming into contact with a component of a gas fireplace. Children sustain most of these injuries. Further, gas fireplaces quickly generate a tremendous amount of heat. Since heat rises, fireplace mantles (and objects resting on the mantles) will frequently melt or burn.

One of my best friends lived in a large and rustic house on a horse farm in Tennessee. His stone fireplace was gorgeous and the opening was five feet wide. He never found a screen large enough to cover the opening. One day on his way home from work, he received that dreaded call by a neighbor. His house was on fire. He lost his entire house in less than thirty minutes. The cause was determined to be a spark that shot out from the fireplace and onto a newspaper he had left on the coffee table. He and I rebuilt his new home on the existing foundation. I visited him soon after that on a cold day.

The fire was roaring! There was no screen between the flames and the living room. I reminded him that he only gets one free rebuild!

## Dryer Lint

Boy Scouts take dryer lint with them on camping trips. Not only is lint one of the most flammable things in a house, it is also light in weight. It is used to start campfires. It burns fast and hot! Every time you use your clothes dryer, wet lint accumulates on the inside of your dryer exhaust duct (hose) similar to the plaque in your arteries. In a few years' time, this highly flammable lint builds up and constricts airflow. The constant and intense heat from a single cycle can cause the lint to catch on fire. Replace, or at least inspect, the dryer exhaust duct every year.

## Aging In Place

Today, Americans are living to ages far in excess of previous generations. Since we are living so much longer, we continue to try and use our homes the same ways we did as young healthy adults. We are learning that how we use the house in our older years differs from the way we did earlier. Elderly Americans can often struggle with the seemingly simplest of tasks, yet fight to stay there as long as possible. Such tasks might include bathing, cooking, or safely passing from one room to another. It makes sense that they do not want to be displaced from their homes any more than younger owners. They have an understandable attachment to the house, neighborhood, and community. The result is that they stay at home and elect to keep their challenges a secret.

Imagine a person reaching across the stovetop to change a clock or grab a saltshaker. Now imagine that same person doing so in pajamas or a loose-sleeved robe. Hanging cloth can easily come into contact with electrical burners or gas flames. Imagine a person lifting a pot of boiling water to drain the excess into the sink. Imagine an unsteady and weaker person attempting the same. Stairs, slick shower floors, overhead cabinetry, and poor lighting can all pose a threat to the quality of life for many seniors. As we age, we get cold faster. Slowing metabolism and thinner skin make electric blankets and space heaters very attractive. Falling asleep in front of a space heater can result in severe burns. A sweeping trend in real estate is that baby boomers, now retiring, are choosing to purchase homes that are single story, smaller, and offer ADA compliant elements. I suggest to anyone over the age of 45 to consider practicality and the future when making a house purchase.

### Smoke Detectors

American codes regulations require builders, landlords, and commercial contractors to install smoke detectors that contain audible alarms. These life-saving devices are useless if they have no power source (dead battery). Batteries must be changed in a smoke detector every year, if not sooner. Many smoke detectors will signal an irritating warning when batteries are at the end of their lives. That screeching noise is intentional. A smoke detector should be tested once a month to make sure it is working correctly. Smoke detectors make a loud noise to wake us up and warn us for the presence of smoke (fire). It must work tonight and next week. Most smoke detectors have a button that reads "Push to Test." If your smoke detector is hooked to your alarm system, make sure to notify local police/fire/emergency personnel prior to performing your test.

If there were ever a single example to define being *proactive* versus *reactive*, this is it.

I have read that many smoke detectors fail without us knowing. This is important. The lens (eye) on some smoke detectors can become milky or clouded as the clear plastic ages. That is why I include the spraying of compressed smoke at the device during testing. Yes, there is actually a product called, "compressed smoke," and no, it has nothing to do with vacuum packed packages of marijuana coming over the southern border.

### Fire Extinguishers

Do you own one? Most homeowners experience some kind of fire over the course of their ownership. When will it be your turn? How big will the fire be? Where will it start and why? What will fuel the flames? I'm just curious. When it happens, will you have access to a fire extinguisher? If so, then consider yourself almost proactive. Almost? Yes. Having a fire extinguisher is important. Knowing that is works is critical. Having one near a likely source of fire can be the difference between a burned couch and a burned down house. The ideal set up is to have fire extinguishers in your bedroom, your kitchen, and in your garage. In America, slightly less than 10% of all homes have a working fire extinguisher. I am a member of the 10%. Witnessing a house fire will do it every time!

Kitchen fires are usually the result of oil reaching a certain temperature called the *flashpoint*. The hot oil can also come into contact with other things and burst into flames. Using water to put out an oil fire will end in an explosive disaster. Keep a small fire extinguisher in your kitchen and several feet away from the stove or oven. Some people opt to extinguish kitchen fires with a wet hand towel, but hand towels are small and mean that you will have to come in contact with the fire. Kitchens are typically centrally located in a house. A kitchen fire can easily spread and rapidly consume an entire house. Know where your extinguishers are. It is bad timing to search for the extinguisher once the fire has started.

Though there are few sources for a fire in your master bedroom, you still need to consider cigarettes, candles, and electronics. Since this is where you sleep, having an extinguisher in your bedroom will make it easier to escape if you are awakened by a fire.

The garage is a great place to have an extinguisher. Many garages are home to gas powered appliances. This means that a flame could be merely feet away from gas, cleaner, or paint fumes. It also means that the flame is right next to your car's gas tank, as well as stored boxes, paper, garbage, and wood.

Most fire extinguishers have a gauge at the top to tell you if the extinguisher is working (pressure and fire retardant). It is a good idea to take the extinguisher outside periodically to make sure it is working. Extinguishers need to be serviced by a professional. The Internet should be able to tell you how often, given the brand and model number.

## Fire Escape Plan

Many homeowners create a plan for escape in case of a fire. Some even practice the drill! But most homeowners devise a plan for when they are sleeping only. They fail to plan for a fire if they are in a basement, bathtub, or kitchen. Most house fire deaths are the result of smoke inhalation. Respirators must be a part of any fire escape plan.

## First Aid Kit

As a builder, it is common for me to keep well-stocked first aid kit in my truck. Most Americans don't own a first aid kit. They may have pieces and parts in one bathroom or in a kitchen cabinet. Most Americans don't have a fresh bottle of hydrogen peroxide. Every homeowner should have a high quality first aid kit. Injuries can happen at any time and in any part of your house. It is a bad thing to have to search in various places for what you may need while injured.

One of my building partners was a paramedic in the Navy as a younger man. It is amazing how many times we relied on him to clean wounds and sew us back together. He kept a professional first aid kit with him at all times. Being part of the remote control aviation crowd, I have witnessed gruesome injuries at various flying fields. I fly the high-speed scale airplanes. These propellers are made of hard plastic or carbon. The RPMs are off the charts. Coming into contact with a moving blade is to lose. Fingers, hands, forearms, necks, legs, and toes frequently get sliced open. That is why I keep a first aid kit with me, even at the park!

## Poison

While still inside the house, let's touch on the subject of poisoning. If I know there will be children in my home, I make sure that their parents know where they are at all times. I need the assurance that children cannot get into my cabinets or closets where harmful cleaners, chemicals, and firearms can be found. Such poisons might be bleach, cleaners, engine lubricants, blinding sprays, and degreasers.

American marketing companies are second to none when knowing how to attract buyers to their products. Television advertising campaigns are a big business. If adults are visually attracted to products on a shelf, then why wouldn't children be? Some of the most toxic products in your home have the most attractive packaging and labeling. Chemicals that unclog drains look like tough toy robots. Small packages of dish detergent look like pieces of Christmas candy. Bleach bottles are light in flowing colors that mirror dairy products. Engine coolant looks like a lemon lime drink and has a sweet taste. This should be changed because many pets consume this liquid and die agonizing deaths from kidney failure. Box stores sell plastic cabinet locks that are inexpensive and easily installed. Garage shelving is a good investment. It keeps poisonous items out of reach from those who can't read.

## Wet Areas

Wet areas refer to any place water can be found. Such places are bathrooms, kitchens, laundry rooms, mudrooms, and outdoor patios.

I would have had a great aunt had she not died as a teenager from drowning in the family bathtub. It sounds next to impossible, I know. As she ran the water to fill the tub, she laid on her back in the tub with her head under the running spout. Her long hair made its way down into the drain and plugged it. The tub filled and she discovered that her hair was caught and there was no escape. The bathroom is the most underrated room in the house when it comes to danger. Many people, especially as they age, are injured in the bathroom. Back in the 1980s, some inventor developed and sold the *Shower Radio*. I thought, "Perfect… I cannot think of a safer place to dance naked than on a slick wet surface next to a glass door.

What could possibly go wrong?" I have never fallen in the shower or tub. Wait, yes I have, but I caught my balance before hitting the ground. The bathroom has to stand up to moisture on all surfaces. That means that the surfaces are likely very hard. Some of those surfaces are sharp too. I refer to faucets, shower door tracks, corners of shower doors, and countertop corners. I believe all bathrooms should have grab bars. Those bars should be in showers/bath walls, on the walls next to the bathtub/shower, and next to the toilets. I am not referring solely to bathrooms in the homes of the elderly among us. I am referring to the healthiest among us as well. I was a highly competitive and successful college athlete. I recall being exhausted and injured after practice or games. Like the other athletes, I headed for the showers. Once there, I would have given anything to have grab bars to steady myself in the warm water while favoring one leg or ankle over the other. I bet Brett Favre and Peyton Manning have grab bars all over their homes!

## Stairs and Handrails

When we are in our teens and 20s, we fly up and down stairs. In our 30s, we begin to walk the stairs. Some of that has to do with the expensive clothes we may be wearing at our new jobs. Most of it has to do with intelligence. When we are in our 40s, we may slip but catch ourselves. In our 50s, we take stair steps in a determined fashion with a keen knowledge of where the handrail is. It is the same when we are in our 60s, but we are slower and climb fewer steps than the 50-somethings. In our 70s, we entertain thoughts of selling our homes in order to buy houses with no stairs at all. If you are in your 80s, stairs can pose quite a threat. If there is no handrail, there is no stepping into a stairway. If in your 90s, you likely never take the stairs. You opt instead to sit downstairs while the teens and 20-somethings annoy the hell out of you by flying up and down the stairs.

One of my friends was a star college pitcher for an SEC baseball team. Today, he is in his late 60s and still has a typical pitcher's frame: tall and strong in the hips. He is an avid runner, golfer, and cyclist. One morning, he was leaving for a long bike ride. The bike and car were in the garage below the house. He opened the door and took his first step into the 13-step stairway down. While stepping, his toe got caught on the step, which resulted in a beautiful swan dive over the remaining 12 steps. Somehow, he landed directly on his knee and on a hard tile floor. It was a gruesome injury and required a long, painful recovery. Had he placed his hand firmly on the handrail at the top, he would have experienced a great day on the bike and a golf-filled summer. Instead, he sat on the couch in the basement watching television for months.

Many homes have long wooden stairways that go to the basement or garage. Many older homes that were built prior to codes regulations and enforcement have long and dangerous stairways that would never comply with today's safety standards. In both of these cases, it is likely that these stairwells are poorly lit. It is a good idea to paint the leading edge of each step with a bright color and with a flat or matte finish. This makes it easier to define the edges of each step, and subsequently, navigate the path safely. If you must paint the entire stair tread, then do so using lighter colors. Make sure the paint finish is flat or matte (as opposed to semi-gloss or high gloss which can be slippery if wet). If you can, mix in with the paint a manufactured texture sold at box stores. If that isn't available, then finish your paint job by applying textured adhesive strips that are designed for stairway steps. This offers your feet a "no slip" surface.

## Guns

I am not a gun expert, but I am an expert on the guns that I own. Knowing and understanding these powerful weapons is the most important aspect to owning or handling one. Most gun accidents are the result of carelessness and ignorance. The gun debate in this country is extremely polarizing. Gun activists and gun grabbers cannot get on the same page and I doubt they ever will. There is nothing I can say or write that will sway you one way or the other. And in the interest of keeping your attention and affection, I will not spend any time on the politics of the issue.

It would be predictable that I would suggest you always keep your guns unloaded and locked in a safe place. It would be predictable that I would suggest you always keep your firearm handy, loaded, hot, and well within reach. Only an idiot would own a firearm without knowing how to care for it, store it, and use it correctly. Only an idiot would steal a gun. If you choose to keep guns in your home, my advice is for you to enroll in a gun safety course that additionally offers tactical training. Seldom will you need to defend yourself while standing in a ready position similar to that at the firing range. As with most things home and safety related, the more knowledge you possess, the better your decisions and outcomes. My belief is that one's quality of life can be negatively impacted by one's death. My further belief is that one's quality of life can be greatly diminished by getting murdered.

## Avoiding Burglaries

Most home invasions and burglaries are avoidable. Despite the fact that a home invasion occurs every fifteen seconds in America, we are targeted based on things we fail to do. These failures attract the burglars. Home invasions are what these bad guys do for a living. They have tremendous experience in their line of work. You don't. The majority of criminals cite avoiding houses that have security systems (during the exit interview I'm sure). Burglars avoid homes where dogs live. They will avoid houses with complex architectural layouts. These homes typically have more doors and windows, but breaking in and guessing where to find valuables can cost burglars a lot of time. *Time* is an enemy to burglars. They want to get in and out quickly.

The average home burglary in America costs victims about $2,000. There could potentially be thousands more in legal expenses resulting from botched prosecution, times where you may need legal defense, and associated work by private investigators. Taking a few extra measures related to your security is far less expensive. Besides, only 10% of home burglaries are ever solved.

30% of those illegally entering your home do so by coming through the front door. 33% of those do so by kicking in the door. Old or hollow doors are easy to kick in. Newer houses are, for the most part, assembled cheaply and locks and doorjambs are fragile and easy to break. When I build a house, I ensure that exterior doors are high in quality and difficult to break. Garage overhead doors and service doors should ideally be made of metal.

If you have a security system with corresponding lawn signs, signs to beware of a dog, keep doors and windows locked, and have quality exterior doors, it is unlikely that you will ever experience a burglary or home invasion.

If your home security system is dependent on a phone landline, it may be useless at the hands of seasoned burglars. They know how to find the network interface and phone line on the exterior of your house. A pair of handheld wire cutters disarms these systems. This might also hamper your ability to call for help. Most of today's home security providers offer wireless systems that cannot be disabled by burglars. The wireless route costs a few dollars more than the wired systems.

With the advent of high-end home electronics and the ever-increasing speed of technology, burglars will *cash in* by taking these items from you. Televisions and computers have highly attractive packaging. When you hang your new flat screen and leave the box by the trashcans, everyone can learn that you have that expensive and brand new item in the house. Burglars also look for toys in the front yard. The presence of toys means that there is a mother living there. Mothers have jewelry.

Since time is of the essence to the average burglar, I like to play a trick on them in case I become a target. I would like for us to keep this between ourselves. Okay? Most homeowners hide a key outside. Popular hiding places are under front door mats, under nearby rocks, in garden hose caddies, or inside an outlet cover. Burglars know the typical places. I hide a key under each doormat. If a burglar lifts the mat, he will try that key in the front door. It will not work. He will take the key to the next exterior door, but it doesn't work there. Because I am a nice guy, I hide a key under the mat at the second door. Sadly, it doesn't work either. So far, the burglar has burned over a minute of time. For added convenience, I leave keys under each doormat. I have a rock near the front door. Under that rock is another key. My home security cameras are in place to catch the burglar's debacle on film! These cameras may not ward off intruders. They are there so that I will have something funny to upload on YouTube. The would be and quite frustrated burglar will quickly leave my property and head for his next intended victim. You see? Home security can be fun!

## Outdoors

I will cover the subject of your yard in the chapter about preventative inspections. For now, let's touch on a few subjects. The addition of outdoor living spaces has become a big deal in America. Homeowners are electing to surrender a portion of their lawn in the back or side yard in exchange for a beautiful and well-landscaped patio that is home to outdoor furniture, cooking areas, appliances, televisions, and even heat. Inside our homes, we are wary of broken glass and pay attention to where we set our drinks down. We keep hallways free of debris, and place our furniture in ways to maximize ease of passage. The same things should apply to exterior living spaces. Toys strewn across a patio can easily trip someone. Glass vessels for beverages are likely to break if dropped. Outside, we have additional threats to plates, glasses, and empty bottles from strong winds. Branches and thorns can cause injuries. It is a good idea to keep exterior living spaces free of toys, debris, errant plants, and toe grabbing ground cover.

In our culture, it is common to go around barefoot. If not barefoot, people wear rubber comfort shoes and sandals that offer little protection from sharp objects and rocks. Keep in mind that when your house was built, workers on the exterior used tools, nails, staplers, and worked with wood, metal, and glass. Construction sites are often messy. After a day's work or upon completion of the house, it is likely that workers cleaned the worksite but only removed the things they could see. But hidden in the flowerbeds, bushes, dirt, and grass may be a virtual landfill. Within fractions of an inch from the bottom of your feet could be rusted nails and utility blades, screws, pieces of sharp metal flashing, wire, machine and tool parts, sharp tool bits, and broken glass. As a child, I was firmly in the barefoot camp! Consequently, I experienced several visits to the emergency room for debris removal and tetanus shots.

Prior to the 1980s, the use of trash dumpsters by residential builders was not all that common. There had yet to be a sweeping public outcry for saving the environment. Some builders would haul construction debris to a dump or landfill, but it was far more common for builders to create a private landfill out of your back yard by burying the trash. Over time, lighter weight metal debris can actually make its way to the surface. These objects are in search of bare feet as they lay in wait. In addition, homeowners spend a lot of time in yards. We drop nails, glass, staples, mower blade chips, and safety pins only to never find them. In high school, I recall surfing across grass in the back yard following a brief yet heavy rainstorm. A toothpick was hidden in the grass and made its way all the way into the bottom of my foot as I slid over it. The lacrosse team captain was a senior and headed for a career as a physician. He was also my ride to practice. He carefully removed the toothpick with a pocketknife and we were off to practice. Thanks Reed, wherever you are!

Potential threats in the yard need to be taken seriously. When I finish a construction project that includes a house exterior, part of the site cleanup requires the use of a large rolling magnet. I roll that magnet across the ground that is within twenty feet of the house or any staging area. These rollers can be rented at many tool rental stores. I strongly urge you to rent or buy one and use it every spring and after every exterior home project. This concept is similar to vacuuming a floor inside after interior projects. You might be surprised at what you find. You may even locate a valuable historical artifact. Make sure to wear gloves. You will be handling the debris that the magnet finds.

Many of us live in historical areas. I do. My driveway was the location of a supply depot for confederate soldiers during the Civil War (Battle of Nashville). My yard has hosted hundreds of metal detector enthusiasts over the years, especially during the construction of my house. Not only were several artifacts located, but it vacuumed my yard too!

Of course metal detectors and magnets will not work on glass, plastic, or toothpicks. But if you have a small enough area where you typically walk without wearing shoes, you can always run a shop-vac over these areas. Keeping grass healthy and cut will help as well. The movement of mower blades creates a vacuum that sucks cut grass (clippings) into the shroud then discharges the grass and debris. Just remember not to point the discharge in areas where you spend time barefoot. The easiest way to avoid foot injuries is to wear shoes. We don't realize how often we use certain parts of our bodies until we no longer have normal use of those parts. If someone accidentally steps on my foot and apologizes, I say, "No worries. I only use the bottoms."

## Skeeters and Flies

What creature kills the largest number of humans? It is the mosquito. A close friend of mine is one our nation's leading authorities on this insect. He has a doctorate in molecular biology from one of the finest science universities in the world. He has been both a great neighbor and my *on air* guest. Though I have learned a great deal about mosquitoes, there is so much more to learn.

Mosquitoes (*"mozzies"* as the Brits call them) love the way we smell and taste. A mosquito can smell us from miles away. They vector towards us by following our exhaled air. Most mosquito bites come from the ones who live near, or at, our properties. They can live and reproduce in a few drops of water. What items at your property catch and hold rainwater? Grills, gutters, toys, planters, garbage, and swing sets are a few such items. If you keep your yard clean and free of standing water, you will have far fewer mosquitoes. I have often wondered why God created the mosquito. The only intelligent answer I come up with is that had it not been for mosquitoes, we wouldn't have invented the screened in porch.

Flies are also masters at spreading diseases. God created them to further the cycle of decomposition. They consume dead animals, feces, dead plants, garbage, and even the food at your picnic. These creatures spend most of their time standing on the poop and then make their way onto the potato salad and hot dogs. Wouldn't it be comforting to know that you remove trash, dead plants, and pet feces from the yard on a regular basis? *Bon Appetit!*

## Decks

Nails and screws are in every square foot of your house. When nails back out of their holes, we tend to hammer them back into place. This solution creates a larger hole that allows the nail to back out faster. When you discover a deck nail that has backed out, remove the nail and replace it with a deck screw. If a deck is built using nails as the material fasteners, most of the nails will eventually back out. Even the tiniest nail head surface can tear skin.

Older decks that have not been maintained or protected may crack and splinter. Pressure treated lumber is used for the construction of exterior decks, furniture, and fences. It can stand up to the weather much better than untreated lumber, but it will still wear if not maintained and protected. And for some reason, splinters from pressure treated wood tend to hurt worse. When you discover deck, stair, and handrail lumber that has worn out, it may be too late for a rescue. The best policy is to replace damaged wood, not try to repair it. Replacing will cost less money and time. If most of the deck flooring is worn out, it is likely that the floor joists underneath have been compromised. If so, it is best to remove the deck entirely. You can choose to rebuild a new deck, pour a concrete patio, or simply give the space back to the grass.

Cleaning a deck is a pretty simple task. Using a deck cleaner found at box stores, water, and a push broom will work, but I prefer to use a pressure washer. It is faster and offers a deeper cleaning. Pressure washers typically come with different colored spray tips. I almost always use the yellow tip. It allows the right amount of water pressure to thoroughly clean without damaging the wood surface. Of course, the closer the spray tip is to a wood or concrete surface, the greater the likelihood of damaging that surface. If you take care of your deck by cleaning and protecting/sealing, it should last you a long time. Just as with the human body, it is easier to maintain than to replace.

Most decks have handrails. Some do not. Handrails are often wobbly and loose. It is a good idea to strengthen the handrail by tightening it or using screws to secure it to adjacent material.

Many people have their decks stained. This is a great idea since almost every deck stain will offer some protection. It can keep the wood young by protecting it from water, wind, and direct sunlight. Protective deck stains come in a variety of colors with different chemicals. Water based deck stains offer tremendous protection and come in semi-transparent and solid colors. Oil based stains typically come in nature based colors (browns, greens, and grays). Unlike most water based stains, oil based stains penetrate wood to a greater depth. Thus, the wood surface is protected, and so is the material beneath the surface.

## Privacy Fences

There is a saying by poet Robert Frost, "Good fences makes good neighbors." Privacy from neighbors is important to most of us. Privacy from the bad guys is important to all of us.

Your privacy fence is likely constructed out of either pressure treated lumber or cedar. Although pretty when they are new, they can weather, deteriorate, and become an eyesore within a couple of years. Just as with any constructed element outside, privacy fences need to be cleaned, protected, and maintained. Doing so will keep the fence, nails/screws, and hardware in safe condition, and will also look better.

Maintaining a privacy fence is easy but time consuming. These fences can also be cleaned with the use of a pressure washer. Protective stains can be applied with a roller, brush, or sprayer. Do not use a sprayer on a windy day. Make sure of what is on the other side of the fence. Stain is expensive, but cheap compared to repainting a neighbor's car or house. When you discover nails that have become loose and backed out, pull them out and throw them away. Replace them with deck screws. A loose nail can catch and tear clothing and skin.

## Digging

Chances are high that you will use a shovel at your property at some point. Before digging, it is a good idea to know what lies beneath the grass or topsoil. Your property may have underground utilities such as high and low voltage electricity, communications cabling, wiring, water or gas conduit, and a host of other possibilities. Such items may be buried and run from the service provider at the street. These utilities may be underground and from house to house or house to garage. Service providers generally know the location of their underground utility lines and pipes. They might not know the location of the things that were buried by your builder or previous owners. Many municipalities/states will offer a service you can call to request service providers to locate and mark the location of their underground utilities at your property. Perform a Google search with the term "Before you dig." Most of us can reach these locater services by dialing 811. Always do this prior to digging on your property.

Utility companies are expedient in marking their underground utilities for you. The water company may know where their water line comes into your property. Typically, they installed a meter when water was run to your property. However, it was likely a plumber who ran the water supply line from their meter into your house. Large electrical wires are typically run from a utility pole to your house by the electric company. They will then connect that large wire to a main cut off on the outside of your house. Gas lines are run from under the street to gas meters found on the outside of houses. Communications cabling is typically run from a utility pole to a network interface box on the outside of your house. But sometimes, all of your utilities are run underground. My point is that the utility companies may be able to locate their utility lines and pipes, but they may not know where tradesmen, builders, and homeowners have buried additional lines and pipes.

There are privately owned companies that specialize in locating additional wires and pipes that were not installed by the utility companies. This is important to know. Homeowners often bury electrical wire carrying thousands of volts of electricity, expensive low voltage wires for lighting and communications, and water supply lines. Sometimes these wires and pipes are just below the surface.

While restoring a historic house, and just prior to digging outside, I called 811 to have the location of all utilities marked and identified. The company representatives were there within a day and marked their respective utilities. The following day, while on a large piece of heavy equipment, I plunged the bucket into the earth alongside the foundation. Upon lifting the bucket full of dirt, a tooth on the leading edge of the bucket snagged and raised a large gray pipe. The pipe suddenly burst and high-pressured natural gas was blowing directly at me in the open cockpit. I jumped from the piece of equipment and called the gas company then waited for their arrival. Since they had failed to locate and mark this gas line, I didn't have to pay to repair the line. I was also grateful to have not perished in a fire or explosion while I was strapped into the large machine.

## Packaging and Plastics

Shoppers and retailers love the lightweight and disposable bags we use to transport our groceries from store to car and car to kitchen. The use of these bags was in response to environmental activists wanting to outlaw paper bags in order to save trees. Today, there is a push by environmental activists to outlaw plastic bags because they take so long to decompose and pose a threat to wildlife. They would like for us to use paper bags or reusable cloth bags. I like paper, plastic, and reusable bags. Give shoppers and retailers a choice.

People like to use the paper bags as garbage containers and for wrapping packages. Children like to use the plastic bags to make parachutes, play games, and school projects. Many children, however, are injured or killed as a result of strangulation with their heads inside plastic bags. My advice is to store plastic shopping bags in a larger bag and keep it out of reach of children.

In closing, though danger and disaster are really not an active part of our daily routines, be assured that they lurk around every corner. I believe that concern for safety is an important trait to incorporate into your life. Be proactive and identify all of the threats to you, your awesome family, and your beautiful home. Apply the knowledge I have shared with you and enjoy your safe and protected quality of life.

# CHAPTER 23
# Your House is A Complex Set of Systems

Your house is the culmination of many systems. Objects that work with other objects in order to function properly represent a system. A roof nail is an object. A roof shingle is an object. Your roof is a system. For the shingle to work properly, there are many other objects within the roof system that must also be working properly. The shingle is only as stable as the roofing nails. Those nails don't fasten properly to rotted plywood under the shingle. The plywood surface doesn't function properly if the roof rafters beneath it are rotted or broken. These elements make up the roof system. The foundation of your house is also a system. Each block is dependent on a strong concrete surface below (the footer). Those blocks are useless unless they are held in place by correctly mixed mortar. The footer, block, and mortar are part of the foundation system. If a contributing member of a system fails, it jeopardizes the integrity of the entire system. In other words, if a soccer team loses its goalie or fullbacks, the success of the whole team is compromised.

Foundations are typically constructed using stone or cement blocks and concrete. The system is designed to evenly withstand the weight of the structure that rests on it without cracking. There are many enemies to a foundation system. Such examples could include earth movement, differing soil conditions from one end of the structure to the other, nearby explosives (blasting), drought, flooding, and poor construction. Damage to a foundation can result in stair-step cracks in the brick veneer of a house. If the foundation moves, it can cause the entire structure to move resulting in cracked drywall, doors and windows that close improperly, door and window trim that has separated from itself, and unleveled floors. Most foundations can be repaired, however. Repairing a cracked foundation is critical if the separation continues over time. If you notice any of the above-mentioned symptoms, you may wish to monitor the movement by measuring the gaps in trim or around doors when closed. These things may change seasonally by shifting back into place one season, then separating during another. A foundation can crack then never move again.

There are various types of home construction methods. What I described in the last paragraph was the foundation of a house over a crawlspace or basement. Some houses are built on a solid concrete slab. The edges of the slab are more robust to support the weight of the exterior walls above. This type of slab is called a "monolithic slab." Developers often choose to build houses on slabs in order to save money during the house construction. Similar to the monolithic slab, a "one stone" foundation consists of large interlocking limestone blocks that form a single body.

Some houses are built on piers that are hydraulically driven into the earth until refusal (rock or undisturbed and supportive matter). This type of construction is typically found in coastal areas where flooding is common, or up in the high country of the Rockies where ideal and level land elevations are sparse.

There has been controversy surrounding manufactured houses. These structures are built in a factory and assembled on a lot and foundation. Traditionally, houses are *stick built*. This means that the raw materials are delivered to a work site and workers build the systems on site. For years, houses that are built in factories carry the stigma that they are cheap and poor in quality. They are compared to mobile homes, which are also built in factories. Though I am a traditional stick builder, I do like the idea of house parts and pieces being constructed in ideal conditions by reliable workers and well-calibrated machinery. These houses are quickly assembled at the work site, leaving less opportunity for flawed measurements, vandalism, injuries, and overhead costs. Given that the Great Recession of 2008 destroyed the American construction labor force, quality labor is difficult to find. It used to be easy to locate and contract with a crew of quality and highly knowledgeable workers. Today, builders have to contract with quality crews months in advance of needing them. There are many less experienced workers available. They are many of the ones you see at job sites today. Having well-built walls, roof systems, and floor systems delivered and assembled by expert tradesmen is becoming more attractive to today's stick builders. I believe the pre-built house industry will eventually become the standard in American home construction.

Your heating, ventilation, and air conditioning (HVAC) is more than a machine in the basement or closet. This complicated system includes elements such as the heater, cooler, evaporator coil, condensing unit, pumps, duct work, thermostats, low and high voltage wiring, and floor/room diffusers (vents). How well this system works is dependent on a host of other factors including the number and placement of windows and doors, direction the house is facing, and the size of the structure it will serve. If any element associated with the HVAC system fails, the entire system usually becomes compromised.

All structurally supporting wood elements in a house are part of the framing system. The floor joists, subfloor, walls, ceiling joists, roof rafters, nails, and screws (fasteners) belong to the framing system. A concrete pad is not a system. A light is not a system. A gutter is not a system. A stairway could be a system if it has treads, risers, runners, and kick plates, but some stairs are made of the steps only.

You do not have to fully understand the elements of each system. But you need to understand that they are systems, and that trade specific contractors will understand all of the their parts.

# CHAPTER 24
# Gilligan's Island

Mary Ann or Ginger?

## CHAPTER 25
# Preventive House inspections

The following are inspections that I perform at my house. These inspections can reveal potential problems long before they become serious issues. I am skilled when it comes to tools, ladders, and inspections. I am able to perform these inspections with minimal chances of being injured because of my knowledge and experience. I do not encourage you to engage in dangerous activities. Qualified professionals should be hired to perform home inspections that could otherwise place you in harm's way. You need to know what inspections these professionals should perform.

### Ceilings

If you notice a spot on the ceiling that is yellow or orange, you likely have a roof or pipe leaking. The leak that is causing it may not be directly above the spot. Water that drips from a roof or pipe could be in another place. Water that gets in through a hole in the roof may roll down a rafter, onto the plywood decking in an attic, then roll for several feet before making its way through insulation and the drywall. Once the water has saturated the drywall, it will reveal itself as a discolored spot or area on the ceiling. If the spot or area is gray or black, you missed the spot when it was yellow.

The leak has probably been happening for some time. The darker color may indicate the presence of mold or wood rot. You may need to replace the drywall and insulation in that area. There is also a chance that you will have to remove the mold and address wood framing that has been compromised. It is a good idea to inspect your ceiling every month. It is as easy as walking through your house and looking up.

## Roof inspection

Roofing material manufacturers and roofing contractors may void your roof warranty if they discover that non-professionals have walked on a roof. I believe the roof is the wrong place for amateurs. Professionals should perform roof inspections. If you want to know what they find, ask them to take pictures. You can discuss the findings on the ground.

## Nails

During the roof inspection, professionals are looking for roof nails that are loose, have backed out, or are no longer coated in silicone. The tiniest hole in a roof can cause massive damage to the interior of the structure. The remedy is for the roofer to fill the hole with special silicone or tar and install a new nail next to the former hole.

## Flashing

The roofer will inspect the integrity of the *flashing*. Flashing is made of metal or plastic and creates a barrier between horizontal and vertical surfaces. An example might be where roof shingles meet a chimney or dormer siding. Flashing is installed so that water is not shed directly into the house where the shingles stop and the bricks or siding begin. Flashing can also be found under shingles of the *starter row*. The starter row refers to the shingles that lean out over the gutter. It is common for flashing to wear out, corrode, and come loose. Reattaching or replacing flashing and sealing the edges with silicone or tar is typically the remedy.

## Trim Surfaces

Roofers will inspect wood trim or accents that come in contact with roof shingles. This usually includes window trim, sills, drip edges (above the window trim), and exterior siding material. Since a roof can be a very hostile place, they will look for silicone or caulk that has become loose/compromised. They look for wood that has been exposed to water or damaged by water. They may close gaps in the trim by adding additional silicone, or by adding more caulk and sealing the caulk with primer and paint. Remember, caulk is a water-based adhesive that adjoins two pieces of material such as trim. Caulk should be painted whether inside or outside. Silicone is oil based and is typically used in wet areas. Most silicone products cannot be painted.

## Venting

Roofers are interested in vents that protrude from the roof. Such vents consist of vent stacks, air vents, and exhaust conduit.

Vent stacks are skinny, PVC or metal tubes that protrude from a roof. They are the conduits that allow air to draw into a drain line. When you flush a toilet or run water in a sink or bathtub, it is deposited into a drain. Gravity is not enough to pull that water through the drainpipes. Air is also needed. To illustrate, if you lower a straw into water and remove the straw, water flows out of the straw. However, if you submerge the straw, cover the top of it with your thumb, and remove the straw, water remains in the straw. When you remove your thumb, water falls out of the tube. Consider the vent stack as a straw. If you cover a vent stack, you will notice that the sink fills or the toilet backs up. Draining water needs air, and it gets it through the vent stack. Vent stacks are stabilized at the rooftop by what are called vent stack boots. They are made of rubber and also prevent water from sneaking in around the vent stack. These boots become compromised over time and water gets inside the house. A roofer can replace the vent stack boot very easily. A vent stack boot typically costs less than $20.

Roofers will also inspect exhaust vents that protrude from the roof. Exhaust vents are where carbon monoxide is removed from inside. Carbon monoxide is a poisonous gas that results from burning natural gas in the water heater and HVAC unit. Exhaust vents are also used to allow hot air to escape from the attic. This is critical because hot attics can cause roof systems to fail. The hot air must be able to escape the attic.

Roofers will also be able to inspect the exterior of a chimney. They are looking for cracks in the brick or mortar and compromised chimney caps. These are places where water can intrude.

### Roof shingles

Roofing materials come in various forms. Roofs can be made from metal, terracotta, clay, wood, and tar shingles. The most common roof shingle is made of tar and fiberglass. These shingles, if installed correctly, can last for decades. They are durable, flexible, and are easily repaired. They do wear out, however. Weather plays a significant role. Direct sunlight is harsh. Hail, rain, snow, ice, foot traffic, branches, and basketballs are enemies to a roof. Cedar shingles are commonly found in the western United States, particularly in the mountains. Cedar shingles are beautiful and durable. Metal roofs are most durable and are among the most expensive to purchase and install. Clay shingles are commonly found in the southwest and in more arid climates. Slate shingles are extremely expensive, durable, and commonly found on castles and high-end houses. All roofs fail with time and abuse. Roofers can identify shingles (or metal) that has been compromised. They can also offer you solutions for repairs and replacement.

## Electrical Riser

The *electrical riser* is the metal tube that protrudes either through or next to a roof. This is where the electrical company delivers electricity to your house. The riser is home to your electrical wires that connect to the wires provided by the electric company. Many roofers will defer to electricians in order to repair or replace anything that comes in contact with the electrical riser. Amateurs should in NO WAY come in contact with any part of the riser or wires.

## Gutters and Downspouts

Any interaction with your gutters should be done by a professional who wears protective gear and has extensive experience working from a ladder.

There are so many different styles of houses. Some house styles perform better in certain parts of the country and fail in others. Steep roofs were designed for, and are intended to handle, the weight of heavy snow. Snow melts slowly and delivers small amounts of water into gutters. However, these steep roofs perform poorly in the southeastern United States, home to heavy downpours. A large volume of water can be delivered in a short span of time, causing gutters to overflow and destroy trim, fascia, and soffits. Shallow pitched roofs tend to perform well, as rainwater sheds at a slower rate. But shallow pitched roofs can suffer under the heavy weight of snow. Metal roofs perform well against rain. Unfortunately, heavy snow can freeze and slide off a metal roof, hurting people, animals, and plants.

Gutters come, or are made, in a variety of sizes. Most gutters prior to 1990 had 4" openings at the top. Today, almost all gutter companies install gutters with 5" and 6" openings. Obviously, the wider the gutter, the more water it can catch, carry, and remove through the attached downspouts. Most of today's gutter installation companies manufacture gutters while at your house. They carry large rolls of aluminum and form the gutters onsite. They then cut the exact length of gutter they will need for a particular run. These gutters are referred to as *seamless* gutters. Seamless gutters perform better since they have fewer joints (only where corners meet). Inside the corners where two pieces are joined, the gutters are screwed together and coated with silicone on the inside. The silicone has a shorter life than the gutter. It needs to be inspected every other year to ensure that it is still in place and watertight.

Gutters can last longer than the structure if they come in contact with nothing but water. Common enemies of gutters are branches, leaves, algae, and roof debris. These things can dent, damage, and clog a gutter. Once a gutter is clogged, it becomes heavy with the weight of trapped water and can begin to pull away from the house. Clogged gutters also back up with water, causing overflow to adjacent surfaces, resulting in wood damage. There are many products designed to protect gutters from clogging. I prefer simple wire mesh. It keeps the trash out while allowing water to fully penetrate into the gutter. If you choose not to cover your gutters with a wire mesh covering, know that gutters need to be inspected or cleaned out at least twice a year if you have trees on your property. I inspect and clean mine every 6 months.

## Water Shedding

People don't consider how damaging water can be to a house. Water that drains off the roof should be delivered to the ground, preferably at least three feet away from the structure, its foundation, sidewalks, and driveways. The main purpose of a gutter is to catch water in order to direct it away from the house. It does so by directing water to downspouts that are strategically installed. Not having gutters or strategically located downspouts will cause erosion of the soil around your house and may eventually compromise your foundation, your basement walls, and the supportive material under driveways, sidewalks, porches, and patios.

Both moisture and the lack of moisture can compromise your foundation and basement walls. Drought can cause supportive soil to pull away from the foundation, leaving it with no lateral support. Likewise, you never want excessive amounts of water to come into contact with your foundation. Not only can water erode the soil, but it can also penetrate the foundation, thereby flooding your basement or crawlspace. If trapped water in the foundation freezes, then your foundation will crack, causing potentially extensive damage to the house.

## The Attic

The attic may be the strangest place in a house. It is mystical and mythical in stories and movies, but an attic can pose more danger than any room in a house. Attics can get hot enough to kill humans. Grabbing anything in the dark often results in spider bites, snakebites, and wasp stings. Breathing attic air is unhealthy. This is because we seldom clean the attic. When air is moved, it kicks up matter from animal and insect carcasses, dust, mold, dirt, and fiberglass that can result in lung infections. People who work in attics without breathing protection (respirators or masks) often end up on oxygen long before their deaths. Attic lighting is typically poor. Attics are home to insect and animal carcasses. The attic is a great place to break a bone if you are into that sort of thing. One misstep in an attic and you can fall into raw lumber, rafters, or through rafters. Knowing how to walk on rafters is an acquired skill. Don't do it.

The condition of an attic can tell us a lot about a house. Because most attic framing is exposed, contractors can easily identify the quality of framing or detect a flaw such as too few nails or evidence of a water leak. He can identify the integrity or amount of insulation. Have your contractor inspect your attic every fall. Doing so will help to keep this important space clean, healthy, and safe. I try to stay out of the attic during the dead of winter so that my movements aren't hampered by bulky clothes or frozen fingers. I stay out in the dead of summer to avoid heat stroke and sweating through my clothes.

During attic inspections, contractors will look for hanging electrical wires that could snag, shock, or cause fires. They will look for the presence of varmints and pests and where they could get in.

Contractors will ensure that your attic is breathing correctly with adequate venting. They will check HVAC ductwork for tears. They will ensure that pipes are fastened correctly. They will check for evidence of a water leak by locating the dark circular spot where the water is entering the attic. They will follow the wood discoloration/water trail to where the water is settling. Contractors are often able to identify mold.

## Fascia and Soffit

Your gutters are nailed or screwed to a trim board called the fascia. This trim board attaches to, and hides, the ends of the roof rafters. The rafters rest on the top plate of exterior walls. Underneath the fascia and gutters is the soffit. The soffit is typically a piece of plywood that is installed horizontally. It extends from the house out to the fascia. If you walk outside and it is raining, snug up to the house and look at the eve above you. You are looking at the soffit. Inspecting the fascia, soffit, and the corners where pieces come together is important. Most of the material you inspect will be in decent condition. When these trim pieces have become compromised by water, the paint may be discolored (gray or black). Paint may be loose or appear like a bubble. This is usually the result of poor gutter fall (inhibiting water to naturally drain toward the downspout), a clogged gutter, or poor roof installation at the starter row of shingles. Water has overflowed the gutters and come in contact with the soffit and fascia material. You either have wood rot or are on the way to having it. A contractor/handyman can remove and replace the rotted material and address any gutter issue.

**Windows**

Windows are engineered to withstand the weather. Newer windows are more efficient and weatherproof than old windows. Replacement windows are, by and large, made of plastic and last far longer than their wooden counterparts.

Like anything else exposed to the elements over a period of time, windows can break down. Glass rarely breaks down, but the wooden frame (sashes) can. Poorly primed and painted wood, if exposed, may rot.

It is important (and included in codes in many cities) that all windows operate properly. The only windows that don't open are referred to as *transom* windows. Having egress in case of a fire or flood is important. If you cannot escape through a door or hallway, you must be able to get out of a house through a window. If windows don't open, there is a strong chance that the sashes have been painted and become glued to the window frame. Banging on the sash is not the way to get them to separate. This usually results in the glass breaking. It is best to use a single–edge razor (box cutter) to gently separate the sash from the frame. Instead of enlisting all of your strength and momentum toward cutting through old paint, it is best to steady the box cutter and tap gently on the top of the box cutter with a medium sized hammer. Take your time.

Windows have several components. The frame and glass is called the *sash*. The sash is raised and lowered where it sits on the *sill*. Above the window, there is usually a piece of material that extends out and past the window frame. This is called the *drip edge*. Below the windowsill is the *brick ledge* or *skirt board*.

The drip edge is there to move falling rain away from window sashes and sills as the water falls. Many windows that were installed in new houses after the 1970s were installed incorrectly. As a result, most of the components of these windows fail. Windows are often installed out of level. Poorly operating sashes, misaligned locking mechanisms, and wood rot are the results. If your windows, sills, and drip edges are out of level, it may be time to get a price from a trusted window installer.

Many homeowners will try to repair wood rot with caulk, auto body filler, or silicone. These remedies are temporary at best. Once the wood components of a window become compromised, water will usually find its way onto the framing, drywall, and floor lumber where it can also rot.

If your windows appear to be in good condition and proper working order, inspect where all window components come into contact with the other window components and the house. If you notice a tiny separation in material or paint, it is a good idea to fill cracks with caulk, then prime and paint. Larger gaps that have led to wood rot mean that new materials should be installed. Always work with a clean surface.

## Exterior Doors

The care, maintenance, functionality, and inspection of exterior doors should be similar to that of windows. Exterior doors get beaten by weather and direct sunlight. Wooden doors can split or rot. Locksets and hardware can corrode. When you examine exterior doors, you are looking for signs of deterioration. If the door is made of wood, you can sand, prime, caulk, and repaint the door. If the door is stained wood, you can sand, fill (wood filler), sand again, then re-stain and seal (polyurethane) the door.

Exterior door hardware (knobs and deadbolts) can fail over time because of direct exposure to rain and sunlight. Cheaper locksets are made from cheaper metal (alloys). They will wear out, corrode, and fail much faster than quality locksets under the same conditions. Your door locks must work properly at all times. You and others may need to get out of the house quickly at some point. You must not have to work to get a door open. I spray a product called DryLube into keyholes and striker hulls (the metal piece that slides in and out of the hole in the door jamb). DryLube is a silicone spray that lubricates internal metal parts without being greasy and attracting dirt. You can also use white lithium spray grease. It works as well, but may be a little messy to work with. Spray the door hinges too.

Some deadbolts require a key to unlock. This is for obvious reasons on the outside of the door. We may feel safer in our homes if a key is required to open the door from the inside as well. Burglars can break door glass, turn a dead bolt knob and walk in. But a potential disaster could arise if you need to escape from a house and do not have a key to unlock the deadbolt. Children, grandma, and guests would be severely at risk in such a scenario. Many metropolitan codes require that deadbolts unlock with a small knob on the inside.

## Basement and Crawlspace

I mentioned how and why the attic can be so dangerous. I believe the second strangest place at a house is the crawlspace. I prefer to spend time in an attic. Crawlspaces tend to be damp, dark, dirty, and cramped. But inspecting your crawlspace is important. It is important to keep this space clean, dry, and safe. Almost everything above the crawlspace is dependent on this. The reason is that dirty and humid air makes its way into the house above. Nearly 50% of the air in your home comes from the crawlspace.

The crawlspace is home to HVAC components, conduit, electrical wiring, water and discharge pipes, framing, the foundation, floor support system, spiders, snakes, and anything else found outside. If a crawlspace is kept clean, well ventilated, and has an airtight access door, we need not worry about bugs and critters. The crawlspace floor should be covered with thick plastic sheeting. This might seem to keep us clean when down there, but it is actually referred to as the *vapor barrier*. The crawlspace can be humid because of water that gets in from the outside or from under it. The plastic sheeting is to keep the humidity levels and mold at a minimum. Nothing except this vapor barrier should be touching the floor of the crawlspace (with the exception of support pillars that are buried into concrete footers). All electrical wires, water pipes, insulation, and HVAC ductwork should be securely fastened to the floor support framing. If these things are near, or on, the floor, they can fail, tear, corrode, and be destroyed by invasive animals.

Foundation vents are the rectangular screens/grates that are installed in the walls of the block foundations (just below the framing). They are designed to allow fresh air to pass in, out, and through the crawlspace. Keeping good airflow will help your framing and foundation to last longer. In extremely humid parts of the country, it is a wise idea to seal the foundation vents and contract to have a full crawlspace encapsulation system installed. This is where a large, air tight membrane is installed to cover the inside of all perimeter walls and floor/dirt of a crawlspace. This keeps the crawlspace air in a manner that enables you to control its humidity and temperature. In this scenario, a crawlspace perimeter sump pump is installed to collect and discharge excessive moisture and water inside the crawl-space, but not into the protective membrane of the encapsulation.

Often, a crawlspace will take on water. This water can come from outside or underneath the crawlspace. The first step to finding a remedy is to address the outside. You may discover that water is spilling out of the gutter and not getting to the downspout. The gutters are probably clogged. You may find that the gutter and downspout are working correctly but that water is making its way back towards the house. If so, then you may need to lengthen the downspout to a point where water will flow away from the foundation. Downspout extensions are available in a few different forms. You may also find that the slope of your yard is directing water towards the house. If so, then you may need to contract with a land-scaper to increase the height of the soil around the perimeter of the foundation. Depending on the slope and amount of water flowing toward the house, it might be time to contract with a foundation specialist to install perimeter drain. If these remedies are not an option, the foundation company may suggest the installation of a perimeter drain with an additional drain inside the perimeter of the foundation that includes an interior sump pump to remove water.

Most builders don't install lighting in crawlspaces. In your time as a homeowner, it is likely that you will require the services of an electrician. If so, ask him to install lights and a light switch in the crawlspace. This can be relatively easy for him, and it is likely that he has everything he will need in his vehicle.

If you live in a part of the country that experiences a lot of rain and humidity, it can be a good idea to close vents and windows in crawlspaces and basements and use dehumidifiers during the warmer months. Within an hour of running a dehumidifier, you should notice a dramatic difference in atmospheric conditions. You would be surprised at the havoc humidity can create for tools, clothes, paper, plastic, ductwork, and electrical connections.

In crawlspaces we rarely look up. That is because of the position your body is in while down there. If you can lie on your back, take your flashlight and look for evidence of a current, or past, water leak. You need only do this under wet areas (bathroom, kitchen, laundry room). If there is/was a leak, you need to know the condition of the subfloor and supporting frame. If wood is compromised, it should be addressed by a licensed handyman or contractor. Doing so will be far less expensive than having to do a repair of floor joists, floor, subfloor, and/or walls.

## Interior Doors

When I walk into a house, the first thing I catch myself doing is looking at corners and door trim. This may sound crazy, but most of us cannot help but take our work with us wherever we go. That is why we seldom smile at someone who we learn is a dentist! I tend to notice corners and door trim because they can tell us so much about the condition of a house from top to bottom.

If drywall mud and tape appear to be coming loose, it is likely that the framers were poor in quality at the time of construction. Wood expands and contracts with changing atmospheric conditions. The frame will move quite a bit if it is not fastened (nailed/screwed) together correctly. The only repair for this involves removal of drywall and strengthening the frame with additional lumber and fasteners.

There may be doors in your house that you rarely open or close. You should open and close all interior doors once in a while to make sure they are operating correctly. Some house settling is normal and should be expected. Newer houses can weigh between 30 and100 tons. Slight movements in the structure can affect how well doors swing or latch. In order to repair such a door, you may need to move the striker plate a little to ensure proper latching. In addition, you should take a look at the door casing (trim). Has it come loose from the wall, doorjamb, or itself? Look at the drywall or plaster around and above the door. Do you notice cracks? This could simply be the result of settling. You can monitor the size of the cracks or door movement over a year or so. If it doesn't get worse, it might be time to patch and paint. If it does get worse, you may have an issue with a roof leak or compromised foundation. The greater the distance from a cracked foundation, the more evidence of it you'll find in the form of trim and drywall cracks upstairs. I explain this to people by asking them to consider how slowly a record spins at the center, but notice how much faster the record appears to spin at the edge. Small movements in a foundation can mean large movements in doors and walls on the second floor.

The sooner you address any problem, especially at your house, the less costly it will be.

## Concrete

Like most things, concrete has a limited life. As it matures, it dries out, hardens, and begins to break down. One day, we begin to notice blemishes, cracks, and loose layers. Concrete can break down for many reasons. Concrete does tend to weaken once it dries completely. Some say that concrete can take sixty years to dry fully. Others say it takes only two years. I suppose failure rates are dependent on many factors, including how knowledgeable the original concrete contractor was. Did he engineer, form, and pour the concrete correctly under ideal conditions? Most of us will never know. But the life of concrete is also dependent on its density, the climate (heat, cold, humidity), and damage. Once thing we do not want to do is to contribute to its premature failure. Further, there are things we can do to elongate the life of our patios, sidewalks, and driveways.

Your concrete is designed to handle compression and weight, but any surface is only as strong as that which supports it. If soil and gravel erode from under concrete, the weight limit of what that concrete can support (including itself) is reduced. It is a good idea to walk the lengths and perimeters of the concrete at your property. If you discover evidence of erosion, then you need to address it immediately. The first step is to identify why the erosion occurred. You will probably discover that water has caused the erosion. You may need to redirect water, ensuring that the water diffuses over a larger area and does not form as a direct stream that hits the concrete and supportive soil. It could be from roof runoff or from the neighbor's back yard. The fix could be as simple as installing a raised flowerbed or more soil and grass. It might also require a visit by a landscape engineer.

It is interesting how strong yet fragile concrete is. One of my favorite pastimes is building and flying high-speed remote control model aircraft. I am careful when transporting and storing these airplanes. Wings, control surfaces, and tail sections can be very fragile. It is astonishing how much punishment they can withstand in the air. In a scale comparison, a human being could never survive the first high-speed turn or maneuver. I recall interacting with my first concrete contractor. I asked a lot of questions. He told me, "All concrete cracks. My job is to control where it cracks."

And as tough as concrete is, it is also quite fragile. All concrete does crack. When a patio or driveway is poured, it is likely that an internal metal frame was added. This metal rebar acts much like a skeleton. It looks like a crude fence when assembled in the hole prior to pouring concrete. The rebar is to give the body of concrete internal strength and minimize the likelihood of the concrete expanding and coming apart in the wrong place. You may also notice grooves that the contractor made in your concrete at the time of the pour. These are called *expansion joints*. They are designed to control the location of a possible crack. Concrete should crack at the expansion joints and nowhere else. Concrete can crack based on supportive soil conditions underneath. One side of the concrete slab may be resting on firm rock, while the other side sits on expansive clay. If the soil on one side shrinks measurably, the concrete can crack.

Concrete gets its strength from many things. But one of the most important factors that affect its integrity and lasting ability is the surface of the concrete. When we stand on concrete, the bottoms of our feet are actually in contact with a very thin and fragile layer of concrete called *portland*. This thin layer is what protects the concrete below. The greatest enemy to the portland is an amateur with a pressure washer. Almost all pressure washers produce enough water pressure to cut right through the top layer (portland). Amateurs will see a dirty concrete surface turn white with the passing of the spray. They believe they are removing the dirt and making progress! What they are doing is killing the concrete. Once the protective layer is removed, the concrete can begin to fail rapidly. Over a short period of time, you may notice the erosion of the surface in the form of a loose gritty texture, deep discoloration, and soon, the surface becomes dirty again. Holes may begin to form where there were subsurface air pockets at the time the concrete was poured and finished. Instead of using a pressure washer to clean concrete, use a good concrete cleanser, water from a garden hose, and scrub with a stiff bristle broom. Of course, this is more labor intensive - but less intensive than removing the concrete and replacing it.

If the top layer of concrete has been compromised, it is a good idea to hire a qualified concrete contractor to clean and etch the surface with muriatic acid and seal it once it has dried.

Asphalt (pavement) is similar to concrete in that it will break down, and in stages. A sign that your asphalt is holding up well is that it is still black with a smooth surface. Once you begin to notice more light color stones than black tar, it means that the protective top layer has worn off. It is probably time to reseal the driveway with a quality tar or oil based sealer. Once you notice holes or cracks in asphalt, you may need a contractor to remove the bad areas and re-fill them before resealing.

Before your asphalt fails to this degree, you have the option to inspect, be proactive, and reseal the asphalt. You can do this yourself, but it will be a dirty and messy job. Box stores and hardware stores sell some good pavement coatings. The coating is applied by rolling, mopping, or brushing it onto the old surface. It will give your asphalt a new look and protect the surface for 3-5 years. Sealant quality is directly proportional to price. I would rather purchase a high quality sealer that lasts five years than save a few dollars and need to reseal every year.

The life of your asphalt will be affected differently depending on where you live. Asphalt lives a shorter life in the harsh weather conditions of Phoenix and Chicago. It tends to last longer in the moderate conditions of Los Angeles and Louisville.

## Decks and Fences

Because wood will break down quickly outside, most decks and privacy fences are made from pressure treated wood. *Pressure treated* means that the wood has undergone a process where pressure forces protectants into the wood. This enables the finished product to withstand sun, wind, and water. When you inspect your decks and fences, you are looking for wood that has split, become loose, or rotted. You will look for algae, mold, and protruding sharp objects such as wooden spears, nails, and screws.

If you come across protruding nails, do not drive them back into place with a hammer. That will make the nail hole larger. Pull them out and replace them with larger deck screws. If you see where wood has broken away from the rest of the board, it is time to remove that board and replace it. Fasten it with deck screws. Handrails should always be tight and strong. If they are loose, remove nails or screws and replace them with larger deck screws. You may have to add additional material to strengthen the existing handrail.

Algae or mold should be removed with a mixture of 1 part water and 3 parts chlorine bleach and a stiff bristle brush. When using chemicals, ALWAYS wear eye protection, breathing protection, and industrial grade rubber gloves. If you come across a board that has split large enough to deposit a quarter, it is time to replace that board, or clean and coat it with a crack-filling deck stain. I have used these products and am impressed. Though the manufacturer warranties are lengthy (over 4 years), I believe they are based on tests that were performed in ideal laboratory conditions.

It is a good idea to clean your deck every year. If you live in a dry climate, you may need only to rinse a deck off. If you live in the south, you may actually have to wash the deck surface twice a year. It can get slippery from sap and insect droppings.

## Bathrooms

**Every homeowner MUST know how to turn off the water supply to the house.**

In older homes (pre-1985), the water shut off to the house is typically down in the water meter in the front yard. You will need a water key to turn off the valve. A water key is a long, steel, T-shaped stick that you can buy at box stores and plumbing supply outlets. This is what you will lower down into the meter and over the valve to turn it on or off. Never put your bare hand into a water meter. In most of the United States, the water meter is home to black widow spiders. Valves can be difficult to turn due to them being open for such long periods of time. Corrosive build up from hard water solidifies the internal gear, making it impossible to turn. Never leave your water meter lid (steel) open and unattended. I have seen people accidentally step into open meter boxes. One of them broke his leg. Modern codes require that the master water shut off valve be located inside the house so that you have easy access to it.

Most bathrooms are similar in that they offer a toilet, sink, and bath/shower. Since all of these items involve water, when you inspect them, begin with the water supply lines. The faucet supply lines will be under the sink and inside the base cabinet. The toilet supply line will be behind the toilet. Some supply lines are made of rubber, while others are made of braided stainless steel. I like the latter since rubber will fail over time. If it happens when you are at work, you will need a canoe to get from room to room when you get home. At the base of supply lines, you will find an on/off valve. If your house is new, you should get into the habit of turning the valve off then on again every month (unless the water to the appliance is treated). This is so the valve doesn't get corroded by hard water to the point that it is locked in the "on" position. Turning it off and on will keep corrosion from forming a solid bond inside the valve. If your house is older, you may not know the last time these valves were closed or opened. If you forcibly close a water supply valve, it may begin to drip water, regardless of whether the valve is in the "off" position or not. If this happens, you will need to call a plumber to replace it - and other valves in your house.

If you take off the top of the toilet tank, you will notice lots of pieces and parts. This isn't a big deal to master. Flush the toilet and become familiar with what's happening. At the bottom of the tank, you will notice a black or red (pink) rubber disk moving up or down as you flush. When you pulled the flush lever on the outside of the tank, that motion moves an arm inside the tank. That arm has a chain on the end of it that is attached to the rubber disk. This disk is called the *flapper*. As the flapper rises, it allows for tank water to leave the tank. That water travels into the toilet bowl and creates enough weight to force waste and water in the toilet bowl down the drain. When you hear water running in the toilet at night, it is probably because the rubber flapper has worn out and tank water is leaking past it and into the toilet bowl. Take a picture of the toilet brand and flapper and take that to the box store. You can buy a replacement flapper for next to nothing and install it yourself. Be sure to turn the water supply off before working on a toilet. The large cylindrical tube to the left or right is called the *flowmaster* valve. It is responsible for delivering the right amount of water back into the tank and bowl after each flush. These wear out as well but are also easily replaced. The Internet offers easy how to videos that explain this simple procedure. Finally, the toilet seat may come loose from time to time. It is fastened to the bowl with plastic bolts and nuts. The reason they are plastic instead of stainless steel is because it is natural for us to over tighten a screw or bolt. If we over tighten a metal bolt, it could easily crack the flat back of the porcelain bowl.

Most of today's sink faucets are similar in design. Most sink faucet bases corrode over time, as it is difficult to clean the area at which the faucet base meets the vanity. Keep it clean and dry before it corrodes and permanent pockmarks appear. If you notice a drip coming from a faucet, it is typically the result of an internal "O-ring" wearing out. These O-rings are black and made of strong rubber. If you want to replace the O-ring, it is simple to do. You will need to turn off both the hot and cold water supply valves prior to doing so. Remember, they are down inside the base cabinet. Before taking a faucet apart, make sure the drains are stopped. Small bolts, tools, and parts can easily slip into a drain. To get the faucet housing loose, you might need a tiny Allen wrench to loosen a small screw. You might need to pry off a plastic label disk at the top of the faucet with a small flat head screwdriver. If you get that far, you should be able to see black O-rings on both the cold and hot side of the fixture. Take a picture of the inside of the faucet and the brand of the faucet to the box store. An employee should be able to help you locate the right O-rings for your particular faucet. O-rings come in a variety pack and cost next to nothing.

When I am in a bathroom, I cannot help but notice how people address cracks in the tile grout or where tile walls meet a tub. People battle against black and reddish stains that appear in these corners. People will clean the cracks as best they can and apply caulk to refill the cracks (wrong… Caulk is for dry areas and should be painted). Some properly use silicone to fill the cracks, but typically make a mess that looks worse than the black and red stains. If you notice grout missing, it is best to remove any other loose grout. Once that is done, you should clean the surface with paper towels and acetone. Once that has dried, you should re-grout the holes between the tiles. Again, I defer to the Internet for how to videos. That black and red stain is likely mold. This means that ventilation is poor in your bathroom, or that you are not using your overhead exhaust fan. Keep shower curtains open when not in the shower. Where the walls meet the tub, you may need to scrape out and remove grout, silicone, or caulk that has become moldy. Once that is done, refill the cracks with silicone or silicone grout found at tile stores.

**Water Heater**

I like both electric and gas water heaters. Electric water heaters are a bit more costly to operate than gas water heaters. Gas water heaters recover more quickly. When electric water heaters fail, it is usually because one or both of the heating elements has failed. Bad heating elements can be removed and replaced relatively easily. They install in the sides of most water heaters. When gas water heaters fail, it is usually because the burner placed at the bottom has burned out. Sediment in our water, such as calcium and lime, forms thick deposits on the burner plates requiring more fire (gas) in order to heat the water in the tank. Water heaters should last fifteen to twenty years. The life of a water heater can be elongated by flushing the inside of its tank every year. Most traditional water heaters have a spigot at the bottom. This is where you would attach a long garden hose in order to drain the water. If the water heater is in a basement, you may have to drain the tank into a large pan and pump the water out of the pan. Prior to draining a tank, you must turn off the electricity or gas to the appliance. Once the tank refills, you can reinstate the power.

Tankless water heaters have made a big splash in America over the last few years. The demand for the tankless application is really heating up. Given how hard the water is across most of America, tankless heaters can fail, resulting from internal corrosion to valves. We have learned to flush/clean our tankless heaters every year. They could last much longer than traditional water heaters.

## Kitchen

We spend a lot of time in the kitchen. Did you ever notice that when you entertain, everyone ends up in the kitchen? It has become the heart of the house, and the most complicated room as well. It is there that we find high and low voltage electrical wiring for lights and appliances, pipes for hot and cold water to serve sinks, water dispensers, icemakers, and dishwashers. The kitchen must also provide for venting for overhead cooking exhausts and HVAC diffusers. The kitchen contains mixed surfaces such as drywall, Formica, tile, wood, granite, hardwoods, steel, and plastics. Of all the rooms in the house, this is the one that must be kept the cleanest. Failure to do so will result in odors, insects (ants and cockroaches), rodents, infectious bacteria, food poisoning, allergic reactions, physical injuries, and damage to appliances and surfaces.

You should check behind and under appliances such as the refrigerator, oven, and dishwasher. Buildup of dust, food, hair, and grease can affect the long-term performance of appliances. It can also attract insects and rodents. Grease can damage grout and hardwood floors. Most refrigerators have water filters. Though these only filter out some forms of chlorine, they should still be changed twice a year.

There are water supply lines and valves for the hot and cold water supply at the sink. There is a cold supply to the refrigerator for the water dispenser and icemaker. Make sure rubber supply lines are not bulging from internal water pressure. These lines should be made out of braided stainless steel. Turn the water valves off and on to fend off internal corrosion that locks the valves in the on position.

Garbage disposal blades should be sharpened twice a year. I suggest that you take a few minutes and input inspection dates and times into your Google calendar. The best way to sharpen your disposal blades is to fill the disposal with lemons and ice. Turn the disposal and cold water on simultaneously. Run the disposal for 20 seconds. Leave the water running for one minute.

Cabinet hardware refers to cabinet doorknobs and drawer pulls. It also includes cabinet door hinges. Pulls and knobs tend to come loose with frequent use. I found that using a drop of Loctite brand thread lock on a bolt prior to screwing into the hardware is the way to keep it from coming loose again. Thread lock comes in two colors. Make sure to use the blue liquid. It will hold tight, but can also be removed with a little extra force.

Once a year, I like to super clean my tile grout. This can be done with steam, bleach, or a lot of hand scrubbing. After I clean the grout, I spray it with water then take a shop-vac over the tile to remove as much moisture and cleanser as possible. Once that is done, I re-apply grout sealer and leave the room for a few hours.

## Laundry Room

This is a *biggie*! The laundry room hosts two of the most dangerous things in your entire home. A friend of mine opened the top of her clothes washer prior to the spin cycle completing. As she leaned forward, her fingers came into contact with the top of the spinning metal basket. Her fingers were sliced and she nearly lost them. That was only the start of her ordeal. She ended up requiring thousands of dollars in antibiotics over a long period of time. You see, the washing machine is host to the most infectious and aggressive bacteria in a house. It is imperative that you spray the inside of the washing machine area with bleach (or appropriate cleaner) every month! Carefully wipe down the surfaces of the bucket. Keep washing machine doors open at all times when not in use. This will inhibit the growth of mold inside the machine.

Your washing machine supply hoses are hooked up to two water supply valves. One is hot and the other is cold. It is a good idea to turn these water valves off when not using the washing machine. If that is not convenient, make sure that these hoses are made out of braided stainless steel. The black rubber supply hoses will eventually burst.

Modern metropolitan codes require that all washing machines are installed in a square plastic or metal pan that has a drain and drain hose. When a washing machine fails and water leaks out, it is captured in the pan and directed to the outside of the house so as not to ruin a floor (and a ceiling below). It is generally easy for a plumber to install such a pan. It is cheap insurance!

I urge you to replace, or at least inspect and clean, your dryer venting duct every year or two. This is the flexible aluminum conduit you attach to the wall for hot air to escape. When you run the dryer, the cycle deposits wet lint onto the interior walls of the tube. That lint is one of the most flammable things in your house. Boy scouts and park rangers keep re-sealable bags full of dryer lint with them as a means to start a fire when in the backcountry.

## HVAC

Heating, cooling, and air conditioning systems may likely be the most complicated system in the house. I would like to give you an example of why changing return air filters is very important. Consider going to the hardware store and purchasing a breathing mask - one of those white, rounded paper masks that are held in place with a rubber band around each ear. These masks are designed to keep particles out of your mouth, nose, and lungs. They prevent dust, pollen, grass, mold, sprays, and wood shavings from getting inside you. Imagine wearing that mask for a period of one month. At the end of the month, what does the mask look and smell like? Now consider keeping that mask in place for another few months to a year. What would the mask look, feel, taste, and smell like? The mere image is disgusting, but a perfect example as to why you should regularly change the return air filters for your HVAC units. The air return and filter is how your HVAC system breathes. Make sure the air that it is breathing is through a clean air filter.

Outside, there is a large metal box containing important fan blades. This is called a condensing unit. The parts that it contains can get dirty from elements in the atmosphere, and from grass clippings that are discharged toward it. Make sure to blow grass clippings away from the condensing unit. During the summer, you may experience that the air blowing from an inside vent is room temperature and not cool. There could be many reasons for this, but there is a good chance that parts of the condensing unit need to be cleaned by an HVAC technician. You may also discover that the system is being overworked because it cannot get enough air through a dirty return air filter.

I like the concept of maintenance contracts between HVAC companies and homeowners. For an annual fee, these companies will routinely inspect your HVAC system. When your system fails on a cold night, it will be comforting for a homeowner to know that he will be placed to the front of the line with more priority than others. I would write down the name of your HVAC system brand, the serial number, and the unit's model number. You should get in contact with the system's manufacturer and ask for a list of every component that is under factory warranty and for how long. Put this paper in a Ziploc bag and tape it to a cool and dry wall on the outside of your HVAC unit. You may be surprised. Some manufacturers warranty parts for up to fifteen years! You need to have this information, especially if the part is expensive to replace, but is still under warranty.

## The Yard

I have covered the topic of the yard in the Home Safety chapter. It is important for you to take a deep look at every square foot of your yard in spring or summer. Keep your yard as clean as possible. When items are left outside, they break down faster. When toys and tools fall apart, they can leave behind sharp objects such as metal spears, wood shards, or plastic pieces. When your house was built or remodeled, there was a lot of trash and debris created. Most of it was removed, but some wasn't. Many builders opt to bury trash and debris in holes that they have dug in the back yard. Smaller items can make their way back to the surface. These items end up in the grass. Every few years, rent a rolling magnet and go over the yard and plant beds. Keep your lawn mowed.

To reduce the pest population at your property, keep up after the pet feces. Make sure there is no standing water for mosquitoes to breed. Toys, planters, and trash can all retain enough standing water for breeding mosquitos.

In closing, routine home inspections are the first step in successfully maintaining your property. Identifying and addressing small problems before they become big ones will increase your quality of life as well as your personal and financial safety. Licensed professionals should perform most house inspections. Now you know what they should look for!

# CHAPTER 26
# Storm Chasers

At some point, it is likely that you will have to address storm damage to your property. The damage could be as simple as a small fallen branch or as life altering as a lightning strike on your house. These events will often result in extreme stress at a time when you will be required to make critical and expensive decisions. Having the following information will help you to make better decisions in your time of need.

The term *storm chasers* refers to people who search for work in your neighborhood following a severely damaging storm. They typically show up within days of a weather related event. Storm chasers, typically, are not from your community, city, or even state. They hunt for easy money among vulnerable homeowners who are in crisis. Few of these outfits are run by people with integrity. They usually represent themselves as delivering quality for a reduced cost. Many storm chasers steal from the homeowners by demanding large amounts of money up front for materials and future labor, then leave town never to be seen again. They convince owners that skilled labor is in short supply, and that they need to secure highly skilled workers, given how important the job is. To be placed at the front of the line will cost more. I have discovered that the greater the damage in a geographical area, the larger the number of storm chasers. Storm chasers can be difficult to spot, and enlist sophisticated strategies designed to fool homeowners.

Storm chasers used to drive around in old trucks with out of state license plates. Their entire crews waited behind in work trucks while the leader knocks on doors to tell homeowners about their services. Today's storm chaser drives around in a newer truck with a magnetic business sign on the side. He drives neighborhoods looking for damage to properties, a process we call *fishing*. The Police call it *canvassing*. Usually, his business card is flimsy and homemade. He is often well dressed, speaks well, and parks his vehicle at the end of the street. This way you can see that the vehicle and magnetic sign look professional, but he is hiding his out of state car tag. If you ask the storm chaser for his business license and proof of insurance, the documents, if any, are fakes. His only referrals are those of your neighbors who have already taken his bait. His goal is to get your money as fast as possible.

Our city went through a horrific hailstorm a few years ago. Hundreds of thousands of roofs and cars sustained damage. Thousands of storm chasers descended upon our large city, made huge profits, then left. Their work was deplorable. During that time, many friends turned to me for guidance and to be a *watchdog* to protect them from storm chasers. You know how you can lead a horse to water but...? I warned neighbors about the storm chasers and how to identify them. I asked for them to keep in contact with other neighbors if any interaction took place with a storm chaser. I asked that they record car models and colors, tag numbers, and physical descriptions of these slick salesmen. I gave people every tool to avoid being ripped off. Some turned a deaf ear to me and fell for the slick presentation and impressive savings. Every friend and neighbor who did ended up getting burned. Every roof had been installed incorrectly from bottom to top and was in need of immediate replacement. They handed over their insurance checks to these con men or paid them in cash. Following these events, most insurance companies required proof of license, insurance, and workman's comp from the contractors prior to beginning the work. The massive numbers of duped homeowners was so large that insurers had to step in to stop the madness.

A contracting license is issued by the state. Do not go to contract with someone who is from another state. Even national companies are licensed in each state where they contract with residents in those states. Make sure to verify that this company is, in fact, addressed to a place in your state or city. Ask for references that go back at least five years. A reference from a neighbor who just bought a new roof from him is not a reliable reference. Ask for the address and phone number of his office. If he tells you that he is headquartered in another state, he is lying or trying to perform work illegally in your state.

Get to know good contractors prior to experiencing natural disasters. It will be valuable for you to be on a first name basis with reliable professionals!

# CHAPTER 27
# Pets

*"For me a house or an apartment becomes a home when you add one set of four legs, a happy tail, and that indescribable measure of love that we call a dog."*

—Roger A. Caras

I opened a broadcast with the following question: "According to every single study ever done, poll ever taken, and survey taken from Gallup to the world of academia, what one thing brings us more joy over any other thing at your house?"

Our pets give us more joy, satisfaction, and unconditional love than any other thing at home. Of course I suspect some of you to defer to God, TV, the kids, or cooking as bringing the most joy. I am a diplomat. I like what you like. But *Google* the importance of pets in our lives. You will be pleased at the related studies and articles. The statistics are overwhelmingly in favor of my opening premise.

I am a dog guy. I *am* a dog according to some. Like most sane Americans, I love animals. Some even taste good. As fickle and uninterested as cats may be, I have met a few good ones along the way. I am not a big fan of having rats and snakes as pets. I find the emotional support peacock strange. The whole pet experience is about interaction and loyal partnership that just seems unlikely with a boa constrictor. Most pet owners consider their furry friends to be a member of the family. We live healthier, longer, and more fulfilling lives when we include pets in them.

I was a breed snob for years. That happens to some of us. I believed that the English Mastiff was the smartest, noblest, and most superior animal ever created by God. After Doc Holliday passed away, I swore to never have another dog. That is, until one hot summer day. A severely injured puppy wandered into my yard (the lost ones always do). He was thrown from a car by thugs a street over. My investigation revealed that he was a bait dog at a pit bull factory. He was tiny, in tremendous distress, and less than a year old. He was a mixed breed of American bulldog (pit) and shepherd of some sort. Since his only likely contact with humans had been negative, he wouldn't allow me to get close to him. He was beaten nearly to death, bleeding from all orifices, and had every possible ailment. With the help of a friend (veterinarian), I tranquilized the puppy and gave the body to my friend. He called me within a few hours and said that the dog had nearly everything wrong with him but no heartworm infection. That dog hit the puppy Powerball that day. Within a couple of months, and with patience on both our parts, we bonded. It happened one afternoon as he sat between my house and the neighbor's. You see, one neighbor called him Rocky. Another called him Charlie. I looked at him, noticing his white feet and said, "Sox." He perked up and came to me with his tail wagging for the first time. That must have been his name somewhere along the way. He grew to be a very powerful, fast, generous, loving, loyal, and intelligent super dog. I was never able to train the animal aggression out of him. He would launch but never bite. His intelligence was stronger than his urge to kill. It helped with the sting of losing Doc, but still hurt when it was time for Sox to move on.

Caring for a pet as carefully as you would a family member will result in a healthier life for *both* of you. Pets will live longer and healthier lives if they are given comfort, training, consistency, shelter, and medical attention. Laws related to pet care are finally coming into the 21$^{st}$ century, thank God. So many people buy pets then forget about them. Having the right accommodations, personal schedules, and time for a pet are all critical, and must be considered before bringing one home.

I am a huge proponent of dog training. It is during this time that you and your dog will bond the most. Since dogs are pack animals, he is looking at you to be the leader and teach him. You have a car, friends, the Internet, smartphone, job, parties, NFL, yoga, and beer! He has you. Since you made the decision to be responsible for another's life, then you believe too that he is worth training so that your time together will be rewarding. He is already genetically programmed to be smart. Train him so that his intelligence and trust is centered on you. Dogs are show offs! Most will read their owners and know when they have succeeded in pleasing them. Your dog's rewards for accomplishments at training are everything to him. Training your dog will teach him that he can trust people. Dogs that attack or viciously bark at people have learned to distrust humans. Untrained dogs can create legal exposure for owners. Training a dog will make him far less likely to bite people and other animals. How well you train your pet will determine how well he will interact with others. Training should encompass more than "sit" or "stay." It should create a rich and healthy psychological framework for the relationship between you two. Training a dog is easy and quick if you are patient and consistent. Besides, you only have to do half the work! He will do the other half. Heck, if I can train the hardheaded Mastiff to do my taxes...

A cat can make a great pet for some. Most rural property owners opt to have a cat or several for rodent control. And despite what people think about "fluffy" the house cat and how sweet she is, make no mistake: genetically, Fluffy is a small lion when nobody is looking. There are so many interesting videos that prove this. People attach small HD cameras onto their cats and let them out at night. Cats travel for miles to kill rodents, snakes, and varmints. Check it out!

# CHAPTER 28
# Painting

The history of paint and its advancements date back to the ancient Egyptians. I find the history of house painting fascinating. The earliest paint was made out of animal fat and blood. This is why early barns and towns were red. In the late 1800s, Henry Sherwin (Sherwin-Williams) invented a superior can and lid that contributed significantly to the marketing of paint. Benjamin Moore made technological advancements that continue to contribute to the paint industry. Early in our nation's history, it was seen as sacrilege or immodest for one to paint a house. Today, we wouldn't consider living in a house that wasn't painted or stained.

Painting and landscaping are the most common "do it yourself" projects. Typically, these are things we can do with little expense or training to add value to our house and home. I don't really care to watch the average person paint. It bores me. I love to watch a professional painter in action! It is amazing how he holds the brush, moves his arms, hands, and elbows as he applies the paint. The brush glides effortlessly, in the straightest line, and delivers the perfect amount of paint on the surface from stroke to stroke. There is no masking tape, drips, or small talk. They dip the brush into the paint can the exact same way every time.

Paint has made huge strides over the last thirty years alone. There are oil-based paints, water-based paints, epoxies, water-based stains, and oil-based stains. For each, there are exterior and interior grade paints. All paints come in different finishes (sheens) such as high gloss or a matte finish. Until recently, almost all stains were oil-based. Today, you can buy virtually any color of water-based stain. The public demanded water-based stains because they are easily applied and easy to clean up. It takes experience to apply oil-based stain or paint correctly. There is a common misconception that a house painted with oil-based paint means a superior result. Oil-based paint offers a superior finish with lasting performance. It can stand up to repeated cleanings. Now, thanks to improvements in technology, there are water-based paints (latex) that can stand up to the harshest weather and to repeated cleanings.

I recall visiting a prospective house customer in need of having his house repainted. The paint was in good shape overall but tired looking, with some evidence of water damage. He informed me that his entire house had been painted years ago and that he preferred oil-based paint. I pressed on one of the front columns and my finger disappeared. The older oil paint held up so well that we couldn't tell the wood behind it had rotted. Latex paint has a quality that allows it to breathe better than cured oil paint. Had my customer originally used latex instead of oil paint, chances are good that he would have caught the water and insect damage to his house prior to us needing to replace a lot of wood before painting.

Interior and exterior paints do have their similarities. They appear to be the same. They apply in similar ways (brush, sprayer, roller). However, exterior paint is a tougher product once cured. It contains volatile organic compounds as well as mold inhibitors and sun blocking ingredients. Interior paints tend to offer more colors and prettier finishes.

## Finish (or sheen)

Paints come in a variety of finishes. People often confuse the finish with color or paint function. There are four basic finishes. They are high gloss (very shiny), semi-gloss (shiny), satin (some shine), and flat (no shine). The variety of finishes offered by manufacturers can differ.

Decades ago, homeowners chose to paint their wet areas and high traffic rooms with high-gloss or semi-gloss paints. They believed that the glossier paints could withstand multiple cleanings and stand up to moisture better than paint with a flat sheen. Back then, their thinking may have been correct. Today, homeowners desire elegant colors with flat finishes throughout the home. There are many top quality paints that provide extremely durable flat finishes. Painting walls with a paint that has a glossy finish is best left to the professional. How the paint is applied and back-rolled will determine the overall outcome and consistent finish once the paint has cured. If applied incorrectly, glossy finish paints will often leave wide streaks and roller marks.

Muscle memory resulting from physical experience is a critical trait to a top-notch painter. Few homeowners are able to readily identify a quality paint job versus one that is pretty good. I think that a sloppy paint job is easy to recognize, and can actually detract from the value of a property. Most of us are not professional painters with the knowledge and skill to deliver an expert paint job.

Physical experience is only one part of what is required to do a paint job correctly. There is so much to know about the world of painting that supersedes our old opinions. I am slow to adopt new products with miraculous claims. Products that are "As Seen On TV" promise amazing results if we buy them. I have bought these products over the years and discovered that some work for a while and some don't work at all. I believe most of them work as promised... Once. Some paint manufacturers now offer paint that comes with the primer already mixed in! Those of us who understand what primer is and when to use it are left with a lot of doubt that paint and primer in one can stand up to anything, on any surface, and for any purpose. We know what kind of primer to use, where to use it, and for what purpose. At present, I will use the primer and paint mix only for interior purposes, or as a means of neutralizing orange, red, and blue colored walls. I have found that using these products on raw materials outside resulted in failure, and in short order.

Primer has several functions. Its basic function is to act as glue. Think of primer as double sided tape. It sticks to a surface and paint sticks to it. Primer also serves as a barrier between paint and a surface so that paint is not absorbed into that surface. Primer helps to inhibit rust. Primer is also used as a means to neutralize certain colors. For example, if you try to change the color of an orange door to white, you will need to neutralize the orange pigment, or it will continue to bleed through the new coat of white paint. People fail to recognize this and become frustrated with each coat of white they add. A light gray primer would neutralize the orange, requiring only one or two topcoats in white.

If I wish to use water-based latex paint to cover a surface that was oil-based, I would first sand the finish of the oil paint and apply a coat of bonding primer (referred to as *elastomeric*) prior to applying the latex paint. If you fail to prepare prior to painting water-based paint onto oil-based paint, it will crack and peel in short order. This is why you would use the elastomeric primer (bonding glue).

## Stain Blocking

I have used a lot of products in attempts to cover stains caused by water, mold, food, and grease. The best way to block stains is to encapsulate them. Using shellac-based or oil-based primer forms an impenetrable coating over the stain. The new paint will then stick to that primer. If you spill these primers onto your clothes or carpet, good luck getting them out!

Some paint manufacturers, in an attempt to lower the cost of production, skimp on the ingredients. This was common years ago at the height of the housing/credit-based recession. Later, these companies would introduce a "top of the line" paint that was, in most cases, the original formula (only now at a premium price!). Using quality paint, primer, and tools is important to me. I don't want to have to chase drips, cover a wall surface over and over, or be called back because the paint didn't stand up to everyday use. As with most products, you get what you pay for. Clever marketing does not a quality product make.

Years ago, I had a client ask me to paint the exterior of her house. She demanded that I use a certain brand that offered a *paint and primer in one* product. She and her husband had relied on this brand for decades. I explained that the brand and the product were wrong for their particular application. I knew that the product would not perform as advertised nor last more than a year or so. I suggested that we use a bonding primer for certain surfaces and her choice on others. I also informed her that I would not be responsible for the surfaces that were painted with her choice of product. Confidently, she agreed. Within a year, the paint she chose was peeling.

In another scenario, we were asked to paint the interior of an extremely high-end home. The owner was adamant that we use her choice in paint brand. At the time, I was a friend to the regional sales manager of that brand. I knew that the quality of that paint had rapidly declined over the previous year due to the housing-based recession. I shared this information with the homeowner but she refused to budge. In my contract, I specifically spelled out that we would apply only two coats of paint to each surface and would not be held responsible for the performance or durability of the paint. After applying two coats of her brand to the walls, the paint hardly covered the original pastel colored surfaces. The paint was drying unevenly and leaving terrible streaks. Given that the customer had to leave town for a week, I matched her color in a quality brand that I prefer. We applied one more coat using my preferred paint brand and the job was finished. Since honesty is the best policy, I shared what I had done with the customer. She was happy that she wouldn't have to keep paying us to apply more coats of paint. In the end, it was yet another example of inexperienced homeowners relying on inaccurate or out of date facts and applying them to, possibly, a completely different product with the same name. Experienced painters know which products are superior.

Another friend of mine decided to help her son by painting the master bedroom in his recently purchased townhouse. The existing walls were blood red and she was painting over them with white. We were hired to handle the upgrades prior to move in. I told my friend how to neutralize the unsettling red color by applying any brand of primer in a lighter shade of gray. I told her that the paint store could tint primer to match certain colors and shades. My advice fell on deaf ears. She painted the room several times over before becoming frustrated and exhausted. The white never covered the red. The red became pink, and the red pigment kept bleeding through the white paint. I asked her why she elected not to neutralize the red with a simple coat of gray primer. She said that she didn't want to spend the extra thirty-five dollars for primer.

If you paint your house, you will have to make a decision as to whether or not to use primer first. If what you plan to paint is a raw material such as wood, stone, drywall, metal, or plastic, you should apply a coat of bonding primer prior to painting it. The surface must be clean and dust free prior to applying primer or paint in order to ensure proper adhesion. If you wish to repaint a surface that is already painted, then you need not apply primer, unless you are planning to paint latex over oil paint.

Most primers can be tinted to a color that matches your finish paint. In most cases, it will not be an exact match, but it will be close. Color similarity makes it easier for the finish coat to cover and offers a more consistent finish.

The tools I use are among the best money can buy. They have to last all day and every day. If a tool breaks down or performs poorly, it could take me much longer to finish a project. If it breaks down, I can lose valuable time chasing down parts or a replacement for the tool. The same thing applies to painting tools. There are a lot of cheap brushes on the market. I use high quality brushes that perform well when applying paint. I can cut straight lines where walls meet trim or the ceiling. I never use painter's tape since the edges can allow paint to bleed onto an adjoining surface (which then needs to be repainted). A good brush will hold the correct amount of paint and distribute the paint onto a surface at the correct rate. When I am finished, I clean my brushes using a stiff wire brush, combing all paint out of the bristles and off the handle. I towel dry the brush and place it back into its form-shaped container (then tuck it in and sing it a lullaby). A good brush will last as long as you need it if you take loving care of it.

A good roller has a handle that doesn't slip from your grip while you roll paint across the wall. A good roller extension is firm and doesn't bend as you apply roller pressure to a wall. A good roller doesn't allow roller covers to slip off. Good rollers, roller covers, and extension poles don't cost much more than the cheap ones, and will last much longer.

There are different types of roller covers. Some are intended for use with oil paints, while others are intended for use with water-based paint. Some roller covers are meant for applying sealers or textures. When I paint with water-based paints, I use lamb's wool covers. They don't come in cheap six packs, and cost only a few bucks more. This type of roller cover applies paint in a uniform fashion without streaks. Cheap roller covers tend to disintegrate during use and leave specs of debris on the walls. Lamb's wool roller covers are cleaned easily and quickly.

I use high quality extension poles. They are great tools. Using a wooden or plastic broom handle is the cheap way to go. It means that you will be a slave to the entire process. You will fight to keep the roller screwed in place. You will be restricted in how much pressure you can apply to a wall surface, and the thing will often break prior to finishing the job. A broom handle is of a finite length. An extension pole easily extends and retracts, making the job go faster.

As easy as painting may appear, it requires knowledge, planning, physical prowess, good tools, and commitment to finish.

Before closing out the painting chapter, I would like to address the subject of painting fences and decks. People frequently paint a fence or deck believing that it will increase visual appeal and durability. After paint is applied, homeowners will become yearly slaves to the deck or fence. Paint does offer protective qualities, but it has no adhesion capability. Painting a raw material such as wood requires initial priming of the surface. You should always use a bonding primer of the highest quality. Exterior wood must be completely dry before priming and painting. Even when homeowners prime and paint decks and fences, the paint tends to wear and break down. Most paints were never intended to support foot traffic or stand up to the blazing sun for long periods of time. As wood shrinks and expands as the result of temperature and humidity changes, paint tends to crack and separate at the joints. Once this happens, the seal is compromised and water can come in contact with the raw wood. Paint peels and the homeowner gets stuck scraping, sanding, and repainting every summer.

Today, there are several companies that manufacture outstanding exterior grade stains designed to adhere to pressure treated or untreated wood. These stains provide long lasting durability and beauty. You must follow the application instructions found on the side of the stain's can. Before scoffing at exterior stains, you might want to know that many of these stains come in transparent *and* solid colors. This means that if you want a white picket fence without having to scrape and repaint every summer, you can elect to stain the fence with a sold white exterior stain. Problem solved!

There is a saying in the music business related to instrument storage and travel: never store your instrument in a place you wouldn't store a child. You would never leave your child in a freezing trunk or hot car. The same thing applies to instruments and paint. When you store paint, it should be in a safe place where there is not fire, excessive heat and humidity, or freezing temperatures. Once paint freezes or cooks, it is destroyed. I suggest that paint (not children) be stored in an interior closet or basement where the atmosphere is livable, consistent, and predictable... Not that I would store a child in a closet. As with any chemical, keep all paints, stains, and sealers out of the reach of children.

Tip: when you are finished with a paint project, either save the lid on the can or take a picture of it. The lid is usually home to the name of the paint brand, color, and finish in the form of a sticker. This way, you can always purchase more of the exact same paint for touch ups. Now get back to work!

# CHAPTER 29
# The Bad Neighbor

*"The size of one's house might bear a relationship to the size of one's opinion of oneself, but it has nothing to do with one's real worth."*

—Alexander McCall Smith, *The Woman Who walked in Sunshine*

Great chapter title isn't it? If you have a heartbeat, then you have a story about a bad neighbor. Even if you *are* the bad neighbor, you have a story about a bad neighbor. I have studied the subject at length academically, intellectually, and though personal experience. I have been in a courtroom and witnessed a neighbor suing a neighbor, and another (me) prosecuting a neighbor. This chapter will cover some basics and offer you guidance through identifying and handling the nightmare neighbor.

Before we start, it is important to point out that most of us are not the size of an NFL Linebacker and highly trained in martial arts. It is never a good idea to get into a physically threatening situation or place yourself or others in danger. Always enlist poise and safety when dealing with bad neighbors and their behaviors. Police like to help with bad neighbors!

In America, homeownership is a highly regarded ingredient in the American Dream. Our homes are referred to as our *castles*. Laws in every corner of our country are written and enforced to better ensure your safety and peace at home. Though we may not protect personal property and possessions with deadly force, we may protect our lives with deadly force in our homes. Your home is a pretty serious place! This applies to renters and owners alike.

There is a specific law that affords and ensures, to all property owners and renters, peace while at home. That protective measure is called the *Covenant of Quiet Enjoyment*. This means that peace and enjoyment are your right at home and that others may not take it from you without risking prosecution or being sued.

Most civilized neighbors will respect your rights as a homeowner. But in every neighborhood, there are bad neighbors. That comes with living in a free society. I imagine that bad neighbors in China or North Korea don't stay in the neighborhood very long. Knowing how to identify a bad neighbor, and how to deal with them and their offenses, can greatly enhance the experiences of homeowners.

Bad neighbors and their respective behaviors can be broken down into a few categories. There are the noisemakers, the self-entitled, the slobs, and the bullies. I submit that the common trait among all of them is a <u>lack of intelligence</u>.

Lack of intelligence is common to the human race and more common in prisons. Intelligence isn't always defined by being good at math. It might describe an uneducated person who walks into a room and intelligently converses with everybody there. I think of actors or founders of corporations. Over eighty percent of millionaires never finished college. Likewise, being dumb doesn't necessarily describe a person who didn't attend college. I know a great physician who cannot balance a simple spreadsheet. It can also describe a highly educated and wealthy jerk that everyone avoids because he doesn't have emotional intelligence and is insecure. When applied to the interpersonal dynamics found in a neighborhood setting, we discover neighbors who are either unaware of their disruptive or rude behavior, or are simply unable to mentally get outside of themselves and in the shoes of others. I find that all examples of bad neighbor behavior are the result of a lack of intelligence on their part. If we approach this subject and offensive neighbors keeping this theory in mind, then we can better identify, understand, and possibly help resolve their bad decisions and behaviors and the impact it has on those around them.

In college, my best friend's father was a recent IBM executive and retired early after his overwhelming success as an Amway distributor. As a college kid with big plans of getting rich quick, I actually enjoyed the clever and positive mantra that motivates prospective Amway distributors. The sayings usually referred to the difference between successful people and losers. They were funny, quick and to the point, and had a southern influence. Listening to my friend's dad reminded me a lot of Ross Perot. When referring to the *doubting Thomases* that are unable to see how rich one can get through multi-level marketing, he would say, "Well... Pigs don't know pigs stink." I grew to see his sentiment in so many people in my life. Psychiatry tells us that the insane don't realize they are insane. Typically, the guy who is concerned about his mental health is the sanest among us. Most idiots don't realize they are idiots. They see themselves through a skewed lens. They interpret their words and actions as cool, funny, smart, or tough. They think everyone else is the idiot (please see: politicians). This is a common trait of the narcissist (a deep psychological disorder). Bad neighbor behavior is the result of one who is unable to see past his own proverbial *mud*. They don't clean up their mud. They cannot see it. That is because they lack intelligence. So my friend's dad was right... Pigs don't know pigs stink!

## The Noise Makers

The Noise Makers are the ones who fire up their loud engines in the early morning hours or late at night. They play loud music all night or in the car with the windows down. Their yelling and screaming can be heard through the walls in the condo next door. Their dogs bark day and night. Sometimes I laugh when I see an old car rolling down the street with tire rims that cost more than my truck. The base is booming from the amplifier and speakers. His window is down and he believes he is cool! I laugh because he is a circus clown and cannot see that everyone else sees him this way. Noisemakers lack intelligence. They haven't the mental aptitude to consider the welfare of other people. This part of their development was arrested at some point during junior high school or earlier. Their intellect and subsequent decisions mirror that of an undeveloped child. It isn't that they are necessarily stupid. Some of these people have the ability to form well-planned bank robbing strategies or Ponzi schemes. In neighborhoods, they just can't mentally keep their behaviors within their own property lines. Most of them enjoy themselves at the expense of others with absolutely no idea that they are doing so. They are not smart enough. This person might leave his barking dog outside all day while at work. This doesn't mean he is a bad person. It means that he lacks information or knowledge of the barking dog and how offensive it is to neighbors. Having information and knowledge are critical ingredients to having intelligence. Children can be extremely loud on the street. Though their noise can be seen as rude and inconsiderate (which it is to thinking adults), there is a chance that they lack intelligence. Further, their parents may live a few blocks over and may have no idea how disruptive and noisy their children are. In this case, the children lack knowledge and their parents lack information (*intelligence* as it is referred to in the military).

If we accept that the behavior of the noisemaker is due to a lack of knowledge, we may discover that the offending neighbor has no idea that he is offending you. Your neighbor Janice may host large and loud parties since she is so popular. Janice may not realize how loud she is being since she is not at your house. You are. How will she learn that her music and guests are negatively impacting your covenant of quiet enjoyment? She is lacking in knowledge, so you may need to become a teacher. If she were intelligent, she would think outside of herself prior to inviting one hundred people over on a Tuesday night. The first action you should take is to confront Janice immediately (unless you don't know her or she is hosting a celebration with dangerous gang members). Your approach should be controlled, emotionless, confident, thorough, and polite. Remember that by approaching her this way, you are in the right. Knock knock knock… (time lapse)… Knock knock knock BANG BANG… "Hello Janice. How are you? Good, wow this looks like a great party. Hey, listen, the music and guests are so loud that my windows are shaking and I have to be up by five in the morning." So far, you have been calm, complimentary, stated the problem, and why it is a problem for you. At this point, you button your mouth, look her in the eye and wait for her to speak. By doing so, you avoid saying anything else that gets her off track and talking about something else. She now needs to come up with an excuse and a solution. I call this the *death pause*. Parents are good at this. Mine were. Janice has two choices. She can apologize and offer a solution, or she can tell you to get off her property. If she offers you a solution, listen and remind her that just so long as you cannot hear it at your house, everything is good and thank her for the help. Her idea of a solution might not solve the problem. That is why you gave her a boundary of "just so long as we cannot hear it." You thank her kindly and will have likely solved the problem. Your visit might also shape the size and times of her future parties. If she tells you to get off her property, do so immediately. This is for the police to handle. You might feel reluctant to report her because you have to live next to her. But since she already exhibits zero respect for you and your quality of life, then do you care if she waves to you next week? She is breaking the law. Chances are, you are not the only one she is offending. It is a good thing that you keep a record of the dates and times Janice hosts these parties.

## The Self-Entitled

The only thing on the radar of these offenders is how much more important, better, and deserving they are than others. They haven't developed the mental capacity to process more than that which involves, or pertains to themselves. Psychiatry refers to this mental disorder as narcissism. The only thing they demand of others is admiration and complete attention. These poor souls live in gaudy houses and yards. They walk in the middle of your street, forcing cars and others to veer around them. They believe that the entire street is an extension of him/herself. They do whatever they want and whenever they want there on all y'all's street. I always wanted to use the term *all y'all's* in a non-fiction book... They host parties and ask their guests to park in front of other houses with little regard for lawns and sprinkler systems. This person might have a dog. If so, they can be found walking their dogs onto neighbors' lawns for the animal to urinate, an act that is illegal in most municipalities. Ironically, the self-entitled are the first to hire a lawyer if they feel offended.

When they break the law, it may be for driving on other's property, cutting you off in traffic, building a fence on your side of the property line, or walking into a garage and taking a tool without asking. Their brainpower is limited due to a lack of development at some early age. These folks are typically extremely insecure. When they drive, they can pose a threat to joggers, mothers with strollers, pets, etc. If any of the above happens on your street, then it is a good idea to contact law enforcement officials for advice or to request extra patrol. You see, the self-entitled driver rolls down the streets without the slightest regard for children, pedestrians, pets, or other drivers. He has yet to master the physical laws of nature, and cannot mentally summon a future picture of the result of speeding where others are present. He is breaking the law. When this happens on my street, I yell, "slow down" or give the international hand signal for slow down (which is also the international hand signal for the dog to lay down). Don't give the hand signal if your dog happens to be in the street at the time. I remain calm and say, "Good morning. Thanks for backing up. I just need to record your license plate number." I walk to the back of his car, get a good look at the number or take a picture of it and tell him that he is excused. I rarely see them on my street again. Of course, the world is a dangerous place, and it is important to remind you that it may not be a good idea for you to handle it as I do. If you notice a particular person or pattern of bad driving on your street, you may need to record tag numbers and assign times to the offenses. Most police will want to help you, and it will be good for them to have patterns and times so that they can set up a speed trap. A street wide petition for speed bumps can work sometimes. As children, we encouraged each other to enlist the use of snowballs to discourage these drivers from speeding on our street. Of course, I would never do that as an adult... Again, the self-entitled people lack intelligence and sometimes you simply cannot fix *stupid*!

My former neighbor grew terminally ill with repeated strokes. I cut his grass and managed the trashcans. It wasn't the prettiest front yard on the street but it wasn't bad. One day, a self-entitled *rumor monger* stopped me and asked how my friend was doing. She was notorious for taking the personal information about others, generating fantastic stories, then spreading them to everyone who would listen to her. I replied, "He is well." She then stared across the street at his yard and said, "I'm considering letting him know that his trees really need some work and the landscaping is dreadful." How mentally disconnected is this woman? I reminded her that her house is by far the ugliest house on the street. It also resulted from the poorest construction I have ever seen. In this case, it was important for her to try and control someone and something else without taking into consideration anything but her self-importance. She acted as the yard police because she lacked intelligence. Looking back, I could have handled the woman with a little more authority and a little less anger. It might have been better to remind her that being nosey and lacking information makes her look unintelligent.

## Slobs

Slobs are easy to identify. Their houses and lives are typically in disrepair. Their yards are trashed. They fail to mow the lawn regularly. They drink beer on the porch and hold contests to see who can throw the empties into the bed of the truck. They leave the cans that don't make it for someone else to pick up at a later date. Slobs have family members who are also slobs. When relatives visit, their cars and trucks leave oil stains behind. Slobs proudly store useless car parts and broken down appliances in their front yards for the world to also enjoy.

Slobs suffer from a lack of consideration of others. They may also possess a twinge of self-entitlement. "It is my property. I can do whatever the hell I want to here on my property." This also makes the slob a bit of a bully, as well. Slobs are human. They can become emotional, indignant, and defiant when reminded about their choices (messes). Slobs view the world one-dimensionally, similar to the self-entitled offenders.

We work hard to build good lives for ourselves and families. We spend thousands of dollars on soap, hair stuff, mowers, and clothes. We want to look nice and see others who look nice. Slobs don't care how they and others appear. They are a tough sell because even if you approach them in the most diplomatic way. There is nothing you can say to convert their behavior to your liking. Additionally, what you regard as tasteless, rusted, and lacking in value may be manly creativity or yard art to the slob.

Unlike the self-entitled, the slob can also be one of the nicest, most genuine, and generous persons on the street. He is likely to offer you a beer from his rusted mini fridge. These slobs are simply naïve. They do lack intelligence, but they live the way they do as a result of laziness. Make no mistake: a nice slob is a bad neighbor. His actions or lack of action impacts your life negatively. We already covered the topic of home values and equity. All zip codes contain slobs. It is all relative. People in beautiful neighborhoods sometimes live next door to them. The slob is the reason that metropolitan mayors and city council members write enforceable property standards and guidelines. The guidelines or rules can apply to grass length, trash in a yard, pet welfare, pest control, dangerous trees, and degree of disrepair to a property, to name a few. There are also laws related to the condition of the inside of a house. There are minimum requirements related to the interior due to health implications. State and local health department officials are eager to help you if you live near a slob. Instead of you becoming a constant babysitter to the slob, why not let trained officials handle it? Slobs respond to hefty fines more quickly than they do your nagging.

## Bullies

Bullies are people who have a very underdeveloped emotional intelligence. Bullies come in all ages. He or she is easy to identify based on their interpersonal relationships with family members, coworkers, neighbors, and other drivers. At some point during their developmental years, their emotions and emotional responses were arrested due to perceived or real traumas, or neglect at the hands of others. They ceased to develop their sense of self-worth and appropriate responses to the perceived threats or criticisms in their lives. They aren't intellectually developed enough to understand that the things they hate or fear in others are simply the things they hate or fear about themselves. They assign and transfer these things onto other people, and attack them for it. In other words, bullies are delusional and terrified. Poor things.

I believe bullies roam the earth searching for people with traits they hate about themselves, perceived or real. They live in fear of others. They puff up physically and vocally in order to scare others. This is an attempt to avoid being hurt. They are unable to see the goodness and potential in others because they cannot identify those qualities in themselves. This makes it nearly impossible for them to love and trust others and form healthy and lasting relationships with them. If they acquire long-term friends, those friends are likely to also be bullies. Some bullies suffer deep mental illness and the prisons are full of them. Remember, the bully is afraid. Their own worst enemies are themselves, and often their momentum can be used against them. The bully is rarely himself and spends almost his entire life acting.

Bullies pick on people in order to control them. Since they have little self-control, they feel the need to control everything and everyone around them. Since the adult child is at constant battle with himself, he has learned to manage chaos and cannot live without it. The only arena where he is truly comfortable is in that of chaos. He will seek a marriage partner who is likely to fuel his inner chaos. He will seek to create fights with neighbors to keep the familiar and manageable chaos alive and well. He will find peace in dominating others while trying to make them feel scared and ashamed of themselves. This is why you should never take bullying personally. Further, this is also where law enforcement may come in to play. You have rights!

Bullying comes in many forms. The most common is that of physical, verbal, or legal threats to others. Of all neighbor types, the bully is the most likely to end up in prison. Prison is where we send people who cannot live peacefully and lawfully among other people (whoa! 1940s news reel guy voice again).

Since most of us operate in a civil fashion, we are not used to having to fist fight in order to maintain control at home. We are not vocally equipped to yell our way through our relationships in order to feel love and belonging. We are not meant to live life walking on eggshells at home. This may be why divorce rates are so high. Fortunately, as a people, we enlist the basic element of civility wherever we go. It is human nature to avoid discomfort both physically and emotionally. We wave to each other. We greet each other. We work to form healthy and supportive relationships with others. That is why it is so easy to spot the bad eggs among us. Most folks just want to get along and pursue the good life. There are physical laws of nature that apply to almost all things in the animal world, specifically survival. Safety in numbers means that we, as a group, are stronger and safer. Offensive neighbors are almost always outnumbered. If you are offended by loud music, trashed yards, and bullies, chances are good that you are not alone. Communication between you and other reasonable neighbors is a viable and reliable avenue for you in keeping peace and maintaining a higher quality of life at home. The more of you, the less powerful the bad ones will be.

Never threaten another person unless you intend to follow through and can afford the results or accept being arrested, beat up, or worse. Again, to threaten someone physically is considered assault in America. Do not allow another person to control your emotions to the point that you behave in a bad way, contrary to the good person you are. Common sense and composure will give you the upper hand when faced with confrontation. Try to remove yourself from the situation either physically or mentally in order to remain objective. If you threaten to sue someone, you must follow through. Be certain that you have the time, money, and proof to successfully sue or prosecute another person. If you threaten legal action and take none, then any subsequent threat to sue will fall on deaf ears. Your threats only encourage further bad behavior by the offender because he now knows that there will be no consequences. If you decide to sue, remember how ugly and expensive a courtroom can be. Long before most court cases are heard, the parties settle out of court, simply wanting their lives and lawyer fees back. If you feel the need to sue based on the behavior of someone else, you might remind the person of how time consuming and expensive court is for both parties. Ask them if this is really what they wish for either of you. In this case, you would be acting as the adult in control by offering the bad neighbor a choice and giving him full control of his destiny, much like you would do for a child.

In today's world, cameras seem to be everywhere. They often catch footage of bad behavior that is admissible as evidence. To date, most homeowners have yet to install fixed security cameras in their homes, but it is catching on. Having video proof of bad neighbor behavior can be extremely useful in bringing the behavior to an end. I have security cameras at my home, and like the idea of you having them as well. Mine are for the purpose of safety and to maintain a good quality of life. I strongly discourage you to follow underage citizens in order to capture them on video. Their parents and officials can accuse you of stalking or being a pervert. Fixed cameras are random and unintentional. Footage captured is the result of the subject's behavior and not yours.

As with almost all bad neighbor behavior, it is your responsibility to respond quickly. A neighbor of mine was spreading rumors/lies about me. I confronted the neighbor by phone. I let him know that I had been made aware that he made a false claim about me. I was specific, which gave him little wiggle room. When finished, I allowed for a *death pause* (getting him out of his comfort and safety zone). I believe he became ashamed since he went into defense mode. In order to deflect, he asked, "Who told you that" then added, "I never said those things and I thought we were friends." His apology was that he was sorry I felt that way. I reminded him that defamation is very serious and that if the rumors persist, I may sue him. This confrontation led to a permanent distance between us. But was this ever a loving, trusting, and supportive relationship in the first place?

I don't ever suggest getting into a physical confrontation. If you are attacked or protecting the innocent, you may be forced to engage physically, but these situations are rare. Nobody wins in an elective physical confrontation. Everyone gets arrested and then has a permanent record of assault. It will negatively impact your future. Understand the difference between assault and self-defense. Both the adult and child bully use the same tired lines such as "What are you gonna' do about it?" I like, "You want a piece of me?" Some things never change. But unlike a dark alley or in the schoolyard outnumbered by a bully and his henchmen, in your front yard, you can choose to end it by simply walking away. Being an intelligent adult does have its advantages. If you perceive a physical threat, you should try to avoid the perpetrator and call the police. If you are verbally threatened but perceive no physical danger, you can simply ignore it and remove yourself from the situation. If you are assaulted physically or verbally, you have not only the right, but also the responsibility to notify law enforcement officials. As uncomfortable as this may feel at the time, your overall comfort at home will increase knowing there is less likelihood of you being robbed, hurt, or killed. This is part of living in our society.

In conclusion, in this chapter, if there is any repeated suggestion I give you related to bad neighbors, it is that you act swiftly when dealing with them. The longer you allow bad behavior, the longer you have to tolerate it. If you work for a boss who brow beats you, it is your responsibility to confront him or her. If you allow it to continue, you are giving his or her inner bully permission to do it over and over. If you confront it quickly, there is a chance that the bullying will discontinue. Remember, they probably report to a superior as well. There is the chance that you will be demoted or fired. But this also brings the bullying to an end.

If you *are* the bully, cut it out!

# CHAPTER 30
# Your Water

*"Human nature is like water. It takes the shape of its container."*

—Wallace Stevens

I hope that by now we all have experience interacting with water! I have learned quite a bit about it, particularly the water in our homes and how important *good* water is to quality of life. Do you know the difference between good and bad water? The answer may seem obvious. I would rather drink from a lake nestled in the Rockies and above the timberline than from a public drinking fountain in some large American cities. I believe that if you don't filter your water, your body will do it for you.

One can survive without oxygen for about three minutes. One can survive without water for about three days, and one can survive without food for about three weeks. Therefore, your air, water, and food should be high quality and readily available. If the air you breathe is full of pollution, carcinogens, or particulates, the results can be manifested over a long term and are serious. People are learning that their public water supply is full of chlorine, drugs, cancer causers, and volatile organic compounds (VOCs). As a result, homeowners increasingly take matters into their own hands by purchasing elaborate water purification and softening systems.

Currently, the EPA sets guidelines for water quality delivered to us by our water utility districts. Their guidelines take into account chlorine levels that are designed to kill bacteria and impurities in the water. These guidelines take into account allowable levels of lead, arsenic, heavy mercury, and chromium 6. There are many other VOCs in our water. The amounts you will find in water vary by provider and location. The chlorine in my city may be higher than that found in a public swimming pool in California. Water in Nashville is known to be among the *hardest* in the country. Meanwhile, Memphis has the *softest* water in the country. *Hardness* refers to the amount of rock, sediment, calcium, and lime found in water. Water providers will often be able to provide you with a list of impurities that are in your water, along with the corresponding amounts. Private water treatment companies such as RainSoft, Echo, and Culligan may visit your house and perform a water test at no charge. These tests will help to determine the levels of chlorine or bleach, the Ph level, hardness, and precipitation (sediment) in your water. It is important for you to know what is in your water before drinking and bathing in it.

## Hard Water

Most of the water that comes into the American home is considered *hard*. Level of hardness is defined by the EPA in "grains per gallon." More grains means harder water. Hard water means that you have a high level of rock, sediment, calcium, and lime in your water. Hard water causes damage to that with which it comes into contact. The interior of your water supply pipes will begin to suffer accumulation (build up) of sediment, similar to a clogging artery. You may notice a white, hard, and chalky build-up around the base and discharge hole of your faucet. The life span of your water heater, dishes, clothes, toilets, and laundry machines can be reduced significantly due to hard water. Your gas or electric bill will be higher because the gas flame or electric elements in your water heater must work harder to heat through the sediment.

## Chlorine, Bleach and VOCs (Volatile Organic Compounds)

Water purification systems can have different functions. They are designed to remove impurities from water. Some filters are carbon-based and remove only chlorine and bleach. But there could be hundreds of other equally dangerous impurities in your water. VOCs refer to gasoline, oil, paint, drugs, stain, etc. There are filtration systems that are designed to remove all of them. The best filters remove chlorine and the VOCs to produce the cleanest and safest water on the planet. The process is called *reverse osmosis*. Many affordable home water filtration systems can produce this excellent water.

Total home filtration systems may seem lavish, but they will increase the life of your appliances, water heaters, and body! Your hair, skin, laundry, and dishes will be cleaner. Soap scum and hard water marks will be gone from showers, faucets, and sinks. You will never notice water spots on your car from washing it. You see, you can only get as clean as the water you are using. If I give you a bar of soap and a salon-grade bottle of shampoo to take with you when you bathe in the catfish pond, how clean will you be when you get out of the pond? You will be only as clean as the pond water. The same thing applies to the water at your property. When in the shower, you know you are clean when you feel squeaky-clean! That squeaky feeling is you rubbing into the rough calcium, lime, and sediment. Your natural skin should feel silky smooth. If you cannot afford a whole house filtration system, look into a smaller one that delivers perfect drinking water in the kitchen.

**Tip:** next time it rains, pour a bowl of water and set it down next to a puddle. Take the dog to the water and see if he drinks from the bowl of tap water or the puddle. The nose knows!

# CHAPTER 31
# Venting

I build the best quality of house I can. I do not take short cuts that will harm or inconvenience the homeowner. A competitor visited one of my projects while I was writing the final punch list. He complimented the house. I told him that the place was so tight it could float. His reply was ridiculous. What he said was true but completely out of context. He said, "Yeah, but a house needs to breathe." In truth, a house does need to breathe. In context, a house should be airtight. Because a house sits on planet earth, it is constantly surrounded by air. Houses breathe when windows or doors are open. They also breathe through the HVAC system. A well-constructed house will have many systems related to the passage of air in and out of the house. This is called *venting*.

## Foundation Vents and Basement Windows

In a crawlspace, you will almost always find foundation vents. They are at the top of the foundation where it meets the brick or siding. In most parts of the country, these vents should be opened in the warmer months and closed in the colder months. These were installed so that fresh and drier air can get in the crawlspace and force out the stale and humid air. Not having this ability can make your crawlspace a mold magnet. In extremely humid regions, the thought is that it is futile to displace humid air with equally humid air. Humidity in a crawlspace or basement means that conduit, electrical wiring, and lumber tend to drip with condensation all summer long. If this is the case at your house, look into *crawlspace encapsulation*. Most foundation repair companies offer this service. Some of the larger extermination companies offer it as well. What's more is that over half of the air in your house comes from the crawlspace. Clean air below means clean air above.

### Windows and Doors

They are good at allowing air in and out of a house. Sorry... Had to include this.

### HVAC (Heating, Ventilating, and Air Conditioning)

Your HVAC system is a complicated one. The HVAC system is to your house what your lungs, brain, and heart are to your breathing. Too bad we can't just smoke and change a filter on our bodies once a month. Most of us believe that the HVAC system is to heat and cool the inside of the house. That is part of its function to be sure, but that is not all it does. Air conditioning actually means *conditioning the air*. Conditioned air contains the right amount of moisture. It is delivered at a certain a temperature and volume. It removes many particulates and dirt. Your system simultaneously removes the humid and dirty air. When your HVAC is having problems, it is often the result of the system not breathing correctly. If you begin to breathe incorrectly, does this rank as serious?

HVAC installers take into account many variables when designing the right system for you. They consider the number of doors and windows and where they are located. They account for the direction your home is facing and the size of rooms inside the house. They consider ceiling heights and hallway widths. They consider foot traffic, elevation, and local climate as well. There may be two identical houses and one sits in the mountains of Montana, while the other sits on Kawai. These houses will likely have very different HVAC systems and duct/register placements.

For the most part, the air that our HVAC systems use comes from inside our homes. It inhales through the return air duct. This is the opening where you install air filters. Keeping the air filters changed (clean) lets your system breathe without struggling. Filters are designed to capture particulates before they get into the system. It is the same reason you might wear a protective breathing mask. The return air filters clog with microorganisms, insects, dust, hair, dander, lint, and most of all human skin that we shed day and night! Depending on how much you use your system, I suggest replacing the filter every month, especially if you buy the cheap ones. There are also filters designed to remove pollen and very small particulates. Their respective manufacturers will suggest that they don't need to be changed as often as the cheap ones. In this scenario, I would choose to buy the filter that has an accordion styled pattern, as opposed to the flat screen. The accordion pattern provides more surface area on the filter for air to pass through and into the system.

## Dryer Exhaust

Your dryer's venting system is likely more neglected than return air filters. We put wet clothes in the dryer and turn it on... The end. Your dryer removes moisture while adding heated air. It forces the hot air through the fabric then out through the discharge tube (duct). That air is full of wet lint that builds up on the inside of the discharge tube over time. This build up is extremely flammable. The fire may stay contained in the tube for a minute or so, but then it will find the end of the tube and come in contact with the exterior of your house. I realize these can be a pain to inspect since it typically means having to get behind the dryer. Since the tube (duct) is so inexpensive, buy an extra and keep it in the laundry room. When you finally get around to inspecting the inside of the old tube, you will be glad you have a replacement on hand.

**Bathroom Exhaust**

Your bathroom is likely to have two venting systems. One is related to plumbing and the other is related to humidity and moisture control. In order for your drains to work, two things are required: one is air and the other is gravity. If you do not know what gravity is, then you are probably a long way from owning a house. Just below a drain hole, there is a curved section of discharge pipe. That is referred to as a *gooseneck*. People think that it is there to catch wedding rings or diamonds that fall off when washing your hands. It is there to hold an amount of water at all times in order to prevent the sewer's methane gas from rising up through drainpipes and into your house. Methane gas is in the sewer air (which stinks, obviously) and can make you very sick. When you run water down the drainpipe, it must be displaced by air inside the tube in order to fall. The air that displaces the water in the pipe comes from a tube that sticks out through your roof. It is called the vent stack. It is important that the tops of these tubes remain free of things that could clog them such as birds, squirrels, and organic matter.

Let me give an example. Let's pretend you invite me over for dinner. I agree because you have promised to serve crab legs, T-bone steaks, and cold beer. Who am I to be unsocial? As we sit down, I pull a straw from my pocket and submerge it into my beer. I place my thumb over the top of the straw and remove it from the beer. What happens to the beer in the straw? Does it simply drain out because of gravity? As long as I keep my thumb covering the opening, the beer will remain in the straw. I find this criminal to some extent, but here is where the story gets interesting! I place the lower end of the straw in my mouth and remove my thumb from the top of the straw. The beer easily falls into my mouth. The beer fell into my mouth because in the straw, it was displaced by air entering the top of the straw. This is how air from the vent stack allows drain water to fall through and out of the drainpipes. It is important to note that most beers and wines will work, should you attempt to try the straw experiment in the privacy of your home.

The other bathroom venting system is the electric exhaust fan system. You will find these in the ceilings and walls of bathrooms. Many people use these fans to displace odor, but the primary function of this fan is to remove humid air from the room while pulling cleaner and dryer air into that same space. The amount of moisture/humidity introduced into the average bathroom during a single shower can be far more than found on a rainy summer day in Cambodia. That moisture hits every surface in the bathroom every day and sometimes more than once. Mold forms and grows as that moisture and humidity sits on these surfaces day after day, month after month, and year after year. Painted walls begin to streak. Countertops begin to feel rough. Metallic objects corrode and mirrors become spotted. Any time you take a bath or shower, the exhaust fan must be on. If you do not have an exhaust fan, it is likely that you have a window. Use it. If you have neither a fan nor window, it is time to call an electrician, plumber, or HVAC technician to install one.

Exhaust fans come in a variety of styles, strengths, and sizes. You can get one that is very powerful or one that is very quiet. You can get the more expensive one that offers both features. When shopping for one, you will see that each fan offers a strength rating called the *CFM*. *CFM* stands for *cubic feet per minute*. *Cubic feet* refers to an amount, and *minute* refers to a measure of time. The higher the CFM, the more air it will displace in a period of one minute. Typically, the higher the CFM, the larger and louder the fan motor will be. There are a few brands that offer high CFM with quiet motors. These are nice, and many come with internal light fixtures. The CFM rating will also be used to describe the power found in a microwave exhaust fan.

## Stove Top Exhaust

This one may seem like a no brainer. I would like to close this chapter now with some parting advice: don't cook cheap meat inside the house.

It is important to exhaust air when cooking. American natives who lived in tepees engineered this unique home design in order to vent efficiently. We all know what the stovetop vent does. What is important to know is why.

When we cook, we create odors. Food smells good. I like the smell. I just don't want to wear it on my business suit all day. When we cook, the air becomes filled with greasy particulates and smoke. These things are actually sticky. They stick to clothes, walls, ceilings, and even skin. You cannot see it at first, but will later. How on earth could upper cabinets get so dirty? Now you know. Also, take a look under the vent hood (over the stove). Nasty!

Any and all venting systems at your home must not end up in the attic. They must exceed the attic and deliver air to the outside of your house. The attic is part of your house. You would be amazed at how many venting systems deliver gasses, smoke, and air into the attic. It is not only ridiculous that builders would cut such corners, but it is also extremely dangerous.

Before I ruin your next dining experience, the next time you are in a restaurant that allows smoking, check out the exhaust intake openings in the ceiling. Chances are they are brown or black. You should have seen them when smoking was allowed in restaurants everywhere. The new way around such malaise is to paint the ceiling black.

## Chimney

The chimney can be the most dangerous thing in your house. When you burn wood or paper, the smoke is supposed to travel up the chimney. If it does not travel up the chimney, then either the fireplace and chimney are faulty or the flue doesn't allow enough air from the room to force smoke up and out of the room/house. If smoke does travel up the chimney, then it is creates a buildup of *creosote* on the inside of the chimney. *Creosote* is a nasty brown and sticky substance that is highly flammable and explosive. If you do not have creosote removed by a licensed chimney sweep, then do not burn wood or paper in the fireplace. Once creosote ignites, it can result in an explosion, thereby cracking bricks and mortar. The gaps in the mortar allow flames to come into contact with the house framing and exterior siding.

I did an in-studio interview with Mark Stoner, President of the Chimney Safety Institute of America. He is a great friend and is a great on air guest. His stories were fascinating. It was interesting to learn about everything that can go wrong with a chimney and fireplace. It is common that chimney sweeps are called to do inspections during colder months, since that is when most people use their fireplaces. Those who have their fireplaces inspected in the autumn often find it unsettling what the inspection reveals. Mark told stories of snakes, living and dead, commonly found in fireplaces and flues. Birds and other small animals often fall down inside the chimney and cannot get out unless it is through the house. You have the choice to not maintain your fireplace system. But if that is your choice, you must never use your fireplace.

**Attic Venting**

Your attic is designed to breathe. If it cannot breathe, the air becomes toxic. In the warmer months, attic heat can become destructive to all contributing members of the roof system.

If you walk up to the side of your house and look up, you are looking at the soffit. You may notice small holes or vents in this horizontally attached piece of material. These are soffit vents. Those holes allow cool air to be drawn into the attic. When the attic exhales, it does so through roof vents or the roof's ridge cap. The roof vents and ridge cap are installed close to the top of a roof because heat rises.

## Radon

In recent years, many houses across America have been tested for the presence of radon. Radon is a naturally occurring gas that spews from the earth. We have learned that exposure to radon causes cancer. There are ways to affordably remediate radon from your property, and the process is pretty simple. A certified technician will encapsulate the earth or concrete under a house with a strong and tight membrane. Air tubes are installed between the membrane and the earth. Radon fills these tubes and is exhausted through a large pipe outside of the house. If you notice a house with a large white PVC tube attached to the side, it is likely that the house has been treated for radon.

## Carbon Monoxide

Many of us use electricity as the energy to heat our houses and water. People in rural areas might use propane as a fuel to heat. But the cleanest, most efficient, and most economical fuel is natural gas. When natural gas burns, it emits carbon monoxide. That gas is highly toxic, and must be vented out of the house. It does so through galvanized exhaust tubes that terminate above the roof.

I recall feeling dizzy and nauseous during the first few weeks after moving into my last house. A good friend and building partner is also an HVAC technician. He suggested that we run air quality tests in the house. One of the tests was done in the mechanical room in the basement. That test revealed dangerous levels of carbon monoxide present in my home and basement. It turns out that a squirrel found the top of the exhaust pipe and decided to climb inside. He nearly made it to the basement before getting stuck. Though it was a terrible death for him, I could have been next. In short order, his body swelled inside the tube, clogging it. Carbon monoxide was not able to vent from the water heater to the house exterior and filled my basement. Within a day or two of removing the carcass, I was back to normal (whatever that means). I strongly urge homeowners to have their entire houses tested for carbon monoxide and dangerous mold. You can purchase permanent carbon monoxide detectors. They are similar in size to smoke detectors, and can be installed near gas HVAC systems and water heaters. By the way, CO2 (Carbon Dioxide) is not dangerous. It is simply in the air we exhale. Trees need it!

## Dehumidifiers

Though this appliance does not transfer air from the inside to the outside of a house, it is designed to remove moisture from the inside air. If you live in a humid climate, it is a good idea to install a dehumidifier in the basement. It is impressive how much moisture it can remove, as is the speed at which it does so. Within a few hours of turning on a dehumidifier, the entire space begins to feel and smell completely different. Using a dehumidifier means that you are removing the moisture that mold needs to survive. Your tools, appliances, electronics, and basement walls tend to corrode quickly in stagnant and humid air. Using a dehumidifier results in a longer, healthier life for not only our belongings, but for us as well.

# CHAPTER 32
# Filling Holes and Cracks: Caulk, Silicone, Fillers

It is common for people to mistake caulk for silicone, or joint compound for fillers. Knowing the difference is simple to learn.

**Caulk** is used to fill gaps that exist between two or more pieces of material that are, or will be, painted. Caulk is found in dry areas since it holds up poorly when in contact with moisture. It can be found where walls meet trim or trim meets trim. Such trim could be crown molding, window casing, or base trim. Caulk can be used outside or inside. To remove the threat of contact with moisture, caulk should be primed then painted. Caulk has an adhesive property, and is applied by using a caulking gun and wet finger (to smooth out the bead).

Similar to caulk, **silicone** is used to fill gaps between two or more materials, but has a waterproof property as well. You will find silicone where the toilet base meets the floor, shower walls meet the tub, covering roof nails, or around the edges of roof flashing. Silicone prevents water from getting into cracks or separations in materials commonly found in wet areas. Silicone is not paintable, and is applied with the use of a caulking gun. Silicone also has adhesive properties.

**Joint compound** (drywall mud) is used to fill gaps, cracks, or holes in drywall. It is also used to fill and cover the joint where one piece of drywall meets another. It is applied with a mud knife. Similar to a large putty knife, the mud knife is typically much wider, and has a smooth metal edge for skimming wet mud across a surface. Once joint compound is dry, it can be sanded to a desired shape or flatness. It should be primed and painted.

**Spackle** is for filling small holes or dents in drywall, wood, and synthetic composites. It too can be sanded and painted. Spackle is typically synthetic, and is more flexible than drywall mud. It is applied using a putty knife.

**Wood filler** is used to fill holes, gaps, and cracks in wood. Most wood fillers can be sanded, stained, or painted after they dry completely.

# CHAPTER 33
# Electricity and the Electrical Panel

*"Electricity is really just organized lightning." -*

—George Carlin

Some of the most potentially dangerous things in our lives are those that simultaneously keep us healthy and alive. I'm thinking of water, fire, food, marriage, and electricity. How we manage these things can mean the difference between life and death. We cannot live but three days without water. But we cannot live more than three minutes submerged under water. Electricity keeps us warm. It keeps our food disease free. It can also burn or kill you instantly. Light switches and outlets are comprised of plastic, metal, and raw electricity. That raw electricity comes to the outlets and switches though wires extending from the electrical panel. Failure at any point in electricity's journey through your house means danger. Licensed electricians are the only people who should ever come into contact with electricity, its wiring, and associated components.

Insulated electrical wiring receives its electricity directly from the electrical panel. Each wire is rated to handle a certain amount of electricity (and no more). Many house fires result from homeowners placing too great a demand on an outlet and its associated internal wiring. Do you recall *A Christmas Story*? Gavin Newsome played the part of the father who knew his house inside and out, and pushed its capability to the limits. He seemed to be at constant war with the house, and for him, it was a source of pride when he won! In the movie, he overloaded outlets with far too many cords and plugs, causing the fuses at the electrical panel to fail. The story takes place in the 1940s. Circuit breakers did not yet exist. Instead, glass fuses governed the flow of electricity from the electrical panel to light switches and outlets. In reality, had the father's fuses not blown, thereby stopping the flow of electricity, the house would have long since burned down. The fuse saved Christmas for Ralphie!

How do you know if a wire or electrical outlet currently carries electricity? I cover the topic of electrical testers in the chapter titled *The Perfect Tool Kit*. Owning a reliable electrical tester is imperative. It will tell you whether or not electricity is present in a wire, outlet, or switch. More complex testers are able to detect *amounts* of electricity.

The electrical panel is almost always installed inside your house, as opposed to outside. It has always been thought that it is a good idea for the homeowner to have quick access to the electrical panel. Electricity from the utility provider comes to your house via big wires that carry raw electricity. Those wires attach to a house at the top of the metal riser found, typically, on the side of a house near the roof. Electricity then travels across the wires on the inside of the riser and down into the electrical panel. When you open the face of the panel, you will see a series of circuit breakers. Breakers look like little black switches. Breakers began to replace fuses in the late 1950s. Fuses were made of thick glass and screwed into the electrical panel like a light bulb. Electricity inside the panel is distributed to the breakers that are secured to the internal frame (the *bus bar*). Each breaker is engineered to distribute a certain amount of electricity through a wire and to an outlet, light switch, or appliance. Picture the circuit breaker acting much like a faucet distributing a certain amount of water into a sink or bathtub. One breaker might be attached to a wire that sends electricity to all of the outlets in your bedroom. Another breaker might send electricity to the garage lights. Other breakers might send electricity to the water heater or clothes dryer. Breakers are also engineered to turn off in the event that electricity is disturbed on its way to, or at, an outlet. Such disturbances might be electricity coming into contact with water, a nail, or fire. Breakers will turn off if the demand placed on an outlet exceeds the size (or rating) of wire carrying the electricity.

Each breaker will have a number printed on it, such as 15, 20, or 30. This number signifies the amount (amperage) of electricity that the breaker, *in-wall* wiring, and electrical appliance/light/etc. can support. A few overhead light bulbs require far less electricity than a space heater or clothes dryer. A series of light bulbs and a desktop computer might need only 15 amps or less of electricity. If the number on the breaker that feeds that room is 15, it is safe. Add a space heater to the equation and chances are high that the breaker will trip (turn off) in order to prevent the electrical wire from overheating and causing a fire inside the walls. In this case, a 20-amp breaker would be ideal if the internal wiring is large enough to carry 20 amps of electricity without overheating. There would be no reason to install a 30-amp breaker to power an overhead light and a few outlets. Larger items such as an HVAC unit will demand more electricity. A 60-amp breaker (or two 30-amp breakers) and large insulated electrical wires might be required to run power to the HVAC unit. To bring the subject of breakers to a tidy conclusion, remember that lights and outlets work off breakers that deliver 120 volts of electricity (110 circuit). A larger item, such as the HVAC unit or clothes dryer, is powered by 240 volts of electricity (220 circuit). Notice that the electrical wire to a light fixture is much smaller than a wire to an HVAC unit. That's because it carries less electricity.

I believe there should be a national codes requirement that all label panels should be legibly marked to identify which breakers go to which room, outlet, or appliance. Inside most electrical panels (inside of the door), there is usually a large sticker with numbers on it. Each number represents a breaker. This is where breaker terminations should be written. It is sad how many of these stickers are blank or sloppily written. Most breaker panels have a dizzying number of breakers, and nobody knows what breaker goes to what outlet. If you decide to change an overhead light in a hallway, how would you know which breaker to turn off prior to removing the old light fixture in the hall? Commonly, homeowners will turn off breaker #1 and walk to the hall to see if that is the right breaker. If not, then the homeowner will go back to the panel, turn #1 back on and turn off #2. He then has to walk back to the hall, only to discover that it isn't breaker #2 either. He then goes after breaker 3, then 4, then 5, and so on. To boot, you have also turned off the microwave, fridge, TV, radio, and stove clock along the way, and need to reset each one of them. I am very strict with my electricians when building or remodeling. I inform them up front that I expect all breaker panels to be filled out with the correct breaker designations and location on the inside of the panel door. It must be printed in English so that everyone can read it. In the world of aviation, all pilots in the world must speak English. Obviously that is for safety reasons.

In your tenure as a homeowner, you should identify which breakers serve the various electrical needs at your house. The good part is that you only have to do this once! Again, inside the breaker panel door, there should be a large white paper sticker. This is where you should write the legend. If you and a friend want to make it easy, turn on all lights in the house and keep a hairdryer or lamp with you. One of you goes to the electrical panel and turns off breaker #1. You then walk through the house to see what lights are off. Plug in the lamp to see if the outlet is hot (or use your electrical tester). When you get to the first room on the left and notice that the light is off and the outlets are dead, then tell your friend to write "bed 1, left, light and outlets" on the line next to the #1 on the legend. Have your friend turn off breaker #2. As you walk through the house and notice the lights are off and the outlets are dead in the master bathroom, then tell your friend to write, "ma ba lights and outlets" in the panel and on the legend next to #2. Easy peasy.

# CHAPTER 34
# Your Trees

*"And the boy loved the tree... Very much. And the tree was happy."*

—Shel Silverstein

We chose to film the pilot episode of my home show (TV) and include a segment about trees. We interviewed a tree expert. A tree expert is an *arborist*. The segment was hilarious and informative.

Like you, trees are tough! They can withstand and master their environments, but also have a limited number of days to live. The ingredients trees need are sunshine, water, $CO_2$, and oxygen. Trees can drown or strangle to death. When the soil around a tree becomes compacted, the roots struggle to get oxygen. When deciduous trees are sick, their leaves form in clumps, as opposed to being evenly distributed along branches. You may notice dead branches. If a tree is sick, an early intervention by an arborist can elongate its life.

When trees become overgrown, we should trim them or hire someone to do it. Having a truck and a chainsaw does not an arborist make. Many of these cats are merely "Yee-Haws with Chainsaws." Arborists are certified, insured, and highly knowledgeable about the trees found in your region. Often, it is the arborist who performs the work done on your trees. Other times, the arborist will represent a company and direct the work being done from the ground.

I rarely work on trees. It takes extensive knowledge, musculature, and specialized equipment. Not having these ingredients can end poorly for amateurs attempting to cut branches from a ladder. Knowing the correct way and time to cut on trees is imperative. If a tree is cut incorrectly, it could easily compromise the health of the tree. If a tree is cut at the wrong time of year, pests can destroy it. When it comes to your tree work, make sure that a licensed arborist directs or performs the work.

I am afraid of heights. Now you know my weakness. I'm not afraid of the fall. The fall can be quite nice if you can find a way to relax as it happens. I'm afraid of the sudden stop at the bottom.

You may have the need or desire to plants trees at your property. I enjoy seeing the yard come to life, but I had to learn some lessons about tree planting the hard way. My first house was a tornado victim that I purchased to restore. The property had many gorgeous and huge maple trees that had been there since just after the Civil War. Those trees were taken by the F-5 tornado, and are probably rotting somewhere in the Carolinas. During the seven years that I lived there, I relished my weekends working in the yard. To me, it is therapeutic and far away from the noise of society. And no... I am not a serial killer, though I ate an entire box of Apple Jacks one night in college. The trees I planted then were small. I knew that I wouldn't get to see them grow to be tall and magnificent. I buried myself in research to find the fastest growing trees available. I discovered the river birch and maple tree. These two are fast growers, and were indigenous to my region. Unfortunately, I planted them too close to the house. Within a few years, my roof became a highway for squirrels and possums. Squirrels threw their trash on the roof, which clogged the gutters. Birds destroyed my roof shingles by doing their business above it. Leaves would fall all year long, and gutter cleaning became a monthly chore.

The solution was to remove the trees and start again. I made another critical error. In my research, I discovered a new genetically modified tree that Australian scientists claimed to be a super tree. The website literature touted that the tree would grow ten feet in height per year. It would grow straight toward the sun! It offered huge leaves to provide shade. If the tree were to grow too large, you could simply cut it down and it would grow back! Given the potential investment opportunity, my mind raced. This wood could be harvested every six years, as opposed to pine, which takes twenty years. It would grow back and there would be no need to till soil and replant pine tree seedlings. The wood weighed 85% less than pine, could be shipped for pennies on the dollar, and was resistant to water and bugs. In the fall, the leaves, high in protein, could be stripped and shipped to farmers as cattle feed. I called my best friend, as well as another friend who had recently retired as the CEO of this country's largest lumber company. We agreed that a trip to Florida was in order to talk to a small grower of the trees. We had the resources to propagate this tree for paper and lumber on a massive scale throughout the entire southeastern United States.

When we arrived at the grove in Florida, I was so impressed with the trees that I purchased six small seedlings. They were five inches in height and fragile. When I got home, I made sure to plant them far away from the house. I had learned my lesson! So, I planted three in the front yard and one in the back. I gave the other two to my buddy next door. Within the first year, they grew to a height of ten feet. They were straight as well. The following summer, they measured at twenty feet tall and were still straight. Do you see any problem yet? By the fourth year, they were easily fifty feet tall and as big around as an eighty-year-old maple tree. Neighbors were impressed with my trees and ordered seedlings for themselves. Within a few years, their roots were surging through their foundations and basements. I had a much larger lot than they did, but knew that disaster at the Taylor crib was not far off. I decided to cut the trees down. It was expensive. Sadly, the literature was true and the things began to grow back. I found a way to destroy the root system and the trees saga ended. I left one of them growing way out near the street when I sold the house. I drove by there recently and saw a utility crew removing it. Poor sewer...

I suppose you wonder whatever happened to our idea of becoming zillionaires by replacing the pine industry. We couldn't find any success stories related to planting these trees and managing groves of that size. It was too risky for our investors. Since that time, there have been success stories (but on a smaller scale). The tree is called the *paulownia*. Its lumber is now used for interior trim. I use it often and with fond memories.

Plant trees that are indigenous to your geographical region. Make sure to plant the trees in the right place. Do your research and ask lots of questions. Trees, chosen and planted correctly, can enhance the value of your property and add to your quality of life. Trees are semi-permanent and expensive to remove. Humans have a lifelong bond with trees. They were with us in the beginning. They held our swings, fostered our climbs, and gave man an excuse to build emergency rooms. They will provide shade, protection, and beauty until we are buried next to them.

# CHAPTER 35
# Your Roof

*"Frisbeetarianism is the belief that when you die, your soul goes up on the roof and gets stuck."*

—George Carlin

Some builders claim that the roof system is the most important system in a house. Others disagree, citing the foundation to be the most important. I would like to play Switzerland and claim that a house with a failing roof or foundation is in trouble.

I come across houses that were framed incorrectly. The house moves. The walls crack. Windows and doors break down. How did you end up with a house like this? Didn't you have a home inspection prior to buying the thing? You did? The only fix is to remove the drywall and reframe the house from the inside out. If it sounds expensive, you are right. This problem isn't specific to inexpensive starter homes. It is common in large, multi-million dollar homes as well. Custom homes cost more because they are built correctly from the bottom of the foundation all the way to the roof peak. The custom builder is hired because he is a master and doesn't cut corners. He is paid for his excellence and experience. Most of you didn't have that luxury.

If a roof is not installed correctly, it will fail in short order. Sometimes roof repairs are possible, but in most cases, the entire roof needs to be replaced. Remember that the roof is a system. If any part of the system fails, then the entire system can become compromised.

There are many different types and styles of roofs. Roof shingles can be made from clay, shale, tar, wood, and even straw. Metal roofs are expensive but extremely durable and can add beauty to a structure. It used to be that the roof had one purpose: to keep water from getting inside. Today, people are choosing highly attractive roofing materials as a means to beautify their properties, which can add value to the house.

The most common roof material is the tar shingle. It contains tar and fiberglass. The fiberglass is to give the tar strength and structure. Most of us grew up in a house with a 3-tab tar shingle roof. The texture of the shingle is grainy like sandpaper on one side and smooth on the other. The 3-tab shingle is becoming a thing of the past. They are being replaced by dimensional tar shingles. Instead of having three tabs as part of the shingle, dimensional shingles come as a solid sheet. On one side, it is still grainy, but offers a decorative finish (as opposed to the monochrome 3-tab color). From a distance, the dimensional shingles appear to be slate. They are more attractive and durable than 3-tab shingles.

Roofing manufacturers offer warranties with their shingles. On the face of the shingle packaging, you will find that warranty. Shingle life is represented by a *20, 30, or 50-year* warranty. This is more to set an expectation about how long the shingle will perform if it is installed correctly. *50-year* shingles will need to be removed and replaced long before 50 years have passed. They do perform better than the *20-year* shingles.

Most roofing material manufacturer's warranties are given to homeowners by certified roof installers. That's right... Just because a contractor installs a new roof on your house, it does not mean that there is a warranty. Your contractor may not be certified by the roof manufacturer to extend a warranty to you. The only roofs I have ever seen installed correctly were by my roof contractor friend, Tom. He costs more than other roofing contractors. Further, he has been certified by roofing material manufacturers to install new roofs and extend the manufacturer's warranty to the homeowner. That is rare. Most roof warranties do not cover labor to remove and reinstall roofing materials. Most roof warranties are deemed void if it is discovered that anyone other than a certified installer has walked on the roof.

A good way for homeowners to tell if the roof is in its final years is to look at it. Faded shingles typically mean that the colorful and protective granules in the tar have come loose and made their way down the gutter downspouts. Frequent roof leaks can result from compromised shingles. This would be the time to get to know a good roofer. It is time to check his references. Prior to going to contract with the roofer, you need to be copied on his license and insurance information so that you can verify it. A roof is too expensive to have to install twice. Ask your roofer for his suggestions related to materials, colors, and brands. <u>Ask if his roof laborers specialize in any other trade.</u> I do this in order to trick them. They will feel proud that their roofers can frame as well! This is the wrong crew for me. I don't want the compressors from the framing job to be used to fasten my shingles. The air pressure in the nail gun will be too high and they will sloppily blow the roof nails through the roof shingle, as opposed to securely fastening the shingles. Your roof will blow off a piece at a time, and in short order.

Ask the roof contractor to describe his typical *starter row*. He will be impressed that you know what this is. The starter row of a roof is the first layer of shingles to be installed (right above the gutters). They are nailed to the plywood but hang over the edge and slightly into the gutters. If he doesn't mention the gutters and proper water shedding, he is not your guy. Too many times, foreign workers lay the shingles on the plywood and start firing numerous nails into the material. The starter row is incorrect and the shingle has been shot by a firing squad. You should also ask about damaged decking and how they handle that. Decking refers to the plywood or sheeting material that the shingles are nailed to. It can become compromised by water or a direct hit. Since he cannot yet see the decking (it is covered with old shingles), he will have a proposed charge for every sheet of plywood that will need to be replaced. You should have access to your attic in order to see where new decking material has been replaced. Sometimes, roofers will charge you for the replacement of several sheets of plywood decking. When you look up in the attic and see there is no new decking, you know he is being dishonest with you. Make sure that if you agree to his proposal, that you be given access to photos of the damaged wood that they removed, as well as pictures of the new wood they installed. Inform the roofer that you would like any flashing addressed with accompanying photos of the failed flashing. Ask him to inspect the vent stack boots and replace them if they are compromised. Vent stack boots are very inexpensive, and you can price them at the box store.

Finally, make sure to get references. References should go back at least five years. A reference of a new roof that has yet to fail is a poor reference. Make sure to check and double-check his workman's compensation and insurance. Qualified roofers will be glad to assist you. They don't like the con men any more than you do.

# CHAPTER 36

# Your Foundation

Most structures have a foundation. Houses built on slabs have foundations that come in the form of thicker concrete around the perimeter in order to support load-bearing walls above. There are different ways to create a foundation. Some foundations are made of poured concrete footer with stone or block walls that rest on them, thereby creating a crawlspace inside its perimeter and beneath the house. Other foundation walls may be poured entirely out of concrete. This is common for houses with basements. There are different thicknesses of foundations depending on where you live. A foundation in Florida may be quite different than a foundation in Newark. It is true that a house built on a solid foundation is superior to a house built on sinking sand. The foundation is the most important system in any structure, since everything above hinges on its integrity.

The idea of a foundation failing can bring terror to any homeowner. Signs of foundation failure are the appearance of stair-stepping cracks in exterior brick or block walls, windows and doors not operating correctly, and/or cracks in the drywall above the windows and doors. The first thing we do is assign the cause to poor construction. But in most cases, this would be incorrect. Most builders follow strict building codes requirements. If the state of Illinois requires that all residential concrete footers are 24" wide and 18" in depth and must be poured only in undisturbed soil, then that is what the builder will do. If, during excavation, the builder digs down and hits solid rock, he may be allowed, by code, to pour the concrete footer directly onto the rock. Codes officials will inspect footer holes prior to them being filled with concrete. They will also re-inspect once the footer is poured. Unless builders test the soil prior to excavation and install supportive piers prior to pouring concrete, there is a reasonable chance that the footer will crack at some point as the soil around it moves. If all builders were to enlist these techniques prior to building a house, they would have to pass that enormous cost along to the buyers (you).

In most cases, concrete footers hold up well, but there are cases where there are differences in soil types from one end of a house to the other. It is common for soil under a house to be a mixture of different soil types. Such soil types could be clay minerals, sandy soil, peaty (perfect soil), or loam (mixture of sand a clay). One end of a house can settle and rotate in one direction because it sits on moisture absorbing clay while the other end, sitting on solid rock, doesn't move at all. Given the sheer weight of a house, the foundation (and house) will often crack. There are remedies that can stabilize, and sometimes restore, a damaged foundation. To date, my preferred method is to have steel underpinnings (piers) installed under the footer and driven to refusal. This almost guarantees that the foundation it supports will never move again.

Basement walls (poured concrete) can provide for a great foundation, but they too can crack, move, and take on water. It is true that drought can be as hard on a foundation as flooding. When basement walls cave in, it is usually a combination of the two. Poor drainage due to faulty gutters and downspouts, the slope of a lot, or excessive rain can cause the soil around a house to expand like a sponge as it absorbs water. This causes excessive pressure on basement walls. But drought can have the opposite effect, causing the soil around a house to contract to the point where it is no longer in contact with the basement walls, leaving them unsupported. If a rainstorm follows a drought, water will fill the void and begin to find its way into the basement. If that water freezes, it can expand, causing basement walls to crack under the tremendous pressure. There are repairs for this kind of damage as well.

# CHAPTER 37
# In Closing

*"Courage is being scared to death but saddling up anyway."*

—John Wayne

You are the person I like having as a neighbor. Sorry to get all Mr. Rogers on you. You reading this book probably means that you care about you, your family, your home, and your quality of life. As I wrote this book, it brought back so many memories. I wish I could share all of them with you, and may do so someday. I also envisioned you as well. I pictured what you may look like and how you would receive and process the information. I pictured you on a plane, on your back porch, and at the kitchen island.

Some of you may have opened the book and read it out of guilt because it was a gift to you. Some of you may have read it because you simply love to read. But most of you read this book (or some of it) because you were curious and needed help. But no matter the reason, no matter your race, religious beliefs, political leanings, or personal preferences, we all have a few things in common. We are human, we succeed, we fail, and we all desire the highest quality of life. You may have already achieved everything in your wildest dreams. Your lifestyle may be perfect. Even still, there is a high probability that you wanted, and have earned, a great quality of life and wish to keep it. We all strive for it. And since everything important to us comes together in the home, our homes should be at the top of our priorities.

There are few problems that a huge check cannot solve. But most of us aren't holding a huge check. I have discovered that the more knowledgeable I become about life, the higher the quality of life I experience. Knowledge leaves us with fewer personal problems. The better we understand our environment, the better we interact with it. It is this way with your job, your car, your family, and your home. When we fail in life, it is not because of things we don't know. We fail because we don't do the things we *do* know. But in the case of the house and home, there are things we simply do not know. My first house was a tornado victim. I bought it midway through the restoration effort. It was early in my life as a contractor. I was left guessing at so many things. The Internet was young. YouTube and Google didn't exist yet. I knew how to use tools, but knew little about planting my proverbial flag on this planet called *home*. I relied on limited experience and advice from my dad and knowledgeable friends. I got ripped off now and then. I won enough times to trudge on. Sometimes I ignored my gut, opting for cheaper prices or quicker solutions when I shouldn't have. There are things we just don't know. These things are foreign to us, and like algebra, we don't know *what* to ask. Since we all learn in different ways, I shared stories, gave examples, and offered guidance. I wish there would have been a book like this when I started out on my journey as a homeowner. It would have solidified my convictions and offered me answers as I sometimes sat frustrated in silence.

Driving home after a day of working at my favorite customer's house, I replayed the conversations she and I had that day. We connect, given that she is a deep soul and wise. She is a former entertainer and is married to a highly respected University Dean. They take an active role in keeping a healthy home. Our communication is mutually rewarding, and I always seem to have the right answers for them. That is rewarding for me. That drive home was the inspiration for this book. Since I cannot do that at your home, then maybe this book will serve you well in my stead and I can rest knowing that, together, we bridged the gap between you and your home.

# Wes